THE '21' COOKBOOK

THE

COOKBOOK

Recipes and Lore from
New York's Fabled Restaurant

MICHAEL LOMONACO

WITH DONNA FORSMAN

AND PHOTOGRAPHS BY CHRISTOPHER BAKER

DOUBLEDAY
New York London Toronto
Sydney Auckland

PUBLISHED BY DOUBLEDAY
a division of Bantam Doubleday Dell Publishing Group, Inc.
1540 Broadway, New York, New York 10036

DOUBLEDAY *and the portrayal of an anchor with a dolphin are trademarks of Doubleday, a division of Bantam Doubleday Dell Publishing Group, Inc.*

The designations '21' and '21' Club are registered trademarks and service marks of '21' Club, Inc.

All of the photos in the color insert, as well as those appearing on the following pages: 11, 25, 31, 36, 37, 57, 121, 132, 184, 213, 231, 246, 283, 303, 380, copyright © 1995 by Christopher Baker.

The "Perfection" crystal water and wine glasses pictured in the color insert are provided by Baccarat.

The mother-of-pearl spoon with sterling silver handle pictured in the color insert is from James Robinson Inc.

Caviarteria provided the crystal and sterling vodka shot glass pictured in the color insert.

Book design by Marysarah Quinn

Library of Congress Cataloging-in-Publication Data
Lomonaco, Michael, 1955–
The '21' cookbook : recipes and lore from New York's fabled restaurant / Michael Lomonaco with Donna Forsman and photographs by Christopher Baker. — 1st ed.
p.   cm.
Includes bibliographical references and index.
1. Cookery.   2. Restaurants—New York.   3. 21 (Restaurant: New York)—History.   I. Forsman, Donna.   II. Title.
III. Title: 'Twenty-one' cookbook.
TX714.L65   1995
641.5'09747'1—dc20   95-5983
                                                                          CIP
ISBN 0-385-47570-5

With love for my wife, Diane, who has
taught me more than books can hold.

M.L.

For Russ and Anna.

D.F.

Illustrator/satirist Russell Patterson captured the fantasy as well as the reality of '21' in this risqué 1950 illustration. (Courtesy of '21')

ACKNOWLEDGMENTS

It takes hundreds of people, working from before dawn to long past midnight, to create the magical experience of dining at '21.' Nearly as many have contributed to this effort to enable you to re-create some part of that magic at home.

Foremost among these has been Stephanie Cogan Golfinos, daughter of '21' owner Marshall Cogan. Her vision, tenacity, and caring have been the engine driving this labor of love. Along with support and insight, she has contributed hundreds of hours coordinating an extensive recipe-testing program to make sure the recipes presented are as practical to make in a home kitchen as they are enjoyable to eat—at home or at '21.' She has dedicated dozens more hours to reviewing the manuscript and suggesting ways to improve and clarify its content.

Patty Abramson deserves more than thanks for her advocacy on behalf of the project, as well as for her role in helping shape the original concept and proposal for the book, and her insightful direction and unwavering support at every step from start through finish.

Marshall and Maureen Cogan must be credited, of course, for their invaluable roles in restoring the '21' Club to the greatness that gained it worldwide fame in the '30s, '40s, and '50s. Credit goes to the late, great interior designer Charles Pfister for his inspired restoration of the club in 1987, to Fred Marcus for his custodianship of the '21' Club and his quiet, steady hand in steering it through occasionally tumultuous times, and to Ken Aretsky, for his years of listening and advice. Thanks, as well, for the assistance and cooperation of '21's hardworking management team: Bruce Snyder, Bryan McGuire, Brad Reynolds, and Walter Rauscher.

A special thank you to Sommelier William Phillips for his knowledgeable contribution of wine recommendations. And to Pastry Chef Andre Bonhomme for his collaboration in perfecting the dessert recipes.

Abundant thanks to all who shared their memories and memorabilia so freely: Jerry Berns, Peter Kriendler, Bruce Snyder, Walter Weiss, President Jimmy Carter, Charles Koppelman, Frank Biondi, Sam Shaw, Pete Gogolak, and many others.

Thanks to our editor, Judy Kern, for her confidence in us. To Design Director Marysarah Quinn and to the Doubleday Art and Production staff for their roles in transforming the many recipes, anecdotes, and visuals into a cohesive whole. Thanks to Judy Hershon at '21' International Holdings Inc. for securing several of the historical photographs reproduced in the book, and to Russell Cherry and Anna Solomon for their research assistance.

Thanks to Christopher Baker for his extraordinary photography. To Connie Yuvan for her encouragement and support, as well as for her visual concepts and direction of photography.

A round of applause to all who volunteered to test recipes: Patty Abramson, Suzanne Barber, Margann Dodge, Beth Eggers, Michael Friedman, Betty Granger, Lisa Karahalios, Jenie Kemp-Magen, David Lambo and friends, Alexandra Lebenthal, Heidi Davidson, Sylvia Norman, Susan Rhodes, Sabrina Sherman, Humaira Sinnott, Lynne Sonntag, Nancy Spetzler, Mary Ellen Swenson, Karin Turner, Connie Yuvan, and Sophia Waggener.

In addition to all those who contributed directly to the book, I want to extend heartfelt personal thanks to my sous chefs over the years: Craig Cupani, James Botsacos, and Denis Williams. To the dedicated crew that has cooked with me for six years. To Mr. Pete and Mr. Jerry—uncles always. To Walter Weiss, Oreste Carnivale, and the devoted service staff who make '21' great every day. To Charles Motola and Pablo Torres for their diligence. To the great and gifted chefs who have guided me and the wonderful cooks who have inspired me: Alain Sailhac, Daniel Boulud, Patrick Clark; to my mother Mary, my mother-in-law Vivian, and Grandma Spadaro. To my father Frank and to my brothers Salvatore and Anthony and their families, their constant encouragement and support has brought me so far, and to my father-in-law Frank, who always keeps me laughing. Finally, to my alma mater, New York City Technical College, and all the chef-instructors who gave me my future.

CONTENTS

THE POWER OF '21'

*Honor, adventure, and sufficient income
was in the air of Twenty-One.*
—NORMAN MAILER, *HARLOT'S GHOST*

Even if you've never set foot in Manhattan, chances are you're not a complete stranger to '21.' Remember the scene in *Rear Window* where the glamorous socialite played by Grace Kelly waltzes into Jimmy Stewart's apartment with a '21' waiter bearing carry-out lobster and champagne? Or the "power lunch" scene in *Wall Street*, where Michael Douglas makes Charlie Sheen an offer he can't refuse, then leaves him to contemplate his raw-egg-topped Steak Tartare?

Incredibly, the reality of '21' is every bit as star-studded as Hollywood's fantasies. Each president since Franklin Roosevelt has dined at '21.' Royalty and heads of state spill out of stretch limos stacked in holding patterns outside. Captains of industry strike up megamergers as readily as $20 cigars. And sables and mink are as ubiquitous as Beluga caviar and Dom Pérignon.

For more than six decades, '21' has continued to be *the* place to meet, to dine, to see, and to be seen: the place to make a deal at lunch under the barroom ceiling's maze of corporate memorabilia. The place to launch a new product to the press in a private room named the Harbor Room by Senator Edward Kennedy. The place to sip a B&B (invented here) by a fireplace in a paneled room full of Remington originals. Or to host a fund-raising gala for hundreds.

What keeps the legend of '21' so alive? Magazines such as *Life, Time, Fortune,* and *Gourmet* have devoted millions of words and hundreds of pictures to explaining the phenomenon. In no small part, of course, it is the excellence of the food—always the best, the freshest, the most difficult to come by—perfectly prepared under the meticulous supervision of '21's celebrated chef, Michael Lomonaco.

'21's wine list is similarly impressive. Private stocks belonging to movie stars, politicians, and pillars of society are stored in '21's fabled wine cellar—once dubbed by *The New York Times*'s Bryan Miller "a marvelous rich man's sandbox."

Yet in spite of its aura of elegance and its steady stream of celebrities, '21' is anything but stodgy. Warm. Comfortable. Homey. These descriptions are closer to the mark. For '21' is as friendly as its service is impeccable. From chairman to doorman to dishwasher, the people who work at '21' have a genuine, unrehearsed affection for people. Captains make it their business to know customers' preferences, to anticipate their needs. No demand is too outrageous. Cary Grant once asked for—and got—a peanut butter and jelly sandwich. When Frank Sinatra ordered pickled cherry peppers, someone made a late-night dash to a deli. Chef Lomonaco has gone out of his way to learn every variation of traditional '21' dishes such as chicken hash, and who prefers which.

During the past seven years, Chef Lomonaco has honed '21's cuisine to an unprecedented level of excellence. His accomplishments have not gone unnoticed. "No one in America does game as well as Lomonaco..." notes John Mariani in *Travel and Leisure*. "...Lomonaco has found a cuisinary balance..." writes Gael Greene in *New York*. In *Gourmet*, Andy Birsh calls him "the right man in the right place at the right time." Chef Lomonaco has appeared on TV innumerable times with Regis and Kathie Lee, David Letterman, and Julia Child; on the *Today* show; and in a special *Smithsonian World* portrait of the restaurant. He's even been invited to the White House as a special consultant.

Art Buchwald and Ethel Kennedy are pictured leaving '21' in a photo that appeared in a 1987 W article on restaurants frequented by New York society.
(Courtesy of WWD)

Here, for the first time, is a book filled with Chef Lomonaco's recipes, menus, and techniques, explained in his own words. Lomonaco has adapted each of the recipes in this book to work as well in a typically equipped home kitchen as it does at '21.' He'll teach you how to "buy smart"—to get the best, the freshest, the healthiest ingredients for your money—the way '21' does. He'll explain why bubbling stock pots are a given in world-class restaurants and show you how to sneak this indispensable trick of the trade into your overcrowded life. He'll even have you cooking from the "new" food pyramid—where meat no longer rules the roost—without feeling you've made a sacrifice.

IF YOU ARE STOPPED AT THE GATE, THREATEN TO
START THE MACHINE WHICH WORKS AS FOLLOWS:
SEAL (*A*) BALANCES BALL (*B*) AND APPLAUDS
HIMSELF, CAUSING STRING (*C*) TO SHOOT BONE (*D*)
FROM PISTOL (*E*) - BONE LANDS ON PLATFORM (*F*) -
DOG (*G*) BENDS HEAD TO PICK UP BONE, CAUSING
CANDLE (*H*) TO SET OFF BOMB (*I*) AND BLOW UP
THE JOINT!

'21'

Rube Goldberg's Surefire Invention for Getting into '21.'
Rube Goldberg's fanciful "machines" were so popular in the '50s that his name become synonymous with anything excessively complicated and confusing. Rube himself had no difficulty getting into '21.' A much-loved customer for many years, he donated cartoons to '21's Iron Gate albums published in 1936 and 1950.
(© KFS)

Sprinkled between the secrets of the culinary rebirth that Michael Lomonaco has brought to the Club are stories from '21's rich and spicy past and present; photographs and works of art from '21's collections; and insights into the reasons for '21's extraordinary staying power in the fickle New York world of "in" places to eat and drink.

THE SPEAKEASY THAT BECAME A RESTAURANT THAT BECAME A LEGEND

How you gonna keep 'em down on the farm,
after they've seen Parie?
—SAM M. LEWIS, JOE YOUNG,
AND WALTER DONALDSON

The First World War (the *Great* War, as they called it then) changed attitudes and lifestyles in America almost as profoundly as it changed the geography of Europe. Hemlines were up. Inhibitions were down. Within two years of war's end, a new decade was ready to roar.

The '20s version of the Moral Majority, however, had other ideas. The Eighteenth Amendment, known then as the Volstead Act, became the law of the land on January 17, 1920. Prohibition, which was supposed to end drunkenness, debauchery, and corruption, promptly made law-breakers of millions of people. Estimates of the number of illegal drinking establishments that sprang up in New York City alone go as high as 32,000—more than twice the number of legal pre-Prohibition drinking places.

Overnight fortunes were made by catering to this insatiable thirst, a fact not lost on cousins Jack Kriendler and Charlie Berns, two collegians who were struggling to make ends meet. Their first speakeasy, The Red Head, sold dollar flasks that customers hid in their coat pockets or poured into teacups, the source of the speakeasy nickname "cup joint." But the atmosphere at Jack and Charlie's had little in common with either a tearoom or the average gin mill. Instead, it felt like one big fraternity party, with live music, gay blades, and liberated flappers doing the Black Bottom and Charleston.

The clubby feeling at each of the "speaks" Jack and Charlie ran before finding their permanent home at 21 West 52nd Street was no fluke. Jack made a conscious effort to "recruit" customers from the Ivy League colleges and to create an environment where the sons of America's first families would feel at home.

Brother can you spare a dime?
When the Roosevelt Administration declared a bank holiday in 1933, Jack and Charlie made sure their business didn't dry up by issuing their own scrip to tide loyal customers over. (Courtesy of '21')

Prices were stratospheric right from the start. But customers got full measure for what they paid. No rotgut hootch. No bathtub gin. Jack and Charlie went directly to Europe and made arrangements to have the likes of Ballantine's Scotch and Hine Cognac smuggled in. They even hired Kaiser Wilhelm's former chef to run the kitchen.

It wasn't only undergraduates who rose to the bait. Writers, artists, movie stars, and adventurers quickly staked claim to the red-and-white-check-clothed tables in Jack and Charlie's barroom. Robert Ruark, Frank Buck, John Steinbeck, and Ernest Hemingway swapped

THE HOUSE THAT
JACK AND CHARLIE BUILT

By the time Jack and Charlie got to 52nd Street, they had some definite ideas about how a speakeasy should be designed. Now, for the first time, because they had purchased '21' outright, they had the opportunity to put their ideas to the test.

Their first line of defense was the iron gates at the property line. Equally sturdy wrought iron grilled the door. But that could only buy time, should the Feds come to call. Inside, Jack, Charlie, and a friend and artist-of-many-talents named Francis Applegate Buchanan devised a system of hidden closets and vaults, drop-away shelving, chutes, and circuitry that defied detection during an eleven-hour raid on June 24, 1932. One of the devices, described the next day in every newspaper in New York, dropped all the bottles behind the bar down a chute to the cellar, where they crashed on iron gratings, releasing their illegal contents into the public sewer system and leaving nothing but aromas to tantalize the frustrated "drys."

Even more ingenious was the concealment of '21's incredible wine cellar, which actually was located under the unoccupied brownstone next door at 19 (which Jack and Charlie had secretly purchased). Frank Buchanan designed a door of solid masonry, twelve inches thick and weighing two and a half tons that was so perfectly balanced it could be swung open by a child—but only if the child knew

In shaping the creation of Jack and Charlie's '21,' Francis Buchanan was artist, architect, engineer, and interior designer. His artwork is still visible on the barroom walls, his inventive 5,000-pound wine cellar door still swings smoothly with merely a gentle nudge. (Courtesy of '21')

where to find the door and how to use its "key." First of all, the door was in what should have been an unbroken foundation wall between two separate houses; not a likely place to look. To obscure it still more, they built a waiters' closet in front of the door, so that the door's edges were hidden by the closet's shelving. The "key" was a long piece of wire—not unlike a straightened-out coat hanger. If inserted just so into a tiny hole between the bricks, it would unlock the door. If poked into any of the other ninety-nine identical-looking little holes, nothing would happen.

...ence of group solidarity
...onal scale?' Are there com-
...s which can bind us effec-
... in spirit into a national
... The answer to this ques-
... determine our course for
... century. Probably it will
...ne our national destiny.''

...hief instrumentality to mold
...pinion in the interest of na-
...goals and to bring about an
...standing and acceptance of
...s designed to achieve them is
...tion, he continued. ''My pro-
...is that education should pro-
... for a congress of social-eco-
...ic scholars who have no axes to
...nd. This congress should set it-
...f the task of telling us what we
...n most safely believe with respect
...those important issues upon which
...r welfare so much depends. This
...cial-economic congress would be to
...ucation what the research depart-
...ents are to the great industrial con-
...erns, or what the technical staffs
...re to the several administrative
...oards of government.''

To the democratic argument that
... people are educated they can be
...rusted to form their own opinions
...n these matters, Dr. Kelly respond-
...d: ''This reason, even if valid
...ecades ago, certainly cannot be ac-
...pted as sound today when the
...uestions involved in almost any of
...he complex social-economic issues
...which face this generation have their
...roots in a mass of data so baffling
...that even those who devote their
...lives to the study of them find it
...well-nigh impossible to encompass
...he necessary information.''

''No field has ever been so rich for
...demagoguery and quackery as the
...social-economic field is today. This
...result is inevitable as long as we
...have to uninformed public opinion
...uestions so complicated as joining
...e League of Nations, inflation of
...e currency, farm relief, unemploy-
...nt insurance, regulation of public
...lities, divorce laws. The question
...omes all the more impossible
...n tremendous financial interests
...involved.

The Need for Experts.

...o not regard it necessary to
... medical journals, the dental
... the mining journals in
...we may have an informed
... these questions. No, we
...ds of scholars in these
... it in the schools. We
...bility of vaccination,
... common drinking
...ention is that the
...'s obligation to
... a nature that
...pon it just as
...nation.''
... hopeful re-
... the present
... speakers
...h opened
... National
...Wil-
...ence
...tes-

numbers of people received something for nothing.

''Children for almost an entire generation were placed before the choice
of 'to have' or 'to be' with the accent on the 'to have,' and with a
supercilious pity for the weak-mind-
ed idealists who still preached that
'being' was infinitely preferable. The
bathroom with running water became the grand and glorious purpose of a life which no longer de-
manded that the austere chamber of
the soul and the intellect should also
be provided with the running water
of criticism and the fresh air of
intellectual independence and cour-
age. This false doctrine has brought
us to the present terrible crisis. We
are not suffering from an overpro-
duction of material goods but from
an under-production of honest think-
ing.''

Dr. Henry Lester Smith, treasurer
of the association, in his keynote ad-
dress declared: ''The school repre-
sents one of the important lines of
defense against reversion in periods
of stress to the earlier and lower
levels of society. At all times, and
particularly in periods of distress, it
should represent a general recon-
struction program. For this task it
should lend itself to necessary over-
hauling.''

Warns on Weakening Education.

Warning against any weakening of
education in this period, he asked,
''May there not be in our own country a more formidable group than
we suspect who, under the guise of
economic stress, desire to reduce the
educational opportunities for the
masses, knowing at the same time
that the privileged classes will not
permit this denial to their own children.?

''Let civilization remember that de-
velopment of children cannot await
the arrival of prosperity. It must
precede and usher in that period.''

The future of radio in education
was discussed by William John Coo-
per, United States Commissioner of
Education. Four chief tasks, he declared, it would probably accomplish
—the bringing into the classroom of
the actual outside world; the making
of more expert teachers; the provid-
ing of better vocational advice by experts in every field, and the supple-
menting of the correspondence school
lesson for children in remote places.

At present, he said, we are afraid
to bring the outside world into the
classroom by radio. ''There are men
who are interested in what goes n
in a classroom and who are interested
in classroom advertising. They would
advertise their goods in schools if
they could do it without getting
caught. Accordingly teachers must
be careful.''

Gets $1,639,507 Tax Adjustment.

WASHINGTON, June 25 (AP).—The
Internal Revenue Bureau today reported a refund of $1,165,295 and a
credit of $474,212 in favor of the
Lehigh and Walkes-Barre Coal Company of Wilkes-Barre. The adjust-
ments, which covered operations for
1920 and 1921, were on account of a
determined overassessment of $1,639,-
7 during those years. The bulk of
... overassessments, the bureau said,
...ted from the redetermin tion of
... liabilities on the b sis of the
...ated net income d invested
... the taxpay and certain
...ations nich filed sepa-

WET SPOT GOES DRY AS RAIDERS ARRIVE

Agents Armed With a Warrant Get a Cordial Welcome at Speakeasy, but No Liquor.

TRICK SHELVES REVEAL WHY

Push-Button Had Dumped Bottles Into Chute and Only Odor Re-mained, Federal Men Complain.

Prohibition agents of the staff of
Administrator Andrew McCampbell
went to the Federal Building yesterday to complain about the way they
had been treated Friday night at an
establishment in West Fifty-second
Street which the agents said was a
speakeasy, but this allegation they
were unable to prove.

The fact that liquid proof was
lacking was the burden of their com-
plaint. However, they were informed
by Thomas E. Dewey, Acting United
States Attorney, and David Marcus,
his assistant, that they could do
nothing about it.

When Montrose Rice, an agent, visited the establishment on June 20
and 22, he swore in an affidavit, he
had been able to buy liquor on both
occasions. Francis A. O'Neill, United
States Commissioner, was sufficiently
satisfied with his story to issue a
search warrant.

Armed with this document, Agents
Benjamin Lippi and Benjamin La
Rosa called at the place on Friday
night. Lippi pressed the doorbell
and waited. In a minute an outer
door opened and a door tender came
out. An inner metal door closed behind him. He asked the agents what
they wanted.

''You sell liquor here,'' said Lippi.
''It's against the law.''

''Yes,'' La Rosa seconded. ''We are
going to search the place. We have
a warrant.''

Another attendant, who had been
listening to the conversation through
a peephole in the inner door, opened
the portal. He was cordial to the
agents and greeted them, they said,
as if they were long-lost friends.

Lippi and La Rosa accepted his invitation to go in. In the barroom,
which supposedly had been well
stocked, the agents found nothing
but a bar and empty shelves. After
looking around, Lippi found a button
in the floor. He pressed it, and all
of the shelves fell flat against the
wall and the bottom of the shelving
dropped downward, revealing a chute
about twenty feet long running into
the basement.

''All they got,'' Mr. Dewey related,
''was a whiff of the liquor running
out of broken bottles. They made no
arrest.''

Senora Calles's Condition Grave.

BOSTON, June 25 (AP).—Señora
Leonor Calles of Mexico City, tonight was still in a grave condition
at Peter Bent Brigham Hospital as
the result of an operation on her
brain for the removal of a tumor.

JUDGE ISAAC BACK... BANKRUPTCY

Says La Guardia Measures... End Virtual Monopol... Receiverships Here...

Special to THE NEW YORK T...

WASHINGTON, June 25...
Max Isaac of New York,...
The American Bankrupto...
today characterized as bo...
tant and far-reaching'' tw...
troduced yesterday by Rep...
La Guardia. One would ...
appointment of corporatio...
tees in bankruptcy and ...
would forbid their appo...
receivers.

Discussing the possib...
the bills, if enacted, J...
who is also secretary-...
the National Associatio...

JR...

CL...

S...

Navy...

ABOVE: *Sommelier William Phillips demonstrates how the "key" to the wine cellar (a thin metal rod) had to be inserted in the correct one of the numerous tiny holes to unlock the masonry door that concealed '21's wine and liquor supplies during Prohibition.*
(Photo: Christopher Baker)

RIGHT: *During Prohibition there were hidden compartments all over '21,' such as this one inside the pantry. (Courtesy of '21')*

tales about the ones that got away. Joan Crawford, Cary Grant, and Myrna Loy commuted from the coast. '21's famous hidden wine cellar—never penetrated by Revenue agents—was one of former New York Mayor James "Gentleman Jim" Walker's favorite spots for clandestine evenings with his mistress.

It was at '21's front door that Clare Boothe Luce reportedly offered to step aside for Dorothy Parker, saying "age before beauty," to which Parker responded, over her shoulder, "pearls before swine." Another evening, humorist Robert Benchley, after closing the bar as he often did, hailed a man in uniform out front: "Call me a cab," instructed Benchley. To which the man replied: "Sir, I am an admiral." "Fine, then call me a battleship," Benchley retorted.

Hail "21"! — with fond memories
of my favorite pin-up, 1941–45!
Dave ("Pvt.") Breger

(Courtesy of '21')

THE END OF AN ERA

When places of entertainment suddenly became legal again in 1934, everyone ran off to explore the glitzy new Stork Club, El Morocco, and the Rainbow Room. But Jack and Charlie hung tough and, slowly but surely, as the novelty of New York's new nightspots began to wear thin, the old-timers came back to the place where they felt most at home.

As '21' expanded, incorporating the town house at 19 West 52nd in 1936 and the one at 17 West 52nd at the end of World War II, the number of Kriendler and Berns family members involved in the operation grew exponentially. Over the years, dozens of relatives of the

ABOVE:

While wartime conditions were far from austere at '21,' the Club did everything it could to contribute, materially as well as spiritually, to the war effort. Here volunteers cart off '21's rubber welcome mat, which was to be converted to urgently needed tires for military trucks and jeeps.
(Courtesy of Daily Mirror, June 1942)

BELOW:

Several thousand miles from their favorite "home away from home," Marine Lieutenant Robert Kriendler and friends raise their glasses in a toast to Jack and Charlie.
(Courtesy of '21')

A MOST FAMILIAR FACE

*F*or its first five years on West 52nd Street, ‘21’ was no more than a twenty-foot-wide town house (except for the clandestine wine cellar under the adjoining property at 19 West 52nd).

In 1935 Jack and Charlie annexed all of number 19. The following year, they acquired number 17 for Charlie's new business: ‘21’ Brands—wholesale distributors of Ballantine Scotch, Hine Cognac, and other imported spirits. But the restaurant's most ambitious remodeling under the Kriendler and Berns families came just after the war, when ‘21’ Brands moved to number 23, and the entire sixty-foot facade was unified by the construction of an enclosed tower of fire stairs and the addition of the ornately grilled stairs and balcony that now give ‘21’s facade its distinctly New Orleans flavor.

Shortly after, ‘21’s iron jockeys took up residence, giving the final touch to the most recognizable restaurant facade in the world.

Before: ‘21’ sports a patriotic facade near the end of World War II. ‘21’ Brands was housed at number 17, at the extreme right of the photo, but renovations had already begun on number 23, in preparation for the big game of musical chairs played out in 1946.
(Photo: Alfred H. Miller Co.)

During: ‘21’ Brands has completed its move to number 23, and the facade of number 17 has been pushed out to the property line to accommodate a tower of fire stairs. Workers are putting the finishing touches on the new stairway and balcony.
(Photo: Standard Studios)

After: The facade created by the 1946 renovation has remained virtually unchanged for the past half century.
(Photo: Standard Studios)

founders have been involved in the '21' Club in one way or another. As Bob Kriendler once put it: "We have tried nepotism, and it works."

During World War II, Ed Sullivan hosted a thirty-nine-week series of CBS broadcasts from the second and third floors of '21,' featuring stars such as Marlene Dietrich, Greer Garson, Humphrey Bogart, Jack Benny, Ethel Merman, and Jeanette MacDonald. Even though '21' rolled up the rubber welcome mat out front and donated it to the war effort, things weren't exactly spartan inside. "We had to do a lot of finagling to go above the rationing to get meat, butter—things like that," recalls Jerry Berns. "We got caviar from Persia instead of Russia. But there was nothing we couldn't get . . . for a price."

THE ADVENT OF
EXPENSE ACCOUNT ENTERTAINING

Within a few years of war's end, '21,' like every other restaurant in New York, had come to depend more on corporate coffers than family fortunes to bankroll its clientele. Broadcasting and publishing were, and are, important neighborhood industries. (The CBS Building is just down the block; the Time Warner Building directly across the street.) More than ever, advertisers sought ways to get '21's cachet to rub off on them.

In the early '60s, American Airlines initiated '21' Club service on its transcontinental Astrojet flights. Menu selections supervised by '21' were served from '21' china and glassware on '21' linens. American even simulated '21's entryway, with iron gates and a jockey in front of the check-in counter.

In 1979, when Backer and Spielvogel, then a brand-new advertising agency with very modest quarters, was asked to pitch the J&B Scotch account, Carl Spielvogel decided to make their presentation at what he calls "the best bar in the world—the '21' Club." "Were it not for the '21' Club," Spielvogel writes, "I am sure we would never have won this very important account."

One of '21's most loyal friends—both personally and professionally—is *Cosmopolitan* editor Helen Gurley Brown. "I knew I had arrived," she is quoted as saying, "when Jerry Berns kissed me." Every Thursday for the past twenty-five years, Brown has hosted a *Cos-*

mopolitan lunch for advertisers in one or another of the restaurant's private banquet rooms, because "it is the one place we can be sure people will *come* to."

GOING ONCE, GOING TWICE, SOLD FOR 21 MILLION DOLLARS

When entrepreneur Marshall Cogan purchased the '21' Club in 1984, it wasn't the first sale of '21,' just the first one that stuck. A 1969 sale to E. (Ralph) Abalon, chairman of the Ogden Corporation, involved $10 million translated into Ogden stock. But when the stock value plummeted, the deal was called off. Then in 1980, the '21' Club announced its sale to Baron Enrico "Ricky" Di Portanova and his Texas millionaire wife, Sandra, for a little over $11 million. But negotiations dragged on so long that the deal ultimately fizzled. During the summer of 1984, Donald Trump spent weeks denying rumors that he was buying '21,' when, in fact, he had been engaged in serious negotiations with '21's owners. "He wanted to pay out in ten or twenty years," explains Jerry Berns, who was then seventy-seven. "We wanted it in five years." So once again, no deal.

Cogan has cited several reasons for purchasing '21,' but the consensus is that his unsuccessful attempt to purchase Sotheby's auction house in 1982 had a great deal to do with it. In Cogan's own words: "We became interested in '21' when we lost Sotheby's. In so many ways, '21' is as important an institution in its field as Sotheby's is in the world of art.

" '21' is probably one of the universal great names—akin to Coca-Cola and General Motors—that's known throughout the world," explains Cogan. "I viewed it as my responsibility to reestablish the legacy, so '21' would once again be as celebrated as it was in the first twenty years of its life."

Cogan and his then-partner Stephen Swid paid $21 million for '21' and invested another $10 million to modernize its systems and restore its interior. "The building was in need of extensive renovation," says Cogan. "But what excited me about acquiring '21' was that, like Sotheby's, it represented an extraordinary institution that was no

longer in ascent, and I believed that I could reinvigorate its spirit and reestablish its preeminent position."

Two people played particularly important roles in the restoration of the building. Foremost was Maureen Cogan, whose vision, love and knowledge of art, and high aesthetic standards set the tone for the at-the-time-controversial renovation. She called in art experts to authenticate the extensive collection of Frederic Remingtons and other paintings, drawings, and sculptures that had been acquired in the purchase. She and Marshall traveled widely in Europe and North America to augment the existing art collection with important new acquisitions. And she personally supervised the renovation of facilities such as the ladies' lounges, which had received little attention under the formerly all-male management team.

Marshall and Maureen Cogan chose their close friend and talented interior designer, Charles Pfister, to oversee the enormous task of refurbishing '21' from the cellar up. His orders were to redo the club in a manner that was respectful of its past and skimped on nothing.

New, custom-designed all-wool carpeting was installed throughout most of the building. Where banquettes had been covered in Naugahide®, they were reupholstered in top-grade leather. Leather-covered upholstered dining chairs of Pfister's own design replaced the existing chairs in the main dining room and adjoining banquet rooms. Walls were covered with fine fabrics. The moldering trophy heads in the old Hunt Room were removed and, at Senator Edward Kennedy's suggestion, the room was restyled as the Harbor Room, featuring a collection of historic paintings of sailing ships searched out and purchased by Maureen and Marshall.

Concurrently, Cogan invited Ken Aretsky and Anne Rosenszweig, founders of Arcadia—a restaurant then (and still) lauded for the excellence and originality of its cuisine—to head up a new management team at '21.' While Pfister orchestrated the round-the-clock restoration of the premises—completed in a remarkable four months—the new CEOs hired Alain Sailhac, then head chef at Le Cirque, to reorganize '21's kitchen. One member of the talented team Sailhac brought with him was a saucier named Michael Lomonaco.

When the renovations were completed and '21' reopened on May 11, 1987, two menus were in place: a still fairly traditional '21' menu downstairs in the barroom, and a more "nouvelle" menu upstairs in the dining room. It was a fiasco because it was confusing. Many regulars, for instance, always ate upstairs, and they always ate steak. But now they were allowed to eat steak only downstairs. Cogan takes complete responsibility: "I made a concerted effort to upgrade the quality of the food. But I did initially make it too frou-frou."

Ultimately it was agreed that Rosenszweig would return to Arcadia. Cogan and Aretsky continued searching for a formula that would both bring in new business and woo back '21's formerly faithful. " '21' requires a very special kind of a person to be its chef," explains Aretsky, who continued as CEO at '21' until early 1995. Unlike most any other restaurant you'll ever go to, you can order anything you want at '21.' A lot of places, if you try to order something off the menu they'll tell you that's too bad, you can't have it. At '21' you can have anything you want. A lot of chefs don't like that."

THE RIGHT CHEF FOR THE JOB

After Alain decided to leave, Michael Lomonaco, who had worked at '21' as saucier under Alain but had left to become sous chef at Maxwell's Plum, showed some interest in returning to '21.' "Michael

Here's One Way to Start a Horse Show

By TOM REILLY.

"HOW does a horse show happen?" The inquisitor was Broadway Bill, the man in the pinched coat. Bill had seen plenty of fights start. He knew that New York kids learned to hunt in a bassinet. But just how people get started into yanking horses over fences for ribbons was beyond him.

So it was only natural to give him the story of the Westchester Embassy Club show, which went over so well for the second time at Armonk, N. Y. This effete exhibition got its start when Jock Whitney stopped in Jack and Charlie's well known cocktail cavern at 21 W. 52nd St. one day to settle up.

The millionaire sportsman had staged a few parties. This was during the great Daiquiri Drought. Consequently the bill wasn't small. In fact, it was large enough to make Jock suspicious. If you remember, at that time all party bills were open to suspicion. So the noted racing man turned to Charlie and said, "How about me paying you in horse flesh?"

* * *

YOU see, Whitney was no chump. He knew more about horses than Charlie did about horses' necks. And Sir Charles knows the value of that palatable drink down to the last lump of ice. Well, after much stalling and good humored haggling the deal was closed. Whitney agreed to send three horses to the Westchester Embassy Club, which is No. 21's summer home. The bill was settled.

When word of this got around the two restaurant proprietors found themselves recipients of a great deal of joshing on the part of the customers. They were accused of serving one of the nags in the caviar, and it was rumored that all three of them had died of acute alcoholism one week after their arrival.

Then Charlie inadvertently let it get around that he was riding one of those horses. That was fatal. The customers were sure he couldn't do it. You see, Charlie is short and weighs some 200 pounds. So one day when he couldn't stand the kidding any more he said he'd prove his ability. He shut up the place on 52nd St. and took every one there up to Armonk to see his exhibition.

Needless to say, it was a success. Charlie only fell off six times. The customers all got to riding horses around. And they liked the place so well they suggested that the proprietors put on a regular show. Taking hints from various horse customers, Jack and Charlie did this. Their show is now one of the best. The big prize in the show is "The 21 Challenge Cup," for hunters. And that's how one horse show started.

* * *

What started as a barroom prank developed into one of the top horse shows of its day. (Courtesy of '21')

HORSING AROUND AT '21,' PART I:

"I'll never get over the shock of finding a horse grazing at '21' . . ." begins Gael Greene's first postrenovation review of '21.' Owner Marshall Cogan must have smiled when he read that line. Cogan bought the horse—a life-size, lifelike eighteenth-century English woodcarving sporting a custom-made '21' horse blanket—specifically for '21,' specifically for that location.

Neither the iconography nor the irreverence are out of keeping for '21.' Jack Kriendler set the tone with his love of horses, riding, and all the trappings attendant to the sport. In the summer of 1931, at the height of the Depression, Jack and Charlie opened '21's country counterpart: the Westchester Embassy Club, which included, in addition to the ubiquitous country club attractions of swimming, tennis, golf, and moonlit dances on the terrace, a stable of riding horses and a show ring for jumping competitions that attracted what one sports writer called "the best hunt team competition of the summer . . . [including] the famous hunting strings of Mrs. John Hay Whitney, Mrs. Bernard F. Gimbel and Mrs. John V. Bouvier, 3rd" (mother of Jacqueline Bouvier Kennedy Onassis).

had a deep love for '21.' Great respect for the place and for the history," continues Aretsky.

"He came in with the right approach, which was: 'I'm not going to teach '21' how to run a restaurant, I'm going to take what they have and enhance it. I'm going to take '21's traditional chicken hash and refine it. I'm going to make the '21' burger the best hamburger in the world. And I'm going to create my own dishes as time goes along.' I give Michael a lot of credit. Michael had the right personality. He worked like a dog. He put together a very good team of people, and it really has worked. It continues to work."

Perhaps the ultimate compliment to Lomonaco's ability to bridge the gap between the old customers and the new cuisine is this confession from Jerry Berns: "Michael's chicken hash is better than ours ever was." To Cogan, of course, the ultimate proof of the pudding is the bottom line: "Since 1987 we've turned the restaurant around completely, from running deeply in the red to solidly in the black."

'21'

Chef Michael Lomonaco, as rendered by Leroy Neiman

$\mathscr{S}$IMPLY THE BEST

*The discovery of a new dish does more for the happiness
than the discovery of a star.*
—ANTHELME BRILLAT-SAVARIN

In 1923 Jack Kriendler and Charlie Berns probably could have made a killing just peddling rotgut booze and bologna sandwiches. But Jack and Charlie had ambitions way beyond that. Right from the start, no expense was too great to insure their whiskey was "the real McCoy." (The expression refers to Captain William McCoy, a rumrunner known for the purity and authenticity of his goods.)

Jack and Charlie's commitment to quality didn't stop at the bar. In the *Fortune* article that included the Margaret Bourke White photograph shown opposite, the writer described how, "At famous '21,' best-known of all speakeasies, wholesale food bills run $50,000 a year, Burgundies arrive at the table lounging properly in silver baskets, and the pressed duck has a city-wide fame."

Jack Kriendler set the standard for the kitchen the day he hired Kaiser Wilhelm's former chef. Cooking for the German head of state had taught Chef Geib a thing or two about European cuisine and quite a bit about catering to a demanding audience. A factor contributing to the continuity of '21's menu over the years has been the continuity of leadership in the kitchen. Henri Geib presided as head chef from the day '21' opened its doors until the mid-1940s, and trained Yves Louis Ploneis to succeed him. Ploneis in turn trained

This photograph by Margaret Bourke White was part of a spread featuring the "best known of all speakeasies" in the June 1933 issue of Fortune *magazine—a full six months before the repeal of Prohibition. Charlie Berns (in the foreground, wearing glasses) and Jack Kriendler (at the rear table, with his hand at his chin) are shown dining in the Tapestry Room, now a private dining room. The stairstep collection of Hine champagne bottles on the mantel (apparently still full at the time) are described in the caption as (smallest to largest): half nip, nip, pint, imperial pint, quart, magnum, jeroboam, rhoboam, methuzelah, salmanazar, and balthazar. Today this collection of historic bottles (which were emptied somewhere along the line) can still be seen displayed on the third-floor landing at '21' (Photo: Time-Life Archives)*

Anthony Pedretti, who came to '21' in 1959 and became *chef du cuisine* following Ploneis's retirement in 1966.

Jack and Charlie—and later brothers Mac, Bob, Pete, and Jerry—went to incredible lengths to get the freshest and the finest for '21.' For example, during hunting season, '21' always served a lot of game, which was flown in fresh from as far away as Scotland at a time when air freight was still in its infancy. At one point '21' even had two wholesale fine foods divisions, Iron Gate Products and Fidelis Trading and Fishing Company, which imported everything from asparagus from Baja and melons from Ecuador to caviar from Russia.

Today many kinds of game are farmed and readily available, so we have included a significant number of game recipes in this book and some suggested resources (page 381) for ordering game and other items you might be unable to find where you live. After all, it wouldn't be a '21' cookbook without recipes for foie gras, morels, caviar, partridge and the like.

'21's menu always has been strongly influenced by the preferences of its owners and friends as well as its chefs. '21' Creamed Spinach (page 252), a favorite of Jack Kriendler's, was referred to for decades as Spinach à la Jack. And '21' Traditional Hunter Salad (page 101), still a popular appetizer at '21,' is named for tennis champion Francis Townsend Hunter, who chaired '21's country club annex, the Westchester Embassy Club, during Prohibition. Along with Chef Lomonaco's own signature dishes, we are pleased to be able to share some of these '21' classics—labeled throughout the book as '21' Traditional recipes.

In recent years, the trend at '21'—as in general—has been toward lighter, more healthful foods. More salads. More vegetables and grains. Vegetables and grains play important roles in the appetizer, soup, and salad chapters of this book as well as in their own chapters. '21' buys organic produce whenever possible. Locally grown, when we can. We seek out free-range veal, poultry, and lamb. Meats that are drug and hormone free. We avoid fish species that are being overharvested, and encourage you to do likewise.

We also encourage you to lobby for better quality and better selections at your local markets. Don't assume they can't, or won't, get

The continuity in '21's kitchen has been extraordinary. During '21's first half century only three people wore the top toque: Chef Henri Geib, shown above at the stove with Jack Kriendler; Chef Yves Louis Ploneis, pictured at right cooking something up for honored guests from the 149th Bombardment Squadron; and Chef Anthony Pedretti, shown below reviewing menus with Pete Kriendler (Photo of Chef Geib by Pix Publishing, Inc.; photo of Chef Plonies courtesy of 149th BOMRONL VaANG; photo of Chef Pedretti courtesy of the Herald-News)

you fresh tomatillas, chanterelles, or mizuna, or that they can't stock organic produce or free-range poultry. '21' hasn't always had some of these things. But it does now.

In the old days, everything on '21's menu was strictly à la carte. If you wanted potatoes or spinach with your steak, you had to order it separately. Today entrées, and even appetizers and salads, are designed to be nutritionally balanced as well as delicious. An appetizer of smoked salmon may be nested in a bed of greens; a serving of double-cut lamb chops flanked by grilled eggplant, tomato, and rosemary; grilled sea bass served with shaved fennel, artichoke, and sun-dried tomato salad.

'21'

Michael Lomonaco, right, takes pride in being a "hands-on" chef. (Photo: Christopher Baker)

We have included suggestions for complementary vegetable and grain dishes at the end of each recipe for meat, fish, poultry, and game, and specific wines for each entrée as well as more generalized rules of thumb for selecting wines to complement appetizers and desserts. Last but not least, the entertainment chapter includes menus that "put it all together" for everything from an intimate candlelight dinner to a New Year's Eve blowout.

Translating the cooking at '21,' where there are dozens of pairs of hands to tend the stoves, into something you can do comfortably at home hasn't been easy. By sheer quantity, restaurant and home cooking are two distinctly different things. So, while all the recipes in this book have appeared on à la carte or banquet menus at '21,' there are other dishes we have not attempted to translate. Recipes also have been simplified—without changing their essential natures—so that their preparation can be accommodated despite the too-busy lives most of us live today.

Even at '21,' where you might expect the presentation to be elaborate, food is not taken to the point where you won't recognize it. "Presentation is important," says Chef Lomonaco, "but I prefer a natural look, one in which all the elements that make up a dish are identifiable. It's a style of presentation with a homey feeling, where taste and the freshness of the ingredients are paramount."

So, browse through the recipes and the wine recommendations. Enjoy the anecdotes, the photographs, the wonderful cartoons and illustrations donated to '21' over the years. Then pick a recipe, a wine, and a night, and treat yourself to a culinary experience that otherwise could happen only at '21.'

'21'

TOOTS SHOR SENT ME . . .

*A*lmost as famous as Jack and Charlie's '21,' Toots Shor and his watering hole of the same name were fellow 52nd Street institutions from 1960 to 1970. Before Toots moved his saloon into the building Jimmy Hoffa had built for him in 1960, Toots's saloon was a block south of '21,' at a location now marked by a bronze plaque. Toots had a management style that was decidedly different from that of the Kriendlers and Bernses, a fact that resulted in '21' securing two of its most valued longtime employees. Walter Weiss, just out of the marines in 1945, lasted less than a week at Toots Shor's. He's been at '21' for more than half a century, working his way through the ranks to become one of the best-known and beloved maître d's in the world. Harry Lavin, originally from Sligo, Ireland, came to '21' from Toots Shor's in 1974. Harry started out serving drinks in '21's lounge, while waiting for an opening for a captain in the upstairs dining room. Within six months an even better opportunity came along: guardianship of '21's front desk. Harry has held the post for twenty years, greeting and guiding guests with his special brand of soft-spoken diplomacy.

*W*hen things weren't too busy at his own place, Toots Shor, second from right, would often stop in for a drink at '21.' In this 1952 photo for a Saturday Evening Post *article entitled "The Speakeasy that Outlived the Ritz," Shor is pictured with, from left to right: Ben Wright, publisher of* Field & Stream; *press agent Larry Hoover; Robert Ruark; Bob Considine; Mac Kriendler; and bartender Emil Bernasconi. (Courtesy of Hans Knopf—Pix)*

On more than a few occasions, guests would navigate the short distance from Toots Shor's to '21' on suspiciously wobbly pins. Along with '21,' Toots Shor's was one of Ernest Hemingway's favorite hangouts. Jackie Gleason was notorious for stoking up at Toots Shor's, then repairing (supposedly for dinner) to '21.' The routine was invariably the same: Take a quiet table in the back (table 30). Order a rib steak and a bottle of Martin Beaujolais to be put on ice. Then drink straight bourbon until he was sound asleep. As best anyone can remember, for all the times Jackie Gleason ordered (and paid for) a rib steak, he never once ate at '21.'

‘21’ Traditional South Side

■

‘21’ Traditional Ramos Gin Fizz

■

‘21’ Traditional Bloody Mary

■

Bloody Bullshot

■

Papa Doble

■

‘21’ Traditional Santa Anita

■

‘21’ Traditional Café Diable

IN THE BEGINNING

*Quick, get me out of this wet coat
and into a dry martini.*

—ROBERT BENCHLEY

Although the succession of clubs Jack and Charlie operated between 1923 and Prohibition's end gained a respectable reputation for the quality of their food, food was hardly the lifeblood of their business. Wines and spirits—the best of both—were '21's earliest claim to fame. Several of '21's traditional drinks are thought to have been invented at the club, among them the Southside, the Bloody Mary, and the Ramos Gin Fizz. The manufacturers of B&B credit '21' with having devised the combination of Benedictine and brandy that became so popular the Benedictines began bottling it premixed in 1937.

Today the most frequently ordered "drink" in '21's barroom—winter or summer—is iced tea. Among alcoholic beverages, wine is the runaway leader, and the bar pours a large, interesting, and ever-changing selection of wines by the glass from all over the world.

'21's legendary wine cellar merits a book all its own. Today the wine cellar and its wonderful door are the subject of a fascinating tour that can be arranged by request. The cellar also hosts spectacular six-course private wine dinners for two to twelve guests. Each wine served is presented with a personal explanation by the sommelier. (We've reprinted a sample menu in the chapter entitled "Entertaining in the '21' Tradition.")

The cellar is laden with tradition, from the booth where New York's former Mayor "Gentleman Jim" Walker entertained his mistress, to the private stock bottles held in reserve for Elizabeth Taylor, Frank Sinatra, President Gerald Ford, and many others. Another such tradition is the laying down of a bottle (generally of cognac or port) when a child is born, to be brought out at his or her twenty-first birthday celebration.

Over the years, the quality of '21's wine cellar has been consistently excellent, with particular strength in Burgundies. Currently the cellar houses approximately 25,000 bottles, including private stock. At any given time, there are about 500 different wines and vintages to choose from on '21's impressive list. These range from good, drinkable table wines priced under $20 to such legends as the Château Lafite Rothschild 1966, listed at $1,400 for a double magnum.

'21' was one of the first important restaurants to showcase California wines, helping to put them on the map internationally as well as on the East Coast. In the wine notes included with the entrée recipes, we have suggested California wines as often as French. We also have made an effort to select wines that should be readily accessible, but in case any of our suggestions are unobtainable in your area, you can use our recommendations simply as guides to direction or style, substituting the same varietal from a different vineyard or even from a different country.

When choosing wine to drink with food, keeping a few simple fundamentals in mind will help you make happier choices. Rather than dogmatically serving red wines with red meats and white wines with poultry and fish, it is more useful to look at the nature and intensity of the food and the wine you propose to serve together. How rich is the dish? How spicy? How light- or heavy-bodied is the wine? Is it fruity and mellow or astringent and assertive?

The most successful wine-food combinations take into account the similarities and contrasts between the two. A similar match might be a high-acid Italian Barbera served with an acidic tomato sauce, or a sweet Sauterne served with rich foie gras. One example of a contrasting pair would be the saltiness of Stilton cheese with the sweetness of a good port; another, the spiciness and piquancy of barbecued pork or venison chili with the freshness of a fruity Beaujolais or Rioja.

Ideally, the combination you choose won't mask the special or subtle tastes of either the food or the wine. If you're unsure, ask. People who work in better wine stores usually do so because they love wines and enjoy sharing their knowledge. Ultimately, no matter what we or anyone else suggest, what tastes best to you is what you should drink. After all, the real name of the game is enjoyment. Cheers!

(© KFS)

'21' Traditional
South Side

SERVES 1

*I*nvented at '21,' this variation on a mint julep
is ordered mainly in the summer.

2 ounces vodka, gin, or rum

Juice of 1 lemon (about 2
   tablespoons)

2 teaspoons granulated sugar

1 tablespoon fresh mint leaves

Combine all ingredients with ice in a shaker. Shake vigorously to
bruise mint leaves. Strain into a chilled Tom Collins glass filled with
ice.

'21' TRADITIONAL RAMOS GIN FIZZ

SERVES 1

Lest you think this a ladies' drink, keep in mind that it was Bogie's standing order at '21.'

2 ounces gin

Juice of 1 lemon (about 2 tablespoons)

1 heaping teaspoon granulated sugar

1 egg white

1 ounce light cream

A few drops of orange-flower water

Club soda

Combine all ingredients except club soda with ice in a shaker. Shake, then strain into a chilled, 12-ounce Tom Collins glass, and add club soda to taste.

THE BACALLING OF BOGIE

Before Lauren Bacall (Betty, as she is affectionately known at '21') came along, Humphrey Bogart wasn't always '21's most welcome guest. True, you'll find his bronze plaque, marked "Bogie's Corner," behind table 30 in the center section of the bar; but in his hard-drinking pre-Bacall days, there were many nights when he was invited to depart sooner rather than later. Bacall had a happily sobering impact on Bogie. They came to '21' often as a couple, and Bacall remains a valued friend of '21' to this day.

'21' TRADITIONAL
BLOODY MARY

SERVES 1

*D*uring World War II, vodka gained enormous popularity, not because it was Russian but because, unlike Scotch, it could be made in America. Following the war, Bloody Marys were so popular at '21' that it wasn't unusual to serve a hundred or more before lunch.

1^1/$_2$ ounces vodka, chilled

2 ounces tomato juice, chilled

Dash of Worcestershire sauce

Dash of celery salt

Dash of Tabasco sauce

Salt and freshly ground black
pepper to taste

Combine all ingredients with ice in a shaker. Shake well and pour into a chilled cocktail glass.

'21'

*L*iving Legends Pete Kriendler, left, and Jerry Berns, right, lunch together at table 1 every day but Thursday. Younger brothers of '21's founding partners, they have been at '21' since 1938, a combined total of more than a century. (Photos: Christopher Baker)

BLOODY BULLSHOT

SERVES 1

*J*ust as the name implies, the Bloody Bullshot (popularized, if not invented, at '21') is a marriage of a Bloody Mary and a Bullshot—both time-honored eye-openers for the morning after.

1 ounce vodka

1 ounce tomato juice

1 ounce beef bouillon

1 drop Tabasco sauce

Dash of Worcestershire sauce

Dash of celery salt

Freshly ground black pepper to taste

Combine all ingredients with ice in a shaker. Shake and serve, ungarnished, straight or over ice.

PAPA DOBLE

SERVES 1

A variation on the frozen daiquiri, the Papa Doble was invented at Havana's La Florida bar and named for the bar's most famous patron and prodigious consumer of the product. (He claimed an all-time record of sixteen at one sitting.) When he was in New York, Papa Hemingway also ordered this potion at '21's "Long Mahogany."

$2^1/_2$ ounces Bacardi White Label Rum

Juice of 2 limes

Juice of $1/_2$ grapefruit

6 drops maraschino juice

In a blender, combine ingredients with crushed ice and blend 15 to 20 seconds. Serve in a large stemware goblet.

LIVING OUTSIDE THE LAW

*W*hen we think of underworld activities during the Prohibition era, Chicago may be the first place to come to mind. But with 32,000 speakeasies, New York also attracted more than its fair share of gangsters. None was more feared than John T. Noland, alias "Legs" Diamond, extortionist and silent partner in numerous speakeasies. Called "The Clay Pigeon" because of the many times he had been shot, Diamond is said to have personally murdered or put out contracts on dozens of gangsters and to have caused the disappearance of ten employees and customers from the Hotsy Totsy Club (a 52nd Street neighbor of the '21' Club) who had the misfortune to witness one of his murders.

LEGS DIAMOND LEGENDS, PART I:
FLIRTING WITH DANGER

*I*n his biography, *Papa Hemingway,* A. E. Hotchner describes how the struggling young writer, behind in his rent and in need of a good meal, was smuggled by Jack Kriendler into a Prohibition-era private party at '21,' where he was introduced to the most beautiful girl he had ever seen. The attraction was mutual, and the pair lingered long past closing time.

"She would not let me take her home, but when I awoke the next day in my Brevoort squirrel cage, my first thought was to find her again. I hurried back to Twenty-One, but as I came in, Jack pulled me to one side. 'Listen, Ernie,' he said, 'you better lay low for a while. I should have warned you—that was Legs Diamond's girl, and he's due back in town at five o'clock.' "

LEGS DIAMOND LEGENDS, PART II:
LITTLE BIG MAN AND THE MOB

*S*hort, stout, bespectacled: Charlie Berns was hardly the stereotypical tough guy. But when three of Legs Diamond's bully boys showed up shortly after Jack and Charlie had settled into their new digs at 21 West 52nd Street—announcing that their boss wanted a piece of the action—Charlie saw red and took a swing. Guardian of the peephole Jimmy Coslove joined Charlie, and together they muscled the bad guys out the door. It wasn't long before word came back that Legs was putting contracts out on Charlie and Jimmy. Fortunately for them, someone got to Legs first, ending Diamond's infamous career on December 18, 1931.

'21' TRADITIONAL
SANTA ANITA

SERVES 1

This sophisticated "snow cone" was named after the California racetrack, but no one seems to remember why.

Shaved ice   2 ounces Scotch whiskey

Fill an Old-Fashioned glass with shaved ice. Top with Scotch.

In Sweet Smell of Success, *filmed in 1957, P.R. flack Sidney Falco, played by Tony Curtis, toadies up to J. J. Hunsecker, most powerful columnist in America, played by Burt Lancaster, as Hunsecker holds court and enjoys a Café Diable at '21.'*
(Courtesy of Photofest)

'21' TRADITIONAL CAFÉ DIABLE

Café Diable used to be a familiar after-dinner ritual at '21,' prepared by the captains at tableside in a special copper bowl and served in tall skinny devil-emblazoned Café Diable cups.

Peel of 1 lemon (removed in a single strip)

Peel of 1 orange (removed in a single strip)

24 whole cloves

2 teaspoons granulated sugar

2 sticks cinnamon

2 ounces brandy

3 cups hot espresso coffee

2 ounces Kirschwasser

Stud the lemon and orange peels with the cloves. Place in a tin-lined copper bowl or chafing dish and add the sugar, cinnamon sticks, and brandy. Cautiously light the brandy, allow to flame for a moment or two, and then add the coffee, which will extinguish the flames. Remove the peels and cinnamon. Add the Kirschwasser and serve immediately in Café Diable or demitasse cups.

'21' TRADITIONAL CRAB CAKE

∎

AMERICAN CAVIAR IN SIMPLE PASTRY CUPS

∎

TEQUILA-CURED SALMON GRAVLAX

∎

SHELLFISH RAVIOLI IN SAFFRON BROTH

∎

SMOKED SALMON AND TROUT WITH CHIVE OIL

∎

ROASTED OYSTERS WITH COUNTRY BACON

∎

SESAME SCALLOPS WITH GINGER DRESSING

∎

TUNA KEBABS WITH WASABI DIPPING SAUCE

∎

MIXED GRILLED VEGETABLE CROSTINI

∎

POLENTA CORN CAKES WITH
WILD MUSHROOM PAN ROAST

∎

PUMPKIN RAVIOLI WITH PROSCIUTTO AND SAGE

∎

'21' TRADITIONAL STEAK TARTARE

∎

FOIE GRAS WITH SWEET AND SOUR CABBAGE

∎

PROSCIUTTO AND PORT-POACHED PEARS

$\mathcal{S}$TARTERS

Even at '21,' where people are more likely to pull out all the stops and indulge themselves than they would be at home, multicourse meals are becoming more the exception than the rule. But that doesn't mean people skip the appetizer section of the menu and go directly to the entrées. Many of the dishes listed as appetizers on '21's menu are equally appropriate as entrées for lunch or a light supper. Some order two appetizers and no entrée. Or a double-portion appetizer as an entrée.

Some of these recipes would be perfect as pregame snacks, picnic food for a lawn concert, finger food for a cocktail party, or a light supper after the theater. And those-that-must-come-first offer inspiration for launching an important dinner party or holiday feast with appropriate panache.

Several can be made ahead so they don't add to your last-minute workload. And several more are light enough in calories not to threaten your waistline. All have been extremely popular with '21's guests. There's every reason to believe they will be popular with yours as well.

If you're planning a multicourse meal—for guests or just for family—choose your entrée *first*, then select an appetizer that will blend well. For instance, if you're serving a meat entrée, choose something

WINE NOTES:

Every course of a meal, be it a simple home-style supper or an elaborate holiday feast, tastes even better with a well-chosen, complementary wine. Thus, each course deserves its fair share of thought and consideration. Whether the opener is a light salad or sautéed foie gras, the distinguishing characteristics of both the food and the wine should be your starting points in choosing what to uncork.

For example: A clean, flinty chablis, or a good bone-dry muscadet would work well with a selection of fresh oysters. The same chablis, with its higher acid and earthy style, would work equally well as a contrast to Polenta Corn Cakes with Wild Mushroom Pan Roast.

(continued on next page)

(continued from previous page)

When the occasion calls for some drama, such as when wild partridge or rack of lamb will be the main dish, you may want to delay the evening's "crescendo" until their presentation. This could mean selecting an unassuming wine to start, so as not to upstage the great, mature Bordeaux that will accompany the lamb or the splendid Taurasi attending the partridge. Many times, the first course ultimately proves to be the most memorable. Be prepared. Don't give short shrift to the selection of its accompanying wine.

'21'

During World War II, apparently not all of the action was on the battlefield. As this photograph testifies, on at least one occasion fourteen stars' worth of general officers converged on '21'.
(Courtesy of '21')

light to start: say a fish or vegetable first course. If your main course is going to be fish or vegetables, you might opt for a richer appetizer, such as foie gras or steak tartare.

You can't menu-plan by a rule book, but in my own planning—both as executive chef at '21' and in my own home—I like to balance a lighter course against a heavier course and avoid overlapping flavors. For instance, if I'm serving a crab cake first, I wouldn't serve a shrimp or lobster entrée. Instead, I would probably choose a lighter fish, such as snapper or sea bass. If I served gravlax first, I wouldn't have grilled salmon afterward. The flavors are too similar. But having said all that, I'll end by saying what I believe most fervently: Trust your own taste; serve what you want and eat what you like.

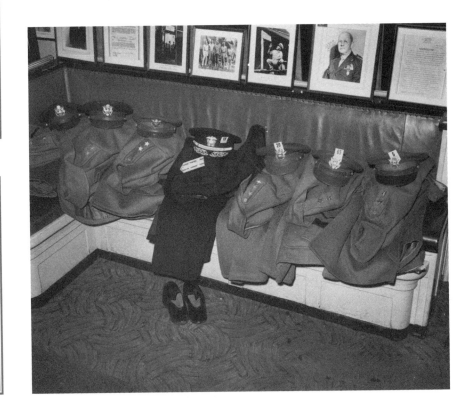

Watercolor of Charlie Berns, which now hangs framed in '21's Puncheon Room, originally appeared as a full-page illustration in Vogue. (Courtesy of '21')

'21' TRADITIONAL
CRAB CAKE

SERVES 8 AS AN APPETIZER, 4 AS AN ENTRÉE

Crab cakes have been a tradition at '21' for many years. The authentic Maryland-style version we serve now is hugely popular, both as an appetizer and as an entrée.

1 pound fresh jumbo lump crabmeat

1 sweet red pepper, diced

1 yellow pepper, diced

1 tablespoon vegetable oil

6 slices fresh white bread, crusts removed

1 tablespoon finely chopped fresh garlic

1–2 jalapeño peppers, seeded and finely chopped

1/4 cup chopped fresh cilantro leaves

1/4 cup mayonnaise

2 tablespoons Old Bay brand seasoning

Salt and freshly ground black pepper to taste

Vegetable oil for sautéing

Clean the crabmeat of all shell fragments but do not crumble the lumps of crab. Sauté the diced sweet peppers in the 1 tablespoon vegetable oil until wilted and set aside to cool. Place the bread in a food processor fitted with a metal blade, and process until finely crumbled. Measure and reserve 2 tablespoons of the bread crumbs to use in the filling. The remaining bread crumbs will be used to coat the crab cakes.

Mix the crabmeat with the sweet peppers, garlic, jalapeño peppers, cilantro leaves, and mayonnaise. Add the seasoning powder, 2 tablespoons of bread crumbs, and salt and pepper. Mix well, then refrigerate 20 minutes before continuing.

Cover a work surface with waxed paper sprinkled with the reserved bread crumbs. Using a 2-ounce ice cream scoop, form 8 equal-size portions of crabmeat. With the palm of your hand, pat each portion into a disk-shaped cake approximately ³/₄-inch thick. It is important for the crab cakes to be the same thickness so that they will cook uniformly. Press each cake into the bread crumbs, turning them so they coat evenly on all sides. Refrigerate at least 1 hour to prevent the cakes from crumbling during cooking.

Preheat the oven to 375°. No more than 30 minutes before you plan to serve the crab cakes, add enough vegetable oil to cover the bottom of an ovenproof sauté pan. Heat until just before it begins to smoke. Add the crab cakes gently, being careful not to crowd the pan. (Cook them in two batches if necessary.) When the crab cakes are well browned on both sides, bake them 6 minutes to ensure that they are fully cooked and hot at the center. Serve with Chili Mayonnaise (page 358), or mayonnaise flavored with mustard or horseradish, and garnish with a small salad.

CHEF'S TIP:

The "secret" of a perfect crab cake is to use the finest, freshest crabmeat money can buy, and plenty of it.

AMERICAN CAVIAR IN SIMPLE PASTRY CUPS

SERVES 4

CHEF'S TIP:

As with jewelry, fine art, and other precious commodities, there is always the temptation for unscrupulous vendors to represent lesser caviars as higher, costlier grades. Your best defense is always to buy your caviar from a dealer of impeccable reputation, and one who is doing enough business to have the frequency of turnover that assures freshness. (See "Resources" for mail-order sources.)

*M*any people are intimidated by caviar, and rightfully so. There is an elaborate mystique associated with the roe (eggs) of certain fish—especially sturgeon—and whole books have been written on the subject. (See pages 49–50 for enough tidbits to get you confidently through a cocktail party conversation on the subject.) For this recipe, suffice it to say that while some caviar (especially Russian beluga) is incredibly expensive, this appetizer need not bust your budget. American sturgeon, salmon, or whitefish caviars are all reasonably priced and delicious. Often they are available in specialty shops and better supermarkets as fresh products and are rarely oversalted. If Russian caviar is within your reach, by all means, indulge yourself and your guests. But if you're looking for good taste at a more down-to-earth price, try some of our homegrown varieties.

1/2 stick (4 tablespoons) melted unsalted butter

3 sheets phyllo dough, thawed according to package directions

1 small red Bermuda onion (about 1/2 cup, finely diced)

1 medium leek (white and light green parts), split, washed, and cut into 1 1/2-inch-long julienne

1/2 cup crème fraîche, sour cream, or plain yogurt

4 ounces caviar

2 tablespoons chopped fresh chives

Preheat the oven to 325°. Lightly brush melted butter onto the sheets of phyllo and stack one atop the other. Cut the resulting stack into 4 equal squares. Brush melted butter into 4 wells of a muffin tin. Place one layered sheet into each well to form a pastry cup with "peaks" that flare out dramatically. Bake the pastry cups 20 minutes, or until they are golden brown and crisp.

Meanwhile, sauté the onion and leek together in the remaining melted butter until wilted but not caramelized. Cool to room temperature.

When the phyllo has baked and the vegetables have cooled, assemble the dish by placing a generous portion of leek/onion mixture on the bottom of each pastry cup. Add 2 tablespoons crème fraîche, sour cream, or yogurt, and top with 1 ounce caviar and $\frac{1}{2}$ tablespoon chives.

'21'

CAVIAR

For the Play I remembered pleas'd not the Million, 'twas Cauiarie to the Generall; but it was . . . an excellent Play.

—HAMLET, *II. II. 457*

While those who aren't hooked on caviar are likely to ask: "Why all the fuss over fish eggs?" the eggs—or roe—of certain fish, particularly sturgeon, can retail for hundreds of dollars a pound. Why? Aficionados' explanations of caviar's appeal border on the mystical. As with sashimi or tapioca, either you get it or you don't.

Those who "get it" have been known to go to great lengths to do so. The most sought-after caviar is made from the roe of four species of sturgeon (sterlet, beluga, osetra, and sevruga) that live in the Caspian Sea. Iranian caviar traditionally has been considered the very finest, not because the sturgeon are different from those harvested by the Russians, but because of the excellence of Iran's processing of the roe. The '21' Club has had a standing order for Iranian caviar for years, but it could be years more before the embargo is lifted.

Sterlet, made from the roe of a small Caspian sturgeon, is so rare you're unlikely ever to find it on the open market. Beluga is next in scarcity. It's available at fine restaurants and in specialty gourmet stores, but only for a formidable price. Osetra and sevruga caviars are also highly prized and fairly expensive.

(continued on next page)

(continued from previous page)

Fortunately, costliest doesn't necessarily mean tastiest. Many prefer the nutty flavor of osetra to the relatively acidic taste of beluga. (Sevruga is the most intensely flavored of the three.) None should taste fishy. If caviar does, it's past its prime, or not the genuine article to begin with. Texture is also important in judging caviar. Beluga eggs are big and firm, bursting most noticably on the tongue. "Pressed caviar," made from broken eggs, is far cheaper, but some would liken it to drinking flat champagne.

Although technically it is salt that transforms roe to caviar, saltier does not mean better. The finest fresh caviar is only lightly salted—*malassol*—a designation that means the caviar contains between 3.5 and 5 percent salt. At the other extreme, lumpfish caviar (with 11 percent salt) is widely available in American supermarkets and reasonably cheap—but not particularly appealing. Fortunately, there are several happy mediums: Fresh American whitefish, sturgeon, and salmon caviars are all deliciously affordable. Whitefish roe is made up of tiny golden yellow beads—very sweet and mild. Salmon roe is larger, fattier, and has a lovely "salmon" color. American sturgeon, if properly processed, is, in my opinion, the equal of Russian sevruga. If your fish supplier doesn't carry any of these, ask if they can be ordered, or check our "Resources" listing. The difference between fresh and pasteurized is worth the wait.

Caviar has always had a place on '21's menu. A 1933 menu lists Imported Makaroff Caviar for $2.25 ($2.50 "aux Blinis"). For comparison, Prime Rib was $1.70 that day. Today the cost ratio is about the same, with an ounce of Russian beluga about twice the price of most of '21's dinner entrées.

During World War II, when Russian sources of caviar dried up, '21' simply shopped the other side of the Caspian, upholding its standards with Persia's best. At war's end, when General Walter Bedel Smith was dispatched as ambassador to Russia, securing a caviar connection for '21' was one of his first unofficial acts.

Caviar service at '21' is a simple, straightforward ritual. Beluga is served tableside by a tuxedoed captain, straight from its original tin—generally a 2-kilo (4.4 pound) tin. The tin is presented on a bed of ice in a silver bowl and spooned out by the captain in 1-ounce portions, using a special mother-of-pearl spoon. Caviar traditionally is served and eaten with a bone or mother-of-pearl spoon rather than a silver spoon: first, to avoid off-flavors caused by the metal tarnishing on contact with the salted roe; and second, to reduce the likelihood of breaking the roe with a metal spoon's sharper edge.

The condiments that traditionally accompany caviar are then offered in separate little dishes, to be served onto the same plate as the caviar. These include chopped egg whites, egg yolks, onion, capers, parsley, sour cream, and toast points. On special occasions I serve caviar with buckwheat blinis, tiny buckwheat pancakes like those shown in the color photograph. Simply follow the buckwheat pancake package directions, adding 3 tablespoons honey for each cup pancake mix. Perfection!

(© WDP)

TEQUILA-CURED
SALMON GRAVLAX

SERVES 6 TO 8 AS AN APPETIZER

*F*ew people realize that gravlax is really quite easy to make, and for a fraction of the price of store-bought gravlax or smoked salmon. Rather than using smoke or heat, this traditional Scandinavian technique uses salt, sugar, alcohol, time, and a pressing weight to produce a silky, moist-textured cured fish that is as versatile and appealing as smoked salmon. In this New World rendition—one of the most popular appetizers served at '21'—tequila replaces aquavit, and cilantro and chives join the traditional dill flavoring.

2 (1-pound) fresh, boneless salmon
fillets (skin on), with all pin
bones removed

CURING INGREDIENTS:

4 tablespoons black peppercorns

1/2 cup firmly packed dark brown
sugar

1/2 cup coarse kosher-style salt

1 cup fresh cilantro leaves, loosely
packed

1/2 cup fresh dill weed

1/2 cup fresh chives

1/2 cup good-quality golden tequila

GARNISH:

1 cup fresh cilantro leaves, loosely
packed

Sliced pumpernickel bread

Spicy mustard

Lime wedges

Culinary-grade cheesecloth to wrap the fillets

Heavy objects to weigh down the salmon as it cures, such as a bag of sugar or flour, bags of dried beans, or a jug of cooking oil

Put the peppercorns in a small plastic bag and crush, using the bottom of a heavy skillet. Add the sugar and salt to the bag and blend well together.

Place 1 cup cilantro and the dill and chives together in the bowl of a food processor fitted with a metal blade and chop fine.

Lay a clean, washed, approximately 16-inch-square single layer of cheesecloth on a clean work surface. Place the fish fillets skin-side down on the cheesecloth. Spread the pepper/sugar/salt mixture evenly over the salmon. Spread the chopped herbs in the same manner and then sprinkle the tequila over the herbs.

Once all the tequila has been absorbed, sandwich the two fillets together, flesh to flesh and skin sides out. Position the fillet "sandwich" in the center of the cloth and wrap as you would a gift, pulling the cloth as tightly as possible around the fillets. Lay the package on a cake cooling rack set in a pan. The rack allows air to circulate for more efficient drying, while the pan will catch the liquid expelled during the 3-day curing period. Put the weight in a second, smaller cake pan and place it on top of the fillets to press out the unwanted water. Place the entire contraption in the bottom of your refrigerator. Turn every 24 hours, replacing the weight each time. At the end of the 3 days, remove the cloth, discard any accumulated liquid, scrape off the herbs, rinse with water, and pat the fish dry.

To serve, finely chop one cup of fresh cilantro and cover the flesh side of the fish. Using a very sharp knife, slice the salmon as thinly as possible, at a 45-degree angle. Your first slices may look a bit rough, but be patient. With a little practice you'll soon be turning out elegant green-edged red ribbons of gravlax. Serve on pumpernickel with spicy mustard and wedges of lime.

SHELLFISH RAVIOLI IN SAFFRON BROTH

SERVES 4

*H*omemade ravioli is remarkably easy to make using fresh wonton wrappers, which are now available in most supermarkets. The ultra-thin wonton skin makes a particularly light and delicate ravioli. In this recipe, the filling is the focus.

RAVIOLI FILLING:

3/4 pound cooked shrimp, crab, and/or lobster meat

3 large eggs

1/4 cup heavy cream

1/2 cup soft white bread crumbs

1/2 teaspoon salt

1/2 teaspoon freshly ground white pepper

2 tablespoons chopped fresh tarragon leaves

1 package wonton wrappers

EGG WASH (TO SEAL RAVIOLI):

1 egg, beaten

3 tablespoons water

BROTH:

4 cups Shellfish Broth (page 340)

1/2 teaspoon saffron threads

GARNISH:

1 small to medium tomato, diced

Chopped fresh herbs such as tarragon or chives

To make the filling, put the cooked shellfish meat and the eggs in a food processor fitted with a metal blade. Pulse until the seafood is coarsely chopped. Scrape the sides. Add the heavy cream, bread crumbs, salt, and pepper and pulse just to combine. Don't overprocess the cream or it will become grainy—or even turn to butter. Remove the mixture to a bowl and add the chopped tarragon leaves, blending them in with a spatula.

Lay out 1 wonton skin on a board. Using a pastry bag or a teaspoon, place approximately 1 teaspoon filling in its center. Brush a second wonton skin with the egg-wash mixture and lay it over the filling, pressing lightly with your fingers to remove any trapped air and to seal the edges of the wonton skins.

The uncooked ravioli can be stored in a covered container up to 2 days in the refrigerator, or for several weeks in the freezer. To freeze, lay the ravioli in a single layer on a wax-paper-lined sheet pan and place in the freezer until frozen. They can then be removed and stored in freezer bags.

In a saucepan, bring the shellfish broth to a boil, reduce the heat to a simmer, and add the saffron. Continue to simmer for 5 minutes while you begin to cook the ravioli.

To cook, place the ravioli in boiling salted water and continue boiling until they begin to float (about 2 to 3 minutes for fresh ravioli, 5 to 6 minutes for frozen ones). Drain and divide among 4 bowls. Add ½ cup Shellfish Broth to each bowl, then garnish with a little diced tomato and some chopped fresh herbs, such as tarragon or chives. Serve hot.

VARIATION:

Shellfish ravioli is also delicious (as an appetizer or an entrée) served with Spicy Tomato, Olive, and Basil Sauce (page 280).

CHEF'S TIP:

Cooked shrimp, crab, and lobster meat are readily available, allowing you to save some time in preparation.

SMOKED SALMON AND TROUT WITH CHIVE OIL

SERVES 4

*H*ere's a colorful, impressive-looking appetizer you can put together in a flash using store-bought smoked salmon and trout. Serve on individual plates as a first course, or arrange on a platter for a buffet.

1/4 to 1/2 pound mesclun *or* your choice of beautiful fresh young salad greens

Juice of 1 lemon (about 2 tablespoons)

1/4 cup Shallot and Champagne Vinaigrette (page 123)

1/2 pound thinly sliced smoked salmon

2 (3- to 4-ounce) smoked trout fillets, skinned and boned

2 ounces tiny nonpareil capers, drained

1 small red onion, finely diced (about 1/3 cup)

4 teaspoons Chive Oil (page 361)

4 teaspoons chopped fresh chives

Country-style pumpernickel bread

Toss the mesclun or your choice of salad greens in a bowl with the lemon juice and the Shallot and Champagne Vinaigrette. Divide onto 4 plates, mounding the greens in the center. Divide the salmon and trout fillets evenly among the plates, arranging them around the greens. Sprinkle the capers and onion over the fish. Drizzle 1 teaspoon Chive Oil over the fish on each plate. Top with some chopped fresh chives and serve with country-style pumpernickel bread.

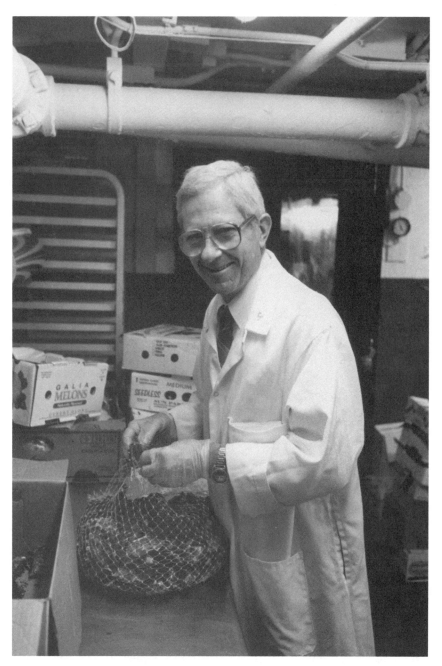

21's chief steward, Charlie Matola, who begins his workday at 6 A.M.,
personally checks the quality of virtually every food item as it arrives at '21.'
(Photo: Christopher Baker)

*W*hen the oysters arrive at '21' each morning, Chief Steward Charlie Matola not only counts them, he clunks them. Grabbing them two by two, he thumps them together close to his ear, listening for a hollow thud that would indicate the presence of mud inside the shell—one sure sign of a dead oyster.

In the old days, the only way to guarantee a fresh oyster was to buy one that had been harvested nearby. Hence in New York one ate Blue Points from Long Island; in Florida, Apalachicolas; in San Francisco, Tomales Bays. Today, with dependable overnight air deliveries, the world is literally '21's oyster. Chilean oysters, for example, are delicious.

Aquaculture also has diversified the readily available bounty. Belons, indigenous to France, are

(continued on next page)

ROASTED OYSTERS WITH COUNTRY BACON

SERVES 4

*Y*es, there is a good reason for the old saw about eating oysters only in months containing the letter R. Oysters spawn when the waters are warm; it changes their texture, makes them milky and flavorless. If you've just got to have oysters in the summertime, look for those from the northernmost waters of the Atlantic or Pacific.

24 fresh oysters, in their shells

2 plum tomatoes

1 tablespoon unsalted butter

3 large shallots, peeled and finely diced (about $1/4$ cup)

$1/4$ cup white wine

$1/4$ cup heavy cream

1 tablespoon chopped fresh tarragon leaves

2 ounces bacon, cooked and chopped

$1/2$ cup steamed spinach (optional)

GARNISH:

Melba Toast, or toast points of brioche or country bread

Preheat the oven to 350°. Using a towel, grasp an oyster in the palm of your hand. Press the oyster, rounded-side down, on a firm surface, still holding it with the towel. Shuck the oyster by wedging the tip of an oyster knife (regular knives are too thin-bladed) between the halves of the shell, at the shell's narrowest end. When the knife tip is securely wedged, rotate the blade to pry open the shell. Slide the knife blade along the length of the shell to open completely. Remove the oyster from the shell and reserve, along with its juice. From each pair of oyster shells, save the one that is most concave on the inside, and discard the one that is flatter. Place the concave shells in a pan of cold water and scrub inside and out. Place the clean oyster shells on a cookie sheet and set aside.

Dip the tomatoes briefly in boiling water to loosen the skins, then in ice water. Peel, cut in half, remove and discard the seeds, and dice.

Have the remaining ingredients measured and ready beside the stove. When you are ready to begin cooking the oysters, place the cookie sheet containing the oyster shells in the oven. On the top of the stove, melt the butter in a hot sauté pan until it begins to foam. Add the shallots, the oysters and their juice, and the white wine. Cook the oysters 30 seconds, then add the heavy cream. Bring to a quick boil, then reduce to a simmer just 1 minute more, or until the oysters' edges begin to curl. Add the tomato, tarragon, and bacon. Heat another 30 seconds, then remove promptly from the heat.

Remove the oyster shells from the oven and arrange 6 on each plate. Spoon 1 oyster into each shell and spoon a little of the sauce over each.

A nice variation of this recipe is to place a "nest" of steamed spinach in each oyster shell before adding the oysters and sauce. Serve with Melba Toast, brioche toast points, or toast points of country bread.

(continued from previous page)

now farmed in Maine, New Hampshire, California, and Washington State. Kumamotos, raised on the West Coast, were introduced from Japan. The Fisher's Island oyster is a relatively new one, grown in Long Island Sound from Atlantic seed stock. Even though it's grown in the same waters as Blue Points, it has the briny flavor characteristic of a Pacific oyster.

In general, Eastern oysters have a more mineral taste than Pacific oysters. Malpeques, from Prince Edward Island, actually have a muddy flavor. Belons are very metallic, almost like iron in the mouth. Another oyster worth looking for is the Olympia, indigenous to Washington State's Puget Sound. The ones I buy for '21' are sometimes no larger than a nickel, and usually no larger than a quarter—so tiny you can open them with a butter knife.

SESAME SCALLOPS WITH GINGER DRESSING

SERVES 4

This spectacular "seafood salad" has become a favorite appetizer at the '21' Club. For hors d'oeuvres, the scallops can be served around a small bowl of the dressing.

MARINADE:

3 large egg whites

1/4 cup low-sodium soy sauce

2 tablespoons Oriental-style sesame oil

1 teaspoon grated fresh ginger

1 scallion, finely chopped

1 pound large, very fresh sea scallops, side muscle removed

GINGER DRESSING:

2 tablespoons grated fresh ginger

1/4 cup low-sodium soy sauce

2 tablespoons dry (*not* cooking) sherry

1 teaspoon chopped fresh garlic

1 teaspoon Oriental-style sesame oil

1/2 teaspoon red chili flakes *or* 1 teaspoon homemade Hot Chili Oil (page 360)

2 scallions, finely chopped

Juice of 1 lemon (about 2 tablespoons)

Juice of 1 orange (about 1/4 cup)

4 tablespoons white sesame seeds,
    mixed with 4 tablespoons
    black sesame seeds

$1/4$ cup canola oil

1 pound fresh spinach, washed,
    dried, and stems removed

Preheat the oven to 350°. Combine the marinade ingredients and whisk together until frothy. Add the scallops and marinate, refrigerated, 30 to 45 minutes.

Meanwhile, prepare the Ginger Dressing. Combine all the ingredients in a saucepan and bring to a boil. Reduce the heat and simmer 5 minutes. Remove from the heat and set aside while preparing the scallops.

Drain the excess liquid from the scallops and dip them in the sesame-seed coating, covering them completely on all sides. Place the scallops in the refrigerator about 30 minutes before cooking to allow the coating to dry.

Heat the canola oil in a heavy skillet. Sauté the scallops on each side until crispy on the outside. Transfer them to a cookie sheet and place in the oven 3 minutes to make sure they are fully cooked in the center. (If you slice the raw scallops so that they are no thicker than $1/2$ inch, this step is not necessary.)

Serve the scallops on a bed of raw spinach leaves and drizzle Ginger Dressing over the top.

Tuna Kebabs with Wasabi Dipping Sauce

Serves 8

*W*asabi *(spicy Japanese horseradish) is traditionally served with sushi. If you're skittish about eating raw fish, here's a recipe for grilling tuna that capitalizes on the flavors and top-quality fish characteristic of sashimi.*

1½ pounds sashimi-grade tuna, deep red in color

16 large shiitake mushrooms, stems removed

2 large sweet red peppers

1 large red Bermuda onion

8 large bamboo skewers, soaked in water

1½ cups Sherry-Soy Marinade (page 344)

1 to 2 teaspoons wasabi paste (depending on how hot you want it)

Cut the tuna into 24 equal-size cubes. Quarter the mushrooms. Cut the peppers and onion into ½-inch squares. Divide the ingredients equally among the 8 skewers, alternating squares of vegetable and tuna. Pour 1 cup of the Sherry-Soy Marinade over the kebabs and marinate, refrigerated, 2 to 3 hours.

Dissolve the wasabi in the remaining ½ cup marinade to make a spicy dipping sauce to serve at the table with the grilled tuna.

On a hot outdoor grill or under a broiler, sear the kebabs 2 to 3 minutes on each side. The tuna should be medium rare—still red in the center—when served with the dipping sauce.

MIXED GRILLED
VEGETABLE CROSTINI
SERVES 6

This simple, rustic dish is particularly flavorful when the vegetables are cooked on an outdoor grill (especially if you add a few chips of fragrant wood, such as apple). If that option is unavailable, a preheated oven broiler or burner-top grill can work nearly as well. The difference between crostini (or croutons) and toast is that toast should still be soft inside, while crostini are baked until crisp clear through.

2 garlic cloves, peeled

1/2 cup extra-virgin olive oil

1 large loaf country-style or
    sourdough bread

1 medium zucchini

1 beefsteak tomato

1 medium eggplant

3 tablespoons chopped mixed fresh
    herbs (such as basil and
    thyme)

2 tablespoons balsamic vinegar

Salt and freshly ground black
    pepper to taste

Cracked black pepper to taste

1/4 cup shaved* Parmesan cheese

Preheat the oven to 375°. Place the garlic cloves and the oil in a saucepan and heat gently 1 or 2 minutes to flavor the oil. Be careful not to burn the garlic or it will turn acrid and bitter. Discard the garlic.

Cut the bread into 1/2-inch-thick slices, brush with the garlic oil, and toast in the oven 10 to 12 minutes, or until golden, turning the slices halfway through the cooking time. Set the bread aside, uncovered, so that it will remain crisp while you prepare the vegetables.

Slice the vegetables lengthwise in $\frac{1}{2}$-inch-thick slices. Brush them with the remaining oil, and grill or broil on both sides until lightly charred but still firm. (Some vegetables will need to come off the grill sooner than others.)

Cool the vegetables for several minutes before roughly chopping and tossing them in a bowl with the herbs, vinegar, and salt and pepper. Serve on the garlic crostini with some cracked black pepper and the shaved Parmesan cheese.

*Sliced very thin with a vegetable slicer or paring knife.

ABOVE:

The first barroom at '21' was a mere twenty feet wide. The fanciest decoration, a round Pabst beer sign, still hangs in the same spot. Below the sign was a not-too-skillfully hidden door to the cellar, "camouflaged" with wine and whiskey labels. (Photo: Standard Flashlight Co., Inc.)

BELOW:

When Prohibition ended '21' "broke through" to the town house next door at number 19. The bar was moved to its present location and banquettes added along the walls, but the Pabst sign, "hidden" cellar door, and remnants of wine labels are still visible. (Courtesy of '21')

At the end of World War II, '21' expanded again, incorporating the town house at number 17. A new sixty-foot bar was installed, the first airplanes had begun to hang from the ceiling, and '21's signature tablecloths had replaced the generic checked cloths of its earliest days; but the old familiar Pabst sign and ship's lanterns were still in place, as they are to this day.
(Courtesy of '21')

POLENTA CORN CAKES WITH WILD MUSHROOM PAN ROAST

SERVES 8

*T*his variation on the basic polenta recipe on page 274 incorporates the fresh taste of corn just off the cob.

POLENTA:

2 ears corn, husked and cleaned of silk

2 cups whole milk

1 cup finely ground cornmeal

2 tablespoons unsalted butter (plus 1 teaspoon to butter pan)

2 ounces Roquefort or other blue cheese, coarsely chopped

MUSHROOMS:

1 tablespoon unsalted butter

1 cup cleaned and sliced mixed fresh wild mushrooms *or* 1 ounce dried, rehydrated 20 minutes in very hot water and sliced

2 tablespoons chopped shallots

$^1/_2$ cup Chicken Stock (page 332) or Vegetable Stock (page 336)

2 tablespoons coarsely chopped fresh thyme

Salt and freshly ground black pepper to taste

GARNISH:

$^1/_3$ cup walnuts or pecans, toasted 4 to 5 minutes at 375°

Roast or broil the ears of corn until lightly browned. Allow to cool, then cut the corn off the cob. Combine the milk and cornmeal in a saucepan. Add the 2 tablespoons butter and the corn kernels and bring quickly to a boil. Reduce the heat and simmer a full 20 minutes, stirring with a wooden spoon to keep the mixture from sticking or burning. If the polenta becomes too thick before the 20 minutes is up, stir in several tablespoons of cold water to loosen it, and continue cooking. At the end of 20 minutes the mixture should be fairly thick. Fold in the cheese and stir until melted. Remove from the heat and pour into a buttered 8-by-8-inch cake pan. Using a spatula, spread the polenta into a thick, even layer. Cool and then refrigerate 2 to 3 hours before unmolding and cutting into triangles or 2-inch squares. (Uncut polenta can be covered with plastic wrap and stored in the refrigerator up to 2 days.)

To prepare the mushrooms, heat the 1 tablespoon butter in a sauté pan, add the mushrooms and shallots, and cook 5 or 6 minutes, until the mushrooms begin to brown. Add the Chicken or Vegetable Stock and cook until the liquid is reduced by half. Remove from the heat and add the chopped thyme and salt and pepper.

Just before serving, place the cut polenta on a cookie sheet in a preheated 350° oven for 10 to 15 minutes to warm, then, if necessary, brown it under a broiler 2 minutes more. To serve, place two pieces of polenta on each plate and spoon some of the mushroom pan roast over them. Garnish with toasted walnuts or pecans.

PUMPKIN RAVIOLI WITH PROSCIUTTO AND SAGE

SERVES 8 TO 10

*T*his shortcut way to make ravioli uses ready-made wonton skins. For the filling, you can use almost any variety of pumpkin or winter squash (such as acorn or butternut) except the traditional jack-o'-lantern pumpkin, which really isn't suitable for cooking because it is so watery and flavorless.

1½ pounds pumpkin or winter squash

1 tablespoon unsalted butter

¼ pound finely chopped prosciutto (optional)

1½ tablespoons chopped fresh sage, plus several whole sage leaves for garnish

1 cup heavy cream

¼ cup freshly grated Parmesan cheese

Salt and freshly ground black pepper to taste

2 (16-ounce) packages wonton skins, at room temperature

Cornstarch for dusting ravioli

1 cup Chicken Stock (page 332)

Preheat the oven to 375°. Split the pumpkins in half, scoop out the seeds, and bake 35 minutes. Remove from the oven and cool to room temperature. Scoop the pumpkin meat out of the skins and discard the skins. Place the pumpkin pulp in the bowl of a food processor fitted with a metal blade and pulse to chop fine. Sauté the pulp in the butter 2 minutes over medium-high heat. Add the prosciutto and chopped sage, and continue cooking 2 minutes more. Reduce the heat to low and add ½ cup of the heavy cream and half of the Parmesan cheese. Slowly reduce by half. Season with salt and lots of freshly ground black pepper and set aside until cool.

Have a cup of water and a pastry brush ready beside your work surface. Lay out a few wonton skins and place 1½ teaspoons of filling on the center of each. Brush all four edges of a second wonton skin with water. Place atop the first and press gently with your fingers to seal the edges and eliminate air pockets. As each wonton is completed, place it on a sheet pan covered with waxed paper lightly coated with cornstarch to prevent sticking. (Alternatively, the ravioli may be dusted with cornstarch.) Cover with plastic wrap and refrigerate until ready to use. They may be stored this way for as long as 2 days.

To make the sauce, simmer the Chicken Stock and the remaining cream and Parmesan cheese in a saucepan over low heat 8 to 10 minutes. While the sauce is cooking, bring a large pot of salted water to a boil. Drop in the ravioli and boil 2 to 3 minutes. Drain and place 5 to 6 ravioli per person on individual plates. Spoon several tablespoons of sauce over each portion. Garnish with sage leaves and freshly ground black pepper.

'21' TRADITIONAL STEAK TARTARE

SERVES 4 TO 6 AS AN APPETIZER

No one who sees the movie Wall Street *is likely to forget the finale to the scene where Gordon Gekko (Michael Douglas) takes Bud Fox (Charlie Sheen) to lunch at '21' and tempts Fox with the opportunity of his avaricious young lifetime, then leaves him face to face with a huge plate of steak tartare, complete with raw egg yolk on top. But you don't have to be a macho Gekko type to appreciate steak tartare. Dinah Shore, the embodiment of grace and femininity, requested it every time she came to '21.' While an entrée-size portion could cost you a week's allowance of cholesterol, an appetizer-size Steak Tartare shouldn't do you in for more than a day.*

1 pound lean (top round) freshly ground beef

2 large egg yolks

2 tablespoons Worcestershire sauce

1 tablespoon Dijon mustard

2 tablespoons chopped capers

2 tablespoons chopped hardboiled egg whites

1 tablespoon finely diced raw red Bermuda onion

1 tablespoon finely diced shallot

1 tablespoon chopped anchovy

2 tablespoons extra-virgin olive oil

1 tablespoon chopped fresh parsley

$1/4$ teaspoon Tabasco sauce, or to taste

Salt and freshly ground black pepper to taste

GARNISH:

$1/4$ cup chopped fresh chives

Toasted sliced rye bread

To retain freshness and color, grind the beef as close to mealtime as possible. Combine all of the ingredients except the beef. Just before serving, fold the beef and the mixed ingredients together. Combine well. Divide into 4 to 6 portions, roughly oval in shape. Garnish with chopped chives and serve with warm toasted rye bread.

'21'

In the 1987 movie Wall Street, *corporate raider Gordon Gekko, played by Michael Douglas, may have believed "Lunch is for wimps," but when the time came to propose a deal to Bud Fox (Charlie Sheen), '21' is where he chose to make the pitch.*
(Courtesy of Photofest)

FOIE GRAS WITH
SWEET AND SOUR
CABBAGE

SERVES 4

*T*his is '21's version of hot dogs and sauerkraut. All kidding aside, fresh foie gras is a luxury everyone should taste at least once in your life. Now that excellent foie gras is being produced in the United States, it is sometimes available raw in specialty butcher shops as well as by air from suppliers listed in the Resources section. It is extremely expensive and may be available only in a larger quantity than this recipe calls for. The "lobe" of fresh foie gras can be divided and the remainder frozen for use at a later time. Less expensive substitutions are discussed at the end of the recipe.

1 tablespoon canola oil

3 shallots, finely diced (about 2 tablespoons)

2 cups shredded Napa cabbage (about half a head)

3 tablespoons honey

3 tablespoons sherry vinegar *or* cider vinegar

$\frac{1}{4}$ cup dried currants or $\frac{1}{4}$ cup raisins

8 ounces fresh foie gras

Salt and freshly ground black pepper to taste

1 tablespoon sesame seeds, toasted 1 minute in a sauté pan

Country bread

Heat the canola oil in a sauté pan over medium heat. Sauté the shallots until translucent. Add the cabbage and sauté quickly until it just begins to wilt. Remove the cabbage and shallots, then add the honey to the pan, allowing it to melt and begin to bubble. Add the vinegar carefully so that the hot honey does not splash. Add the currants and cook just long enough to plump them. Remove from the heat and set aside.

The fresh, raw duck or goose liver known as foie gras is generally sold as grades A, B, or C; Grade A is the best and most expensive. Grade A foie gras is also free of most blemishes and imperfections, so it requires the least time to clean of veins and bile. All three grades will require some hand cleaning with a small paring knife. (A cooperative butcher would be a great help.) After the foie gras has been cleaned, it should be cut into 4 1/2-inch-thick slices weighing approximately 2 ounces each.

Season the foie gras with salt and pepper. Heat a clean sauté pan until very hot. Add the foie gras to the pan and sear quickly on both sides. Place the cabbage on a heated platter. Lay the foie gras on top of the cabbage and pour the currant sauce over the top of the foie gras. Sprinkle with sesame seeds.

At '21' we serve foie gras and cabbage with a pepper brioche bread, but any toasted fresh country bread would be wonderful.

'21'

CHEF'S TIP:

If fresh foie gras is simply not in the cards, there are two alternative strategies worth pursuing. Either use canned foie gras, sliced and sautéed quickly, or use fresh duck or chicken livers. The sweet-and-sour cabbage makes a nice counterpoint to balance the richness of any type of liver.

PROSCIUTTO AND PORT-POACHED PEARS

SERVES 8

If domestic or imported Italian prosciutto is unavailable, this dish is equally delicious made with Westphalian or real Virginia ham. If you choose Virginia ham, just remember that it must be fully cooked first.

3 cups water

$1/2$ cup dry white wine

$1/2$ cup good port wine

2 tablespoons granulated sugar

1 cinnamon stick

2 or 3 whole cloves

$1/4$ teaspoon red pepper flakes

4 firm pears (such as Bosc)

GARNISH:

$1/2$ cup extra-virgin olive oil

$1/4$ cup balsamic vinegar

$1/4$ pound Gorgonzola or other blue cheese

$1/2$ pound mesclun or your choice of fresh young salad greens

$1/2$ pound thinly sliced prosciutto, Westphalian, or real Virginia ham—properly cooked and cooled

Bring the water, wine, sugar, and spices to a boil in a pot just large enough to hold the pears. Lower the heat and simmer 5 minutes.

While the poaching liquid is cooking, peel but do not core the pears. (Use a vegetable peeler for the neatest job with the least waste.)

Poach the pears, uncovered, 20 minutes, or until they are just tender to the tip of a knife. Remove from the heat and cool the pears in the liquid another 20 minutes. You can then refrigerate them (still in the liquid) for later use. When ready to serve, remove the pears from the liquid, cut in half lengthwise, and remove the core with a teaspoon. With a sharp knife, slice each pear half into $\frac{1}{4}$-inch-thick lengthwise slices, leaving the neck of the pear unsliced so that you can "fan" the pear half on its serving plate.

Make the garnish by combining the oil and vinegar in a bowl with the crumbled Gorgonzola. Add the mesclun and toss.

On each serving plate, place a pear half at the six o'clock position, "fanning" it across the plate. Divide the prosciutto into 8 portions and drape one portion across the middle of each serving plate, covering the top half of the pear fan. Garnish each plate with $\frac{1}{4}$ cup dressed greens, placed in the twelve o'clock position, above the prosciutto.

'21' TRADITIONAL MANHATTAN CLAM CHOWDER

■

'21' TRADITIONAL CUBAN BLACK BEAN SOUP

■

YELLOW PEPPER GAZPACHO WITH
SEARED SHRIMP AND HOT CHILI OIL

■

'21' TRADITIONAL SENEGALESE SOUP

■

POTATO AND LEEK SOUP, TWO WAYS

■

FULTON MARKET FISH CHOWDER

■

PUMPKIN SOUP WITH APPLE SCHNITZ CROUTONS

■

ROASTED CORN CHOWDER WITH
COUNTRY CHEDDAR CHEESE

■

WHITE BEAN AND CABBAGE SOUP

*S*OUPS AND CHOWDERS

The day has the color and the sound of winter.
Thoughts turn to chowder. . . .
Chowder breathes reassurance. It steams consolation.
—CLEMENTINE PADDLEFORD

Inherently egalitarian, soup traditionally has been both the mainstay of the humblest peasant kitchen and an indispensable feature of formal "soup-to-nuts" dining in the manor house.

Earlier in '21's history, as many as twenty to twenty-five soups would be available on a given day. At that time '21's kitchen was run in the classical French manner described by Auguste Escoffier. Several basic soups would be offered with variations in their serving temperature or garnish, and each variation had a different name—such as Consommé Celestine (beef consommé with crêpe), Consommé Julienne (vegetable julienne), or Jellied Consommé Madrilene (chilled consommé with tomato).

Soups are a telling barometer of the tastes of their times. A 1933 '21' menu featured Green Turtle Soup with Sherry, Petite Marmite Bouchère, and Madrilene en Gelée. By the '60s, Manhattan Clam Chowder, Lobster Bisque, and Vichyssoise were favored by diners shifting away from six-course lunches toward soup and salad—albeit still washed down by three martinis!

Today three-martini lunches are a thing of the past. And soups—like everything else—have lightened up still more. Cholesterol-loaded cream soups are sharing the table with soups thickened with high-fiber vegetables such as beans, potatoes, and pumpkin. And while the use of meat-based stocks is a wonderful technique for enriching flavors, it is also a significant source of cholesterol and fat. For that reason, water or vegetable stock may be substituted wherever stock is called for in these recipes. Just keep in mind that they will yield a slightly different result both in taste and texture.

(Courtesy of '21')

'21' TRADITIONAL MANHATTAN CLAM CHOWDER

SERVES 4 TO 6

New Yorkers are fiercely loyal to their namesake's chowder. If it's Friday, there's sure to be a pot simmering at '21.'

1/4 pound fresh bacon, diced

4 carrots, peeled and diced

1 large onion, peeled and diced

4 celery stalks, diced

2 tablespoons dried oregano

2 bay leaves

2 tablespoons chopped garlic

1 teaspoon cayenne pepper

1 pint (about 2 dozen) cleaned, shucked, coarsely chopped chowder clams and their juices

1 (10-ounce) can plum tomatoes, drained and crushed

2 quarts water

2 Russet or Idaho potatoes (about 3/4 pound), cleaned, peeled, and diced

Salt and freshly ground black pepper to taste

GARNISH:
Freshly grated horseradish to taste

In a heavy-bottomed soup pot, cook the bacon until its fat begins to render. Add the diced vegetables and sauté until wilted. Add the oregano, bay leaves, garlic, and cayenne. Stir in the clams with their juice and continue to sauté 2 minutes. Add the crushed tomato and water, and bring to a boil. Reduce the heat and simmer 1 hour. Add the potatoes and continue to simmer another 30 minutes. Season with freshly ground pepper. Taste, and salt if necessary. Serve hot, with freshly grated horseradish as a garnish.

'21' TRADITIONAL CUBAN BLACK BEAN SOUP

YIELD: 10 TO 12 SIX-OUNCE PORTIONS

Cigars aren't the only Cuban tradition associated with the '21' Club. This hearty—but not excessively spicy— soup is another long-standing favorite.

1 pound dried black (turtle) beans	3 tablespoons ground cumin
3 tablespoons pure olive oil	2 tablespoons finely chopped garlic
3 medium white onions, chopped (about 1½ cups)	¼ cup tomato paste
2 large sweet red peppers, chopped	4 quarts cold water
3 stalks celery, chopped	Salt and freshly ground black pepper to taste
3 tablespoons chili powder	¼ cup dry (not cooking) sherry

GARNISH:

Sour cream   Chopped scallions or chives

Sort the beans carefully to remove any debris. Rinse and then soak the beans overnight in cold water, refrigerated. If any water remains after soaking, drain before adding the beans to the soup pot.

In a large soup pot with a heavy bottom, heat the olive oil. Add the onions, peppers, celery, chili, and cumin, and sauté over medium heat until the vegetables wilt. Add the garlic and tomato paste and cook an additional 3 minutes, stirring to make sure you don't burn the tomato or garlic. Add the water and bring to a boil.

Add the black beans, return to a boil, then lower to a simmer and cook 2 to 2½ hours, or until the beans are tender. Remove from the heat, season with salt and pepper to taste, and cool 30 minutes before pureeing in small batches in a blender or food processor.

If you are serving immediately, return the soup to a boil and add the sherry. Cook 2 minutes more. Ladle into bowls and garnish each serving with 1 tablespoon sour cream and a sprinkling of scallions or chives. If you are preparing the soup ahead of time, cool thoroughly after blending, transfer to a container with a tightly fitting lid, and store in the refrigerator up to a week. Add the sherry after reheating the soup to serve.

'21'

CHEF'S TIP:

For maximum flavor, the vegetables used in soup-making (except potatoes) should be "sweated" or "wilted" by sautéing in oil until limp and translucent before adding water.

Yellow Pepper Gazpacho with Seared Shrimp and Hot Chili Oil

SERVES 4 TO 6

Although gazpacho can, of course, be made with red tomatoes, this frosty variation is a spectacular summer refresher when made with vine-ripened, low-acid yellow tomatoes.

6 large yellow tomatoes (2^1/$_2$ to 3 pounds), ripe but still firm

1 sweet red pepper, seeded and cut into chunks

1 sweet yellow pepper, seeded and cut into chunks

1 large European cucumber, preferably seedless, skinned, split in half, seeded, and cut into chunks

1 medium red onion, peeled and cut into chunks

1 fresh jalapeño pepper, stemmed and seeded

2 cloves garlic, peeled

^{1}/$_4$ cup pure olive oil

^{1}/$_4$ cup sherry vinegar *or* balsamic vinegar

^{1}/$_2$ cup bottled tomato juice

1 small bunch fresh cilantro leaves

1 teaspoon salt

^{1}/$_2$ teaspoon freshly ground black pepper

GARNISH:

^{1}/$_2$ pound tiny salad shrimp (generally flash frozen), defrosted

1 clove garlic, peeled and chopped

1 tablespoon extra-virgin olive oil

2 tablespoons dry (not cooking) sherry

^{1}/$_2$ teaspoon Hot Chili Oil (page 360) per serving

Dip the tomatoes briefly in boiling water to loosen the skins, then in an ice-water bath. Peel, cut in half, remove and discard the seeds, and dice.

Finely dice approximately ½ cup each of the tomato, peppers, and cucumbers, and ¼ cup of the onion to reserve for garnish. (These can be combined in a single bowl and refrigerated until needed.) Place the remaining vegetables along with the remaining gazpacho ingredients in the bowl of a food processor fitted with a steel blade. (A blender can be used, but it incorporates more air, making the soup less colorful.) Process until smooth. Place in a covered container and refrigerate 45 minutes to 1 hour before serving. (Gazpacho will keep approximately 3 days refrigerated.)

While the soup is chilling, make the garnish by sautéing the shrimp and garlic in the olive oil 2 minutes. Remove the shrimp from the pan and cool. Ladle the cold soup into chilled bowls. Garnish each bowl with the reserved diced vegetables, the sherry, the Hot Chili Oil, and the seared shrimp, and serve immediately.

CHEF'S TIP:

To seed tomatoes, cut them into a top and bottom half. Hold half the tomato cut side down over the trash and squeeze the tomato gently. The seeds and some pulp will drop right out.

'21' TRADITIONAL SENEGALESE SOUP

SERVES 4 TO 6

This rich, cold curried soup is more familiar in Europe (especially England) than in the United States. It has been served at '21' for years, and we may be one of the few restaurants in this country where you can still find it. At '21,' the classic garnish for this soup is diced poached chicken. This version substitutes 1/2 teaspoon chutney instead.

2 tablespoons unsalted butter

1 large white onion, peeled and chopped

1 clove garlic, peeled and chopped

3 apples, peeled, cored, and chopped

1/4 cup raisins

2 carrots, peeled and chopped

3 tablespoons curry powder

2 tablespoons unbleached white flour

2 quarts hot Chicken Stock (page 332)

1 tablespoon tomato puree

1/2 cup heavy cream

GARNISH:

2 to 3 teaspoons mango chutney

Melt the butter in a heavy-bottomed soup pot. Add the onion, garlic, apples, raisins, and carrots, and sauté over medium heat 10 to 12 minutes, until the vegetables begin to wilt. Add the curry powder and stir 1 minute to release its flavor. Add the flour and cook 2 to 3 minutes before adding the hot Chicken Stock and tomato puree. Lower the heat and simmer 1 1/2 hours. Add the cream during the last 10 minutes of cooking. Remove from the heat and cool in an ice-water bath until a comfortable temperature to work with, then process until smooth in a food processor fitted with a metal blade or blender. Strain into a clean container and chill several hours before serving. Garnish with 1/2 teaspoon chutney per serving.

The '21' kitchen as it appeared in 1949, just after its postwar remodeling. (Photo: Barrett Gallagher)

POTATO AND LEEK SOUP, TWO WAYS

SERVES 6 TO 8

*I*n *France, hot potato and leek soup is known as potage santé (health soup), the Gallic equivalent of chicken soup. The cold summer version is pureed into the elegant creamed soup known on French and Continental menus as vichyssoise.*

2 quarts Chicken Stock (page 332) or water

3 tablespoons unsalted butter

4 large leeks, split, washed, and diced (about 3 cups)

2 large white onions, peeled and chopped (about 2 cups)

1 teaspoon dried thyme

2 bay leaves

2 cloves garlic, peeled and chopped

$^1/_2$ teaspoon salt, plus additional to taste

$^1/_2$ teaspoon ground white pepper, plus additional to taste

4 raw Idaho potatoes (about 2 pounds), peeled and diced

1 cup heavy cream (for the cold soup) *or* nonfat yogurt (if you are counting fat grams)

GARNISH:

3 tablespoons chopped chives (for the cold soup)

French bread croutons (for the hot soup)

While the Chicken Stock is preheating in one pot, melt the butter in another large, heavy-bottomed soup pot. Add the leeks, onions, thyme, bay leaves, garlic, $^1/_2$ teaspoon salt and $^1/_2$ teaspoon ground white pepper, and sauté over medium heat until the vegetables are wilted, about 10 minutes. Add the preheated Chicken Stock to the vegetables and bring to a boil. Reduce to a simmer and cook 30 to 35 minutes.

Add the potatoes, return the soup to a boil, then reduce to a simmer again. Continue to cook 20 minutes more, or until the potatoes are tender. Remove the bay leaves. Salt and white pepper to taste, and serve hot, with some croutons of French bread toasted with olive oil as a delicious chunky peasant *potage santé*.

For vichyssoise (cold potato and leek soup), cool the soup in an ice-water bath, then puree in a blender, strain through a fine sieve, pressing the solids to extract maximum flavor, and chill thoroughly. To serve as a refreshing summer soup, blend in the cup of cold heavy cream and garnish with chopped chives.

FULTON MARKET FISH CHOWDER

SERVES 4 TO 6

*L*oosely based on bouillabaisse, this chowder should be concocted from the freshest, most readily available fish.

1/2 cup pure olive oil

2 large onions, diced
(about 1 1/2 cups)

2 leeks, white and light green parts only, split, cleaned, and diced (about 2 1/2 cups)

5 stalks celery, diced (about 1 cup)

1/4 cup finely chopped garlic

1 cup canned plum tomatoes, drained, seeded, and diced

1 teaspoon saffron threads

2 bay leaves

1 tablespoon dried thyme

1 1/2 teaspoons salt

1 teaspoon freshly ground black pepper

1/2 cup dry white wine

2 quarts Roasted Shellfish Broth (page 340) or Fish Stock (page 331)

2 Idaho potatoes (about 1 pound), peeled and diced

1/2 to 3/4 pound mixed fish (any variety or mixture will do) cleaned, peeled or boned, and cut into small cubes

PEPPERY CROUTONS:

French baguette, sliced 1/4-inch thick (about 3 to 4 slices per person)

1/4 cup extra-virgin olive oil

1 to 2 teaspoons cracked black peppercorns

Heat the olive oil in a large, heavy-bottomed soup pot, add the onions, leeks, and celery, and sauté until translucent, about 6 minutes. Add the garlic, tomatoes, saffron, and seasonings. Stir about 2 minutes, then add the white wine and cook 4 to 5 minutes, or until almost all the liquid has evaporated, before adding the shellfish broth. Bring to a boil, then reduce to a simmer and cook 45 minutes. At the end of 45 minutes, add the potatoes and cook 20 minutes longer, or until the potatoes are tender.

Preheat the oven to 300°. While the broth is simmering, make the Peppery Croutons: Brush one side of each French bread slice with olive oil, sprinkle with cracked pepper, and toast in the oven until crisp (about 12 minutes).

After the potatoes have simmered 20 minutes, add the fish. Reheat to just below a boil and cook at a strong simmer 3 to 5 minutes, until the fish is cooked but not yet flaking apart. Remove the bay leaves, taste for seasoning, and serve immediately, garnished with the Peppery Croutons.

CHEF'S TIP:

This recipe can be made very economically if you buy trimmings from your fish dealer, or save and freeze fish trimmings when you've caught or purchased fish for other uses.

PUMPKIN SOUP WITH APPLE SCHNITZ CROUTONS

SERVES 10 TO 12

*T*his soup can be made with nearly any variety of pumpkin or winter squash, except *the traditional jack-o'-lantern pumpkin, which really isn't suitable for cooking because it is so watery and flavorless. Apple Schnitz is a time-honored Pennsylvania Dutch way of preserving apples. It makes a tasty, healthful snack as well as a garnish.*

4 pounds whole pumpkin or winter squash such as butternut or Hubbard (should yield 6 to 8 cups baked pumpkin pulp)

2 tablespoons unsalted butter

3 large carrots, diced

4 stalks celery, diced

2 large onions, diced

1 leek, split, washed, and diced

3 quarts Chicken Stock (page 332) or water

2 teaspoons ground cinnamon

$1/2$ teaspoon ground nutmeg

$1/4$ cup maple syrup

1 cup heavy cream

APPLE SCHNITZ CROUTONS:

2 tart apples, such as Granny Smith

$1/2$ cup firmly packed light brown sugar

Preheat the oven to 350°. Cut the pumpkin or winter squash in half and remove all seeds. Place cut-side up on a cookie sheet and bake 45 minutes, or until soft. Remove the pulp from the shell, puree in a food processor fitted with a metal blade, and reserve.

Heat the butter in a large, heavy-bottomed soup pot until foamy. Add all of the vegetables (except the reserved pumpkin or winter squash) and sauté 10 minutes. Add the Chicken Stock and bring to a boil. Reduce to a simmer, then add the pumpkin puree and the spices. Cook 45 minutes, adding the maple syrup and heavy cream in the last 5 minutes of cooking.

While the soup is cooking, make the Apple Schnitz Croutons: Peel and core the apples and slice into paper-thin rings using a food processor fitted with the vegetable slicing disk. Spread the slices on a nonstick cookie sheet or one lined with parchment paper. Dust with light brown sugar, and dry in a preheated 300° oven approximately 25 to 30 minutes, or until crisp.

When the soup has finished cooking, cool several minutes before pureeing in small batches in a blender or food processor. Serve immediately, garnished with the Apple Schnitz Croutons.

'21'

The late Bob Kriendler welcomes Western singer and film star Gene Autry to '21's old first-floor dining room.
(Courtesy of '21')

Roasted Corn Chowder with Country Cheddar Cheese

Serves 8 to 10

Corn cobs are the secret ingredient in this just-picked-tasting harvest chowder. The luscious milk that remains when the corn is cut from the cob adds texture and creaminess to the soup, along with a wallop of corn flavor.

6 ears fresh sweet corn, brushed lightly with butter and grilled or broiled until toasted on all sides (about 3 cups cut corn)

2 tablespoons unsalted butter

1 large onion, peeled and diced (about 1 cup)

2 celery stalks, diced

1 leek, split, cleaned, and diced

1 large sweet red pepper, diced

2 teaspoons ground cumin

1 teaspoon ground coriander

$1/2$ teaspoon salt

$1/2$ teaspoon cayenne pepper

2 quarts Chicken Stock (page 332)

8 ounces white or yellow cheddar cheese, preferably extra-sharp, grated

Cut the roasted corn off of their cobs, reserving the cobs. Melt the butter in a large, heavy-bottomed soup pot. Add the corn, the diced vegetables, and the seasonings, and sauté until the vegetables are soft but not browned. Add the Chicken Stock. Bring to a boil, then reduce to a simmer and add the reserved corn cobs. Cook 40 to 45 minutes, remove the cobs, and stir in the grated cheese. Serve immediately.

White Bean and Cabbage Soup

SERVES 4 TO 6

A hearty chill-chaser for cold autumn or winter days.

1 tablespoon vegetable oil

1 small head white cabbage (about 2 pounds), outer leaves and core removed, diced

3 large carrots, peeled and diced (about 1 cup)

4 celery stalks, diced (about 1 cup)

3 leeks, split, cleaned, and diced (about 2 cups)

2 medium-size white onions, peeled and diced (about 1 cup)

3 tablespoons finely chopped garlic

1 tablespoon dried thyme

2 bay leaves

Freshly ground black pepper to taste

2 quarts Chicken Stock (page 332) or Vegetable Stock (page 336)

1 pound white Navy or pea beans

1 teaspoon salt

1 cup diced smoked ham

Sort the beans carefully to remove any debris. Rinse and then soak the beans overnight in cold water, refrigerated.

Heat the oil in a large, heavy-bottomed soup pot. Add all of the vegetables except the beans and all of the dry spices except the salt. Sauté the vegetables over medium heat until they wilt. Add the Chicken Stock and bring to a boil. Drain the beans and add them to the pot. Reduce to a simmer and cook 1³/₄ to 2 hours, or until the beans are tender. Add the salt in the final 15 minutes of cooking. Remove the bay leaves. Stir in the ham and serve promptly. This soup freezes well.

CHEF'S TIP:

Salt tends to toughen beans if added too soon in the cooking process, so wait until the final 15 minutes of cooking to add salt to taste.

'21' TRADITIONAL SUNSET SALAD

■

'21' TRADITIONAL HUNTER SALAD

■

MICHAEL'S CAESAR SALAD

■

COBB SALAD

■

ENDIVE, WALNUT, AND BLUE CHEESE SALAD

■

SHAVED FRESH FENNEL WITH
SUN-DRIED TOMATOES

■

MÂCHE AND ENDIVE WITH
STILTON CRUMBLE AND PORT

■

GRILLED MUSHROOM SALAD

■

ROASTED TOMATO AND GOAT CHEESE SALAD

■

GRILLED VEGETABLE SALAD WITH
BULGUR WHEAT TABOULI

■

WHOLE MAINE LOBSTER SALAD

■

WARM FRESH TUNA SALAD WITH
ROASTED PEPPERS

■

GRILLED SWORDFISH SALAD

■

GRILLED SHRIMP AND SCALLOP SALAD

■

'21' TRADITIONAL LORENZO DRESSING

■

'21' HOUSE DRESSING: FRESH HERB VINAIGRETTE

■

SHALLOT AND CHAMPAGNE VINAIGRETTE

■

CHUNKY BLUE CHEESE AND WALNUT DRESSING

■

CITRUS GINGER DRESSING

■

BASIL AND ROASTED PEPPER VINAIGRETTE

■

FRESH RASPBERRY VINAIGRETTE

SALADS, VINAIGRETTES, AND DRESSINGS

Lettuce, like conversation, requires a good deal of oil,
to avoid friction, and keep the company smooth.

—DUDLEY WARNER

Salads are, and always have been, an important part of '21's menu. Several of '21's most popular salads, such as Hunter Salad and Sunset Salad, were invented here. Others, such as Cobb Salad and Caesar Salad, were invented by other famous restaurateurs. Today the definition of "salad" has expanded so much that it's impossible to confine them to just this one chapter of the book. Several of the appetizers in the "Starters" chapter either rest on or are garnished with salad greens. You'll also find salad components sprinkled throughout the various entrée chapters. And several salads in this chapter make substantial main courses themselves. Today's salads often incorporate warm as well as cold elements. I think these are especially delightful with fish or meat prepared on an outdoor grill.

More and more varieties of lettuce are becoming available in specialty produce stores and large supermarkets. Some are sweet and delicately flavored. Others, such as arugula, are unmistakably assertive. Some are a little tart. Some are peppery. Some have a bitter edge to them.

This burgeoning selection of "greens" actually includes a kaleidoscope of colors, from red, pink, purple, blue, and white, to every imaginable shade of green. The selection of textures and shapes is equally impressive. Lacy frisée and convoluted escarole. Silky endive and tender red oak. Spiky mizuna, toothsome kale.

Combined, young spring lettuces make a colorful, beautiful, flavorful salad that is sometimes called a mesclun, or field greens salad. Mesclun is a fairly common market item throughout France and certain other parts of Europe. It also is becoming increasingly popular and more widely accessible in the United States. While the price per pound for mesclun may seem high, remember that these lettuces are prewashed, sorted, dried, and then mixed together, so there is no waste—and no labor on your part. Four to 6 ounces of mesclun are more than adequate for a small salad serving six to eight people or a larger salad for four to five.

For those of you who would prefer to construct your own custom blend, the following descriptions may help guide your selection.

Arugula: A distinctive, bitter-peppery green native to the Mediterranean region. You'll find it called rocket in old cookbooks.

Belgian endive: Crunchy and bittersweet, Belgian endive is the forced root of witloof chicory, grown completely in the dark.

Bibb lettuce: Also called limestone lettuce. Delicate, but more substantial and deeper green than Boston.

Boston lettuce: Soft and delicate, loose headed, and pale in color. Also called butter lettuce.

Chicory: Also known as curly endive. Slightly bitter, with a toothy texture and upstanding crenelations.

Escarole: Also from the chicory family. The flavor is similar, but the dark-green leaves are broad and flat rather than curly.

Frisée: This lacy, pale-green lettuce is mildly flavored. An indispensable component of mesclun.

Iceberg lettuce: Twenty-five years ago, if you asked for lettuce almost anywhere in the United States, iceberg is what you got. Poor old iceberg's reputation has taken quite a hit in recent years, but it's still an indispensable ingredient in '21' Traditional Sunset and Hunter salads.

Mâche: Also called lamb's lettuce, these dark green leaves have a distinctive sharp flavor.

Mizuna: A spiky-leafed, mild-flavored green with a crisp stem. Great in stir-fries as well.

Radicchio: A tight-headed Italian chicory with beautiful ruby-colored leaves, creamy white ribs, and slightly bitter taste.

Red oakleaf lettuce: A mild, tender, loose-leaf lettuce visually reminiscent of oak leaves in autumn.

Romaine: Mild flavored but boldly crunchy inner leaves. There would be no such thing as Caesar Salad without it. It stands up well to all dressings.

Watercress: Distinctly peppery, with soft leaves, crunchy stems, and deep-green color. The first fresh green of spring.

'21' TRADITIONAL
SUNSET SALAD

SERVES 4

*S*unset Salad originated at the '21' Club early in its history. *Jerry Berns says the name comes from the sunsetlike colors of its ingredients. Sunset Salad is most often served with Lorenzo Dressing, also invented at '21' by a waiter of that name. Together with a bowl of Gazpacho (page 84) or cold Potato and Leek Soup (page 88), this is a quintessential '21' lunch.*

2 cups finely shredded green
    cabbage

2 cups finely shredded iceberg
    lettuce

1^1/2 cups cooked, diced, smoked
    beef tongue (about 1 pound)

2 cups diced cold poached chicken
    breast (about 1^1/2 pounds)

^{1}/2 recipe Lorenzo Dressing
    (page 119)

Combine all salad ingredients and toss with the dressing just before serving.

'21' TRADITIONAL HUNTER SALAD

SERVES 4 TO 6

*T*he Hunter Salad is named for Francis (Frank) Townsend Hunter, a tennis star and big-game hunter who became chairman of Jack and Charlie's Prohibition Era summer retreat, the Westchester Embassy Club, and eventually the president of '21' Brands (wholesale liquor distributors).

A classic '21' dish, it harkens back to a simpler time in the culinary tradition of the club when this salad represented a healthful lunch. The classic Hunter Salad is comprised of raw fresh vegetables, all cut about one-quarter to half an inch in size, presented by the captain in a colorful pinwheel arrangement of vegetables over greens, then mixed with shredded Bibb and iceberg lettuces and tossed with the dressing of the diner's choice—usually Lorenzo Dressing.

There always have been numerous variations on Hunter Salad. Some customers prefer one dressing over another: Blue Cheese or Lorenzo, or a simple Vinaigrette. Some customers are even more creative, adding shrimp or crab meat, chicken or avocado. Hunter Salad was a do-it-yourself invention before the days of salad bars.

½ cup each diced carrot, celery, fresh-cooked beets, red peppers, yellow peppers, cucumbers, and tomatoes

1 small Bibb lettuce, washed, dried, and torn into bite-size pieces

1½ cups shredded iceberg lettuce

½ recipe (¾ cup) Lorenzo Dressing (page 119)

Serve as you would any tossed salad.

MICHAEL'S
CAESAR SALAD

SERVES 4

Although '21' served Caesar Salad long before my arrival, the version served at '21' today is a recipe I began making when I worked at a private club where New York's then mayor, Ed Koch, sometimes dined. Koch, who is well known for his love of garlic, asked that the recipe be given to his chef at Gracie Mansion, and a framed copy was hung at City Hall for a time.

DRESSING:

2 large raw egg yolks (optional)

5 large cloves garlic, peeled

3 tablespoons Dijon mustard

1/4 cup fresh lemon juice

2 tablespoons red wine vinegar

1 tablespoon Worcestershire sauce

1 cup extra-virgin olive oil

1 (2-ounce) can anchovy fillets, chopped

Salt and freshly ground black pepper to taste

1 head romaine lettuce, cleaned, dried, and torn

GARNISH:

1/2 cup freshly grated Parmesan cheese

1 cup toasted croutons

CHEF'S TIP:

You can make your own croutons from day-old sliced French or country bread brushed with olive oil and toasted in a 250° oven until golden.

In the bowl of a food processor fitted with a metal blade, combine the egg yolks, garlic, mustard, lemon juice, vinegar, and Worcestershire. Pulse the mixture together until the garlic is finely chopped. Then, while continuing to pulse, add the olive oil in *a very patient, slow, steady stream* to produce a smooth, creamy mayonnaiselike emulsion. Add the anchovies, pulse for 30 seconds, and season with salt and pepper to taste. This makes enough dressing for 8 servings. The extra dressing can be stored covered in the refrigerator 3 to 4 days.

To serve, place the romaine in a large salad bowl. Add the Parmesan cheese and half the dressing. Crumble the toasted croutons roughly over the salad. Toss thoroughly to coat the greens evenly.

Prince Valiant takes the long count at "21"

(© KFS)

COBB SALAD

SERVES 4

*T*his classic originated at The Brown Derby Restaurant in Hollywood, whose founder was named Cobb. We most often serve Cobb Salad as a complete luncheon entrée, but I also like to serve it as a dinner appetizer, with several deep-fried oysters as a garnish.

$1/2$ head Bibb lettuce, washed, dried, and chopped

2 cups chopped watercress, coarse bottom stems removed

1 cup diced poached chicken breast meat

2 large ripe avocados, peeled, pit removed, and diced

$1/4$ cup chopped cooked bacon

1 small red onion, peeled and diced (about $1/2$ cup)

3 tablespoons tiny nonpareil capers

1 small cucumber, peeled, seeded, and diced (about $1/2$ cup)

Combine all the ingredients in a salad bowl and toss with your favorite dressing. Blue cheese dressing is traditional for a Cobb Salad. The salad would be delicious served with Chunky Blue Cheese and Walnut Dressing (page 124).

Endive, Walnut, and Blue Cheese Salad

Serves 4

$^1/_2$ head red leaf lettuce, washed and dried

4 large Belgian endive heads, cut lengthwise into julienne strips

$^1/_2$ cup shelled walnut halves, toasted at 250° for 15 minutes

$^1/_2$ cup Shallot and Champagne Vinaigrette (page 123)

1 cup chunked Roquefort or other blue cheese

2 tablespoons chopped fresh chives

GARNISH:

2 fresh, ripe tomatoes, sliced

Place several lettuce leaves on each of 4 plates. Toss the julienned endive with the toasted walnuts. Combine the vinaigrette with the cheese, and mix with the endive and toasted walnuts. Divide among the 4 plates. Sprinkle $^1/_2$ tablespoon chives on each serving. Garnish with fresh, ripe tomato slices.

SHAVED FRESH FENNEL WITH SUN-DRIED TOMATOES

SERVES 4 TO 6

*F*resh *fennel can be cooked many ways: sautéed, braised, poached, steamed, and grilled. It also can be served raw, as in this refreshing salad. Fennel's aniselike flavor lends itself well to all varieties of fish as well as to pork and chicken.*

1/2 cup julienned sun-dried tomatoes

2 large bulbs fresh fennel (about 3/4 pound)

2 tablespoons chopped fresh basil leaves

3 tablespoons pitted, chopped Niçoise or Kalamata olives

1/4 cup extra-virgin olive oil

1/4 teaspoon salt

1/4 teaspoon freshly ground black pepper

Either purchase sun-dried tomatoes that are already rehydrated and packed in olive oil, or rehydrate the less-expensive still-dry tomatoes in hot water 20 minutes and pat them dry before slicing into thin julienne strips. (Any extras can be stored in your own olive oil.)

Cut the fennel bulbs in half. Using a very sharp knife or a vegetable slicer such as a mandolin, cut or shave paper-thin lengthwise slices of fennel into a bowl. Combine all the remaining ingredients with the fennel in the bowl and toss together. Marinate just a few minutes, then serve with Grilled Shrimp (page 160).

'21'

CHEF'S TIP:

To pit ripe olives easily, lay them on a wooden board, and, with the palm of your hand, press on each olive to break the skin. Squeeze the olives between your fingers to remove the pits.

MÂCHE AND ENDIVE
WITH STILTON
CRUMBLE AND PORT

SERVES 4

1/4 pound English Stilton, crumbled into bits

4 tablespoons good, nonvintage port wine

2 washed Belgian endive heads, separated into leaves

2 cups washed, dried mâche (lamb's lettuce) leaves

1/4 cup hazelnut oil

Crumble the Stilton into a small bowl. Pour the port over it and allow the cheese to marinate while you prepare the lettuces. Arrange the endive leaves decoratively on 4 salad plates. Toss the mâche leaves with the hazelnut oil, and place a small mound of mâche on top of the endive leaves in the center of each plate. Sprinkle the marinated cheese over the salads and drizzle with the remaining port.

GRILLED MUSHROOM
SALAD

The key to this dish is to use the freshest, most flavorful berries at the height of their season and to prepare the vinaigrette immediately before serving.

3 tablespoons extra-virgin olive oil

2 cloves garlic, peeled and finely minced

$1/4$ teaspoon ground coriander seed

Juice of $1/2$ lemon (about 1 tablespoon)

1 to $1^{1}/_{2}$ pounds shiitake or Portobello mushrooms,

cleaned of all dirt and stems removed

2 cups torn frisée lettuce or fresh chicory leaves, washed and dried

1 recipe Raspberry Vinaigrette (page 127)

To prepare the mushrooms, whisk together the olive oil with the garlic, coriander, and lemon juice. Brush onto the mushroom caps and grill or broil them until done, about 3 minutes per side for the shiitakes, 4 to 5 minutes for the Portobellos.

While the mushrooms are still warm, slice them coarsely into large chunky slices. Combine the mushrooms with the frisée lettuce or chicory and toss with the Raspberry Vinaigrette.

ROASTED TOMATO AND GOAT CHEESE SALAD

SERVES 4

This is a perfect accompaniment for lamb or roast chicken.

2 large beefsteak tomatoes (about 12 ounces each)

Salt and freshly ground black pepper to taste

1/2 cup extra-virgin olive oil

3 tablespoons balsamic vinegar

2 tablespoons each chopped fresh thyme, sage, oregano, and basil

1 (12-ounce) log Montrachet goat cheese

2 cups mixed salad greens

CHEF'S TIP:

To seed tomatoes, cut them into a top and bottom half. Hold half the tomato cut-side down over the trash and squeeze the tomato gently. The seeds and some pulp will drop right out.

Preheat the oven to 300°. Halve and seed the tomatoes and season with salt and pepper. Lay the tomatoes on a baking rack set over a cookie sheet in oven for 20 minutes, or until the skins slip off easily. Meanwhile, combine the oil, vinegar, and chopped herbs. Remove the tomatoes from the oven, slip off their skins, and brush the tomato halves lightly with this vinaigrette. Return the tomatoes to the oven to roast 1 hour more.

Meanwhile, slice the Montrachet log into 12 equal-size disks. Brush each disk with the vinaigrette. Remove the tomatoes from the oven and divide them among 4 salad plates, alternating slices of goat cheese and roasted tomato halves.

Toss the greens with the remaining vinaigrette and place 1/2 cup alongside each serving of tomatoes and cheese.

GRILLED VEGETABLE SALAD WITH BULGUR WHEAT TABOULI

SERVES 4 TO 6

*I*nstant tabouli, which is quite good,
makes this salad very simple to prepare.

TABOULI SALAD:

1 cup instant tabouli, prepared according to package directions (omit any seasoning packets that may be included) *or* 2 cups cooked bulgur wheat ($^3/_4$ cup uncooked)

2 tablespoons grated lemon zest

Juice of 2 lemons (about $^1/_4$ cup)

$^1/_4$ cup chopped flat-leaf parsley

2 cloves garlic, peeled and finely minced

$^1/_3$ cup extra-virgin olive oil

1 large beefsteak tomato, peeled, seeded, and coarsely chopped

$^1/_4$ teaspoon ground coriander seed

$^1/_4$ teaspoon ground cumin

Salt and freshly ground black pepper to taste

GRILLED VEGETABLES:

2 medium zucchini

4 heads Belgian endive

2 large Portobello mushrooms, cleaned and stems removed

1 small eggplant

1 large red onion, peeled

1 sweet red pepper

1 sweet yellow pepper

2 tablespoons extra-virgin olive oil

Salt and freshly ground black pepper to taste

3 tablespoons chopped fresh herbs: thyme, tarragon, chives, oregano, and sage in any combination

MARINADE:

$^1/_4$ cup extra-virgin olive oil

2 tablespoons balsamic vinegar

Combine the tabouli salad ingredients and set aside to marinate while preparing the grilled vegetables.

Slice the zucchini and endive in half lengthwise. Leave the mushroom caps whole. Cut the eggplant into $1/4$-inch-thick, round slices. Cut the onion into $1/2$-inch-thick slices. Split the peppers in half lengthwise and remove the seeds, stem, and ribs. Brush the vegetables with 2 tablespoons olive oil. Season with salt and pepper, and place on a hot outdoor grill or under a broiler. Cook the vegetables until well charred on all sides, then remove and cool.

When the vegetables have cooled, cut into slices or cubes. Add 3 tablespoons freshly chopped herbs and toss with the marinade of olive oil and balsamic vinegar. Adjust the salt and pepper seasoning, and set aside to marinate at room temperature.

Both the tabouli and the vegetable salad can be made hours in advance. When ready to serve, spoon several tablespoons of the seasoned tabouli onto a plate and top with several tablespoons of the mixed grilled vegetables. A lemon wedge and extra-virgin olive oil in a cruet make a nice accompaniment.

CHEF'S TIP:

To seed tomatoes, cut them into a top and bottom half. Hold half the tomato cut-side down over the trash and squeeze the tomato gently. The seeds and some pulp will drop right out.

HAIL TO THE CHIEFS

"There aren't too many presidents you get to know in your life," Pete Kriendler told Sharon Rosenthal in a 1980 *Daily News* interview. "I'm fortunate," he continued. "I've known them all." And he met them all at '21.' Every president since Franklin D. Roosevelt has dined at '21' either before, during, or after his presidency. FDR came when he was governor of New York, Clinton while governor of Arkansas.

As long as the formal upstairs dining room was still open to the public, '21's "Presidential Table" was number 120, where Roosevelt, Truman, and Kennedy all dined at one time or another. When it was only he and Bess, Truman would sit at table 121. It was also at table 121 that, remarkably, JFK dined alone a night or two before his inauguration.

Eisenhower came to '21' both as President of the United States and, even more frequently, as president of Columbia University. Nixon came more often than any other president, often sat in the barroom, and never left without sticking his head in the kitchen to thank the help. Nixon also had a private stock of La Tache in '21's wine cellar, courtesy of Frank Sinatra.

President Reagan came to '21' only after he had left the White House. His wife, Nancy, however, came more than once while she was First Lady. George and Barbara Bush showed up on short notice in 1993 and paid their bill with an American Express card. Gerald Ford came for lunch in the summer of 1994 and ordered chicken salad from the $19.94 Prix Fixe menu.

President Carter, who during his presidency had attended only private parties at '21,' assumed it was a private club. After Marshall Cogan purchased the restaurant in 1984, Carter called him to find out whether it would be possible to arrange an invitation for him and Rosalynn. It was the beginning of an ongoing friendship between the two families.

In a letter to Cogan, Carter describes his most vivid memory of '21'

as when I had just returned from one of my visits to the Middle East—to Israel, the West Bank and Gaza, Jordan, Lebanon, Syria, and Egypt. You wanted me to give a report to about 15 or 20 of your friends, who were assembled for a late breakfast in one of the private rooms. . . . I described my unpublicized meetings with Arafat and other PLO leaders on the trip, expecting to be chastised by the Jewish leaders for doing so. On the contrary, there seemed to be unanimous encouragment for me to keep open the lines of communication with both Israelis and Palestinians, which I have done ever since that day.

ABOVE:

*Jimmy Carter confers with Daniel Patrick Moynihan in the midst of a 1976 Democratic Convention week fund-raising event at the '21' Club.
(Photo: Robert Knudsen)*

BELOW:

*Richard Nixon visited '21' more often than any other president. He and his wife, Pat, are pictured here in 1969 with '21's Bob Kriendler and Bruce Snyder.
(Courtesy of Bruce Snyder)*

How to Select, Clean, Cook, and Shell Lobsters

At '21,' we demand lobsters that are not only live but also straight from the ocean, rather than being held in tanks. Even though you'll see live lobsters in tanks in supermarkets and some restaurants, their quality begins to deteriorate as soon as they are put in a tank, because the tanks cannot provide lobsters with all the nutrients they need to thrive. Be sure to ask for fresh-delivery lobsters rather than storage lobsters. They're expensive either way, so it's worth insisting on the very best.

To prepare four $1\frac{1}{2}$ pounds lobsters for lobster salad, first wash them under cold running water. Place a double recipe of Court Bouillon (page 335) into a pot large enough to hold the Court Bouillon as well as the lobsters.

Bring the Court Bouillon to a boil. Place the whole lobsters in the pot, cover with a lid, and cook 12 to 14 minutes, until the shells are completely bright red. Remove the lobsters from the Court Bouillon and allow them to cool enough so that you can handle them with your bare hands. The Court Bouillon can be strained, cooled, and refrigerated or frozen to use again.

Break off the tail, claws, and knuckles that are attached to the claws. If you intend to stuff the cooked lobster, split the body in half by laying it shell-side down on a work space. Place a sharp heavy knife between the small legs on the underside of the body and split the body completely in half. Remove the long black intestinal tract as well as the stomach sack, and, with a spoon, remove the body meat and any red roe, reserving them for use in your salad or another lobster dish.

At the top, toward the head, find, remove, and discard the feathery gills. The green tamale (or liver) can be discarded if desired. Separate the claws from the knuckle shells and crack the claws straight across with the back of a sharp knife. Separate the claw shell and remove and save the claw meat. Crack the knuckle shells with a nutcracker and remove as much of the tiny nuggets of meat as possible.

Take the tail shell in the palm of your hand and squeeze firmly. This will help to loosen the tail meat. Then, using sharp scissors, cut through the length of the soft undershell. Spread the hard shell apart and remove the tail meat intact. Split the tail meat in half and remove and discard any remaining intestinal tract. Chill the lobster meat for use in lobster salad, use in another lobster recipe such as Shellfish Ravioli in Saffron Broth (page 54) or sauté it briefly and combine with risotto or pasta.

WHOLE MAINE
LOBSTER SALAD

SERVES 8 AS AN APPETIZER, 4 AS AN ENTRÉE

*The key to this dish is fresh, live lobsters,
simply cooked and simply served.*

4 (1½-pound) lobsters

2 recipes Court Bouillon (page 335)

2 cups mixed salad greens (pages 98–99)

½ cup Shallot and Champagne Vinaigrette (page 123) or other vinaigrette

1 cup sliced radishes

½ cup peeled, seeded, and diced cucumber

2 large beefsteak tomatoes, cut into eighths

2 avocados, peeled and pit removed

½ recipe Green Herb Mayonnaise (page 359)

Prepare the lobsters in the Court Bouillon according to the directions on page 114.

Toss the salad greens with half the vinaigrette. Divide them equally among 4 or 8 plates. Scatter the radish, cucumber, and tomato on and around the greens. Slice the avocados thin and place on top of the greens. Arrange the lobster meat on top of the avocado. Drizzle with the remaining vinaigrette and serve with the Green Herb Mayonnaise on the side.

'21'

CHEF'S TIP:

After removing the lobster meat used in this recipe, reserve the lobster bodies and shells to make lobster broth. If you don't have time to make it right away, toss them in a plastic bag and store them in the freezer for later use.

WARM FRESH TUNA SALAD WITH ROASTED PEPPERS

SERVES 4

1 pound fresh, center-cut tuna steak, cut 1-inch thick

3 tablespoons extra-virgin olive oil

Salt and freshly ground black pepper to taste

2 cups mixed lettuce leaves, washed and dried

1/4 cup Niçoise or Kalamata olives, pitted and chopped

2 tablespoons tiny nonpareil capers

6 fresh plum tomatoes, sliced, *or* 1/2 pint fresh cherry tomatoes, quartered (whichever is ripest)

6 anchovy fillets with excess salt washed off, chopped

1 cup unpeeled diced boiled new potatoes, such as Red Bliss

1 large sweet red pepper and 1 large sweet yellow pepper, roasted, peeled and seeded, and cut in julienne strips

3 tablespoons chopped fresh herbs, such as parsley, chives, and thyme

1/2 cup plus 4 teaspoons Basil and Roasted Pepper Vinaigrette (page 126)

Brush the tuna with olive oil, season with salt and pepper, and sear well on all sides on an outdoor grill or under the broiler. Searing 3 minutes on each side will leave the inside of the tuna a nice pink medium-rare.

Set the tuna aside to cool slightly while preparing the salad. Toss the remaining ingredients, including 1/2 cup of the vinaigrette, together in a bowl.

Divide the tossed salad onto 4 dinner plates. Cut the tuna, which should be still warm but not hot, into 4 equal portions. Place 1 portion of tuna on top of each salad, drizzle 1 teaspoon vinaigrette over the tuna, and serve promptly.

'21'

CHEF'S TIP:

To pit ripe olives easily, lay them on a wooden board and, with the palm of your hand, press on each olive to break the skin. Squeeze the olives between your fingers to remove the pits.

GRILLED
SWORDFISH SALAD

SERVES 4

4 (6-ounce) swordfish steaks

1 recipe Ginger-Pepper Marinade
    (page 343)

6 cups mixed greens, such as
    radicchio, arugula, mâche,
    frisée, and Bibb lettuce

2 pints ripe cherry tomatoes,
    cut in half

$^2/_3$ cup Fresh Herb Vinaigrette
    (page 122)

Rub the swordfish steaks with the marinade. Cover and marinate, refrigerated, overnight. The next day, prepare an outdoor grill for cooking. (In case of rain, you could broil the swordfish instead, but it won't be quite as wonderful.) Right before serving, toss the greens and tomatoes with half the dressing, and divide among 4 serving plates. When the grill is hot, grill the swordfish until it is well colored on both sides and the interior is medium (about 4 minutes total). Remove from the grill and cut each swordfish steak into 3 slices. Place 3 slices on each plate of salad, drizzle the additional vinaigrette over the fish, and serve while still warm.

GRILLED SHRIMP AND SCALLOP SALAD

SERVES 4

16 whole large raw shrimp (about 1 pound), tails on, shells removed

8 large sea scallops

¼ cup Lemon and Garlic Marinade (page 342)

Salt and freshly ground black pepper to taste

1 cup mixed salad greens

½ cup Citrus Ginger Dressing (page 125)

SPECIAL EQUIPMENT:
4 bamboo skewers, soaked in water

Place 4 shrimp and 2 scallops on each of 4 skewers. Brush the Lemon and Garlic Marinade onto the skewered shellfish. Marinate, covered and refrigerated, 2 hours. Just before cooking, season with salt and pepper. Grill over a hot fire (or broil) for 5 minutes on each side, or until fully cooked. Divide the salad greens among 4 plates, top with the skewered seafood, and drizzle with Citrus Ginger Dressing.

FRESH FRUIT IN A COOL GINGER BROTH

**PORT-LACED CHOCOLATE MOCHA TERRINE WITH BROWNIES,
CHOCOLATE TRUFFLES, AND LINZER SQUARES**

POACHED PEARS IN A PHYLLO OVERCOAT

BELUGA CAVIAR SERVED WITH BUCKWHEAT BLINI,
CRÈME FRAÎCHE, AND TRADITIONAL ACCOMPANIMENTS

TEQUILA-CURED SALMON GRAVLAX

WHOLE MAINE LOBSTER SALAD

**DUCK BREAST WITH BALSAMIC VINEGAR GLAZE
AND GINGER-CHESTNUT DRESSING**

SOFT-SHELL CRAB CLUB SANDWICH WITH SHOESTRING FRIES
(THE BEVERAGE IS A SOUTHSIDE)

'21' TRADITIONAL
LORENZO DRESSING

YIELD: 1½ CUPS

During most of '21's history, virtually all the salads (and many of the other dishes) were prepared by captains or waiters in the dining room. This unusual salad dressing was invented by one of those waiters, whose first name, not surprisingly, was Lorenzo. Prepared chili sauce (a mild, chunky tomato sauce) is a table condiment that was once nearly as common as ketchup.

1 teaspoon dry English mustard, dissolved in 2 tablespoons water

½ teaspoon salt

½ teaspoon freshly ground black pepper

¼ cup red wine vinegar

⅔ cup pure olive oil

¼ cup prepared chili sauce

¼ cup finely chopped watercress leaves

¼ cup chopped cooked bacon

In the bowl of a food processor fitted with a steel blade, combine the mustard paste, salt, and pepper. Pulse the mixture together briefly. Then add the vinegar a little at a time. While continuing to pulse, add the olive oil *in a very patient, slow, steady stream* to produce a smooth, creamy mayonnaiselike emulsion. At this point, the dressing can be refrigerated for up to 1 week. When ready to serve, stir in the chili sauce, watercress, and bacon to complete the classic '21' Lorenzo Dressing.

DRESSING THE HOUSE

*N*o protocol officer ever had a more challenging job than Walter Weiss. Or less time to get it right. From 10 A.M. to noon each morning, Walter is seated at table 1, right next to the kitchen door, a steadily ringing phone by his side and chits of paper everywhere. Between calls he performs the intricate ritual called "dressing the house." One hundred fifty almost-equally powerful people are due to begin arriving when the clock strikes twelve. Each is accustomed to leading, being deferred to, getting his or her own way. Many have been coming to '21' their entire lives, as their parents and grandparents did before them. Some come every day; some also come back for dinner two or three times a week.

So how does Walter decide who sits where? Tradition plays a big part; if someone has sat at the same table for lunch every day for the past two decades, there's little question where he or she will be seated. But "dressing the house" also requires a decorator's touch. As an interior designer might make a famous painting the focus of a room and brighten a niche with an object of especial beauty, Walter may seat Arthur Schlesinger at table 1—readily visible to everyone entering the room—and a stunning young fashion executive in a bright red dress at table 12, just inside the entrance.

The tripartite barroom divides inevitably along the structural supports that demarcate the three town houses: 21, 19, and 17, which together make up the '21' Club. "17" used to be the nonsmoking section. "19" includes "Bogie's Corner" and the movie character J. J. Hunsecker's table in *Sweet Smell of Success*. The oldest, "21" section, is where many of the regulars congregate.

Some care more about where they're placed than others. "I go out of my way *not* to request a regular table," says Viacom CEO Frank Biondi. "I hate that," he continues, but then confesses: "They give me a nice table because I know Marshall."

Mama Gabor (center) flanked by two of her three famous daughters, Zsa Zsa at our left, and Magda at our right. Photographed during an era when ladies lunched wearing hats and gloves. (United Press Photo)

Unquestionably the best in their profession, Maîtres d'hotel Walter Weiss, left, and Oreste Carnivale, right, flank the entrance to '21's famed barroom. Semiretired, Walter works only from 10 A.M. to 4 P.M., while Oreste, who came to '21' from The Four Seasons in 1993, typically works twelve to fourteen hours a day, not unusual in the restaurant business. (Photo: Christopher Baker)

'21' HOUSE DRESSING:
FRESH HERB
VINAIGRETTE

YIELD: 1½ CUPS

$^1/_3$ cup balsamic vinegar

3 tablespoons Dijon mustard

2 tablespoons fresh thyme leaves

2 tablespoons fresh oregano leaves

$^1/_4$ cup fresh basil leaves

1 cup extra-virgin olive oil

Salt and freshly ground black
    pepper to taste

Combine the vinegar and mustard in the bowl of a food processor fitted with a metal blade. Pulse briefly, then add the herbs. Pulse again until coarsely chopped. With the processor running, add the olive oil *very slowly* so that the mixture will emulsify into a smooth blend. Season with salt and freshly ground pepper to taste. This dressing will keep, covered, up to 10 days in the refrigerator.

SHALLOT AND CHAMPAGNE VINAIGRETTE

YIELD: 1 CUP

This elegant vinaigrette is also the foundation for the Chunky Blue Cheese and Walnut Dressing and the Citrus Ginger Dressing.

$1/4$ cup champagne vinegar

1 tablespoon Dijon mustard

1 tablespoon granulated sugar

4 large, peeled shallots

$1/4$ teaspoon salt

$1/4$ teaspoon ground white pepper

$3/4$ cup extra-virgin olive oil

In the bowl of a food processor fitted with a metal blade, process the vinegar, mustard, sugar, shallots, salt, and pepper until the shallots are finely chopped. With the processor running, add the oil *very slowly* in a small stream until all the oil has been incorporated and the dressing has achieved a silky, smooth texture. The dressing may be stored, covered, up to 2 weeks in the refrigerator but should be brought to room temperature before using.

'21'

CHEF'S TIP:

True champagne vinegar is produced from champagne grapes. If unavailable, a good white wine vinegar may be substituted.

Chunky Blue Cheese and Walnut Dressing

Yield: 1½ cups

¼ pound smoked slab bacon, cut in
 ½-inch dice

1 cup Shallot and Champagne
 Vinaigrette (page 123)

¼ pound strong blue cheese,
 crumbled into chunks

¼ cup chopped walnut pieces,
 toasted 15 minutes in a 250°
 oven

In a large frying pan, cook the diced bacon over medium heat until crispy but not burned. Drain and discard the rendered bacon grease and allow the bacon cubes to cool. In a stainless-steel bowl, whisk together all of the remaining ingredients. Add the cooled bacon just before dressing the salad.

CITRUS GINGER DRESSING

YIELD: 1½ CUPS

2 blood or navel oranges

1 lemon

1 pink grapefruit

2 limes

2 tablespoons grated fresh ginger

½ teaspoon ground cumin

3 scallions, finely chopped

1 cup Shallot and Champagne
 Vinaigrette (page 123)

SPECIAL EQUIPMENT:

Citrus zester (an inexpensive,
 handy kitchen tool available
 in most houseware
 departments)

Run the citrus zester along the skins of each fruit, being careful not to cut so deeply as to remove any of the white pith. Place 3 tablespoons of the resulting julienne shreds of zest in a mixing bowl. With a very sharp paring knife, peel the fruit and discard the skin and white pith. Slice the peeled fruit into ¼-inch slices, capturing as much of their juice as possible. Combine the fruit slices and juice and the remaining ingredients in the bowl with the zest, and allow to macerate 1 hour before serving.

If you prefer, you can chop the fruit slightly before adding it to the vinaigrette; however, don't overdo this because part of the appeal of this dressing is the visual impact of the vibrantly colored fruit segments.

'21'

CHEF'S TIP:

Slice the fruit over the mixing bowl in order to catch as much of the juices as possible.

BASIL AND ROASTED PEPPER VINAIGRETTE

YIELD: 1¾ CUPS

1 sweet red pepper and 1 sweet yellow pepper, roasted, peeled, seeded, and julienned

¼ cup roughly chopped fresh basil leaves

2 tablespoons chopped shallots

2 tablespoons pitted and chopped Niçoise olives

¼ cup balsamic vinegar

1 cup extra-virgin olive oil

Salt and freshly ground black pepper to taste

Combine all of the ingredients except the olive oil and salt and pepper. Whisk in the olive oil *very slowly* so that the mixture will emulsify into a smooth blend. Season to taste with salt and pepper. This dressing will keep several days refrigerated in a covered jar.

FRESH RASPBERRY
VINAIGRETTE

YIELD 1¼ CUPS

*I*nstead of using raspberry vinegar, this vinaigrette uses fresh raspberries. Fragrant, extra-virgin olive oil has a potent synergy with the berries. Whisk everything together at the last possible moment to bring the full impact of the combined aromas to the table.

1 tablespoon Dijon mustard

½ pint fresh raspberries

½ cup fragrant, extra-virgin
   olive oil

3 tablespoons sherry wine vinegar

Combine all the ingredients, and whisk together until the raspberries just begin to break apart. Serve with Grilled Mushroom Salad (page 108), on grilled chicken, duck, or quail salads, or on a salad of mixed greens.

CHEF'S TIP:

This is a terrific use for day-old or slightly overripe and soft raspberries or blackberries.

'21'

HORSING AROUND AT '21,' PART II:

*A*lways the extrovert, '21' founder Jack Kriendler rode in many a New York parade. According to Jerry Berns, Jack owned one hundred custom-made Western outfits, twenty-five each of four different styles. But his most prized and flamboyant piece of Western finery was the famous Mission Saddle that Jack and his brother Pete bought at a bankruptcy auction in California and promptly insured for $25,000.

The Mission Saddle was made in Los Angeles by saddlemakers commissioned by Marco Hellman of San Francisco. The hand-tooled Mexican leather saddle, which took three years to make, is studded with sterling silver conchos depicting each of the Spanish missions along the California Mission Trail. In 1956 *Argosy* magazine featured the Mission Saddle on its cover, calling it the "World's Finest Saddle." While at '21,' the saddle was displayed in a steel and glass case built specially for it. About twenty-five years ago, at Pete Kriendler's direction, the Mission Saddle was given to the Buffalo Bill Museum in Cody, Wyoming, where it is currently on display.

Only a few examples of Jack's Western paraphernalia are still on display at '21,' mostly in the Winchester Room, one of the Club's private banquet rooms. Included are two pairs of his boots, one with appliquéd leather Ks, and a pistol holster studded with sterling miniatures of '21's iron gates.

ABOVE:

*T*he Mission Saddle was a fixture in '21's lobby for many years. Here, Jack Kriendler allows a guest to try it out. (Photo: Eric Schaal—Pix)

CENTER:

*J*ack in the saddle again. The caption on the back of this postcard reads in part: "Two-Trigger Jack" Kriendler, Baron of Manhattan's noted "21" Club and one of the West's most colorful horsemen, is shown with his famous California Mission Saddle, during his participation in a typically Western Rodeo recently held at the B-Bar-H Ranch, Palm Springs, Calif." (Courtesy of '21')

BOTTOM:

*'21'*s famed Mission Saddle was studded with solid silver conchos depicting each of California's twenty-three Spanish colonial missions. (Photo: HPK Cody)

PAN-ROASTED SALMON WITH
COUSCOUS AND CHILI OIL

■

'21' TRADITIONAL COLD POACHED SALMON
WITH PRESSED CUCUMBERS

■

PAN-ROASTED RED SNAPPER WITH
BASIL OIL AND SUN-DRIED TOMATOES

■

SEA BASS POACHED WITH
LEMON GRASS AND CHILI COCONUT BROTH

■

GRILLED RED SNAPPER WITH
ROASTED EGGPLANT AND PEPPERS

■

PEPPERED TUNA STEAK

■

BROILED RAINBOW TROUT WITH
PINE NUT STUFFING AND SAGE BUTTER

■

FARM-RAISED STRIPED BASS WITH
CHILI PEANUT SAUCE AND
STIR-FRIED NAPA CABBAGE

■

WHITEFISH FILLETS WITH
MORELS AND ASPARAGUS

■

PAN-ROASTED HALIBUT WITH
SEARED TOMATOES AND LEEKS

■

'21' TRADITIONAL BAY SCALLOPS WITH
LEMON BUTTER

■

GIANT BLUE PRAWNS WITH GARLIC RISOTTO

■

GRILLED SHRIMP ON SKEWERS

■

CURRIED SHRIMP WITH ALMONDS

■

SOFT-SHELL CRAB CLUB SANDWICH

■

LOBSTER POT PIE WITH TARRAGON BISCUITS

FISH AND SHELLFISH

Is this a Fast, to keep
The Larder leane? And cleane . . .
Yet still to fill
The Platter high with Fish?

—ROBERT HERRICK

Seafood has always been an important part of the '21' dining experience; from caviar, oysters on the half shell, and Norwegian smoked salmon to Dover sole, grilled swordfish, and Maine lobster. Today, like restaurants all over America, '21' is selling more seafood—and more different *kinds* of seafood—than ever before. People have discovered both seafood's health benefits and its appetite appeal. And overnight air freight has made fresh delicacies from afar as readily available as the local catch.

The most important criterion in shopping for fish is to consider the source. A reputable fish dealer, or fishmonger as they're called in England, is essential. Ask your friends where they buy fish and compare. Ask questions at the market. And let your eyes and nose tell you whether you've found a store that deserves your trust. For instance, a fresh fish's eyes should still be clear, its gills bright red, and its aroma sweet.

In seafood, freshness is all-important. In cooking, it's better to substitute the freshest available fish than to slavishly follow a recipe when that might mean using something less than fresh. It is better to substitute a similar type of fish (oily for oily; white-fleshed for white-fleshed; or flaky for flaky).

At '21,' we always use the freshest, seasonally available fish in our cooking. The flavor, texture, sweet aroma, and overall success of each dish is founded on this principle.

In some parts of the country, there is little fresh fish available. If frozen is your only reasonable alternative, the integrity of your fish dealer is again key. Insist on fish flash-frozen as it is caught. This shipboard technique has been improved greatly in recent years and can result in a good product. Bear in mind that you always should defrost frozen fish in the refrigerator for twenty-four to thirty-six hours to preserve its texture and avoid mushy, soggy, inferior results.

'21'

Chef Michael Lomonaco adds final garnishes to a plate of Broiled Rainbow Trout (recipe page 144). (Photo: Chirstopher Baker)

1 3 2

PAN-ROASTED SALMON WITH COUSCOUS AND CHILI OIL

SERVES 4

I like to serve fish with its skin intact to preserve the healthful, delicious oils that are just below the skin. The crispy skin of a well-sautéed fish adds texture as well as taste and aroma.

4 (5- to 6-ounce) fresh salmon steaks, skin on

Salt and freshly ground black pepper to taste

2 tablespoons canola oil

2 large shallots, peeled and finely chopped (about 1/4 cup)

3 tablespoons tiny nonpareil capers, coarsely chopped

1/4 cup Niçoise or Kalamata olives, pitted and chopped

Juice of 1 lemon (about 2 tablespoons)

1/4 cup dry white wine

1 recipe Couscous with Roasted Tomato (page 277)

4 teaspoons Hot Chili Oil (page 360)

Season the salmon steaks with salt and pepper. Heat the canola oil in a sauté pan or skillet over medium heat 1 minute. Add the salmon steaks, skin-side down, and cook 4 to 5 minutes, until the skin is nicely browned and crispy.

Turn the salmon steaks over and sauté another 4 to 5 minutes. Add the shallots to the pan and cook together with the salmon 1 minute. Add the capers, olives, lemon juice, and white wine. Cover the pan, lower the heat, and cook 3 minutes. Remove from the heat and serve immediately on a bed of Roasted Tomato Couscous. Drizzle 1 teaspoon Chili Oil over each salmon steak just before serving. Serve with Braised Kale with Garlic and Red Wine (page 254).

WINE NOTES:

Choose a crisp refreshing white or a light-styled red such as a Pinot Noir from the Sancerre region of France's Loire Valley to balance the salmon's natural oils and cool the fire of the chili oil.

Chalone Pinot Blanc, California. While this doesn't have the massive flavor of a Chardonnay, it does have the body and acidity to stand up to the richness of the salmon.

Sancerre Rouge "Cuvée Prestige" L. Crochet, Loire Region, France. This rich 100 percent Pinot Noir from the Loire region would be terrific with this highly flavored dish.

'21' TRADITIONAL COLD POACHED SALMON WITH PRESSED CUCUMBERS

SERVES 4

*T*he pressed cucumbers for this recipe should be started at least 4 to 5 hours before you plan to serve or, preferably, the night before.

PRESSED CUCUMBERS:

2 large cucumbers, peeled, split down the middle, seeds removed with a spoon

3 tablespoons salt

Freshly ground white pepper

1 recipe Court Bouillon: (page 335)

4 (5-ounce) fresh salmon steaks, all skin and bones removed

Bibb Lettuce

1 recipe Green Herb Mayonnaise (page 359)

Cut the halved cucumbers into ¼-inch slices resembling half-moons. Place the cucumbers in the bottom of a colander and sprinkle thoroughly with salt. Cover with paper towels. Place the colander in a bowl so that when the cucumbers drain, the bowl will catch the liquid. On top of the paper towels, place a saucepan large enough to cover the entire surface of the cucumber slices, and weight the pan with liquid or anything heavy. The idea is to press the cucumbers with the weight. The combination of the weight and the salt will draw all of the excess moisture out of the cucumbers. Allow to drain, refrigerated, overnight, or at least 4 to 5 hours before serving.

Remove the paper towels and rinse the cucumbers with fresh water to remove any remaining salt. Shake the colander to remove excess moisture, then turn the cucumber slices out onto paper towels to absorb any remaining moisture.

Season the cucumbers with a little freshly ground pepper. Refrigerate, covered, until ready to serve. If you prefer, they can be dressed with mayonnaise and chopped dill, or sprinkled with some white wine vinegar.

Bring the Court Bouillon to a boil. Reduce to a simmer and add the salmon steaks. Simmer, covered, 10 to 12 minutes. Turn off the heat and allow the salmon to cool in the bouillon. When completely cold, remove the salmon from the bouillon. Drain on paper towels to dry completely. Cover the fish with plastic wrap, and place it in the refrigerator to chill 1 to 2 hours, or until ready to serve.

Serve the cold poached salmon on a bed of lettuce along with the pressed cucumbers. The Green Herb Mayonnaise may be passed in a sauce boat or served in small individual ramekins on the side.

PAN-ROASTED RED SNAPPER WITH BASIL OIL AND SUN-DRIED TOMATOES

SERVES 4

WINE NOTES:

These two lighter-bodied reds stand up well to the fresh herbs and the acidity of the tomatoes in this recipe, and go well with fish in general.

Barbera M. Chiarlo, Italy. A light, fresh red, but with lots of bracing acidity that echoes the acidity of the tomatoes.

Moulin-à-Vent Beaujolais, Georges Duboeuf, France. A fresh, lively Gamay. Often the boldest of the Beaujolais. Serve slightly chilled.

4 (5-ounce) pieces red snapper fillet, skin on, but with all pin bones removed

Salt and freshly ground black pepper to taste

2 tablespoons olive or vegetable oil

¼ cup sun-dried tomatoes, soaked in hot water, drained, and julienned

1 clove garlic, finely minced

2 tablespoons chopped fresh thyme

2 tablespoons chopped fresh oregano

3 tablespoons finely chopped shallots

4 teaspoons Basil Oil (page 361)

Season the snapper fillets with salt and pepper. Preheat a sauté pan with the olive oil until the oil is hot, 1 to 2 minutes. Add the snapper to the hot pan, flesh-side down, and cook over medium heat 4 to 5 minutes. Turn to cook the skin side an additional 3 to 4 minutes. The fillets will curl inward briefly, but once they have cooked 1 minute, they will begin to relax and lay flat again, allowing you to cook the skin side to a crispy texture.

Lift out the snapper with a slotted spatula, leaving the juices and oil in the pan. Add the sun-dried tomatoes, garlic, and shallots, and sauté together 2 minutes. Add the fresh herbs to the pan. Stir quickly, just to heat the herbs enough to release their aromas. Pour the sun-dried tomato and herb mixture over the snapper. Then drizzle 1 teaspoon Basil Oil over each fillet and around the dish. Serve with Tuscan White Beans with Olive Oil (page 256).

PLAYROOM FOR THE POWERFUL

"The ceiling's covered with toys!" blurted one surprised first-time visitor to '21's barroom. Well, not exactly. The model airplanes, trucks, and football helmet-stalactites that obscure '21's barroom ceiling are actually corporate mementos, gifts from the captains of industry who consider '21' their neighborhood pub. The flying boat that launched the tradition was donated by Imperial (now British) Airways. Pan Am's Juan Trippe saw it and asked '21' to hang a Pan Am Clipper. C. R. Smith chipped in an American DC-3. Howard Hughes upped the ante with a TWA model. And on it went, with trucks and ships and soccer balls and hardhats joining the crowd.

And each one tells a story. A model of the *PT 109*, donated by John F. Kennedy, hangs over table 28, where Kennedy used to sit when he was fresh out of Harvard. An Owens-Illinois tractor trailer commemorates a specific event that occurred at the table below it: the deal separating Owens Fiberglass and the Illinois Glass Company.

Some of the mementos are more personal than others. Chris Evert's tennis racket, tenor Lauritz Melchior's horned Wagnerian helmet, one of Dorothy Hamill's ice skates. Others are evocative of '21's macho roots: a silver bullet from Teddy Roosevelt's Rough Riders, a noose from who knows where, and an elephant tusk donated by one-eyed hunter Green Annen. Tom Stanley, an architect from Texas, created the bronze Pony Express rider specifically for '21'.

Henry Zbikiewicz presided as '21's head bartender for forty-one years, until his retirement in 1987. Here he serves a crowd that includes then-owners Jerry Berns, Pete Kriendler, and Sheldon Tannen. (Photo: Maxwell Coplan)

SEA BASS POACHED WITH LEMON GRASS AND CHILI COCONUT BROTH

SERVES 4

*T*his is a lower-fat dish, delightful and refreshing with its combination of coconut and chili flavors. A small container of Thai curry paste will go a long way and is a great addition to the seasoning shelf in your cupboard. Lemon grass can be found in the produce section of Oriental grocery stores and some supermarkets. It is an herb that has a lemonlike aroma and flavor without containing citric acid. If you can't locate lemon grass, substitute 1 teaspoon lemon juice for each stalk of lemon grass.

1 stalk fresh lemon grass, cut into 1-inch sections

1 cup Ginger and Soy Broth (page 338)

$1/4$ cup unsweetened shredded coconut (optional due to fat content)

1 teaspoon Oriental chili paste (found in specialty food markets)

$1/4$ cup dry (*not* cooking) sherry

8 large shiitake mushrooms, julienned

4 6-ounce sea bass fillets, *or* red snapper, orange roughy, or flounder

1 recipe Saffron Basmati Rice (page 287)

GARNISH:

12 basil leaves

1 large tomato, seeded and diced

$1/4$ cup chopped scallions

Crush the lemon grass with the back of a knife to release its oils. Combine all ingredients except the fish and rice in a lidded 10- or 12-

inch skillet. The skillet should be large enough so that when the fillets are placed in the broth, they are covered only halfway. Before adding the fish, bring the other ingredients to a boil, reduce the heat, and simmer gently 15 minutes.

After placing the fish fillets in the broth, lower the heat to a very low simmer. Cover and poach gently 8 to 9 minutes. Remove from the heat, place the fish fillets on a bed of Saffron Basmati Rice (page 287), and strain the broth. Discard the lemon grass, but arrange the mushrooms on top of the fish fillets. Ladle a little of the broth over the top. Garnish each serving with 3 basil leaves, diced tomato, and scatter chopped scallions freely over the fillets.

A chilled Beaujolais, a light, easy-drinking Italian, or a Chilean red would also be delicious with this Mediterranean-style classic.

Verdicchio di Matelica, Bisci, Italy. Mouth-wateringly fresh, dry wine, with a touch of Malvasia blended in for additional fruit.

Arneis B. Giacosa, Italy. The Arneis grape in this Piedmont white is full, rich, gloriously fruity, even unctuous. Difficult to find, but worth the effort.

GRILLED RED SNAPPER WITH ROASTED EGGPLANT AND PEPPERS

SERVES 4

*T*his makes a wonderful, easy-to-prepare outdoor supper, since the fish and the vegetables are roasted side by side over the same charcoal fire.

1 to 1$\frac{1}{2}$ pounds tiny baby eggplant or purple Oriental eggplant, halved

2 to 3 fresh sweet red peppers, cored and quartered

$\frac{1}{3}$ cup pure olive oil, plus olive oil to brush on grill

2 (2$\frac{1}{2}$ to 3 pound) whole red snappers*

8 sprigs fresh rosemary

3 cloves garlic, finely chopped

Salt and freshly ground black pepper to taste

Prepare an outdoor barbecue grill with good charcoal briquets or wood chips stacked against one side of the grill and let them burn until ash white. Brush the grill lightly with olive oil, then brush the eggplant and peppers lightly with the oil. Place them skin-side-down on the opposite side of the grill—not over direct heat. Roast 4 to 5 minutes on each side, until well grilled and cooked. Remove to a warm platter and reserve while grilling the fish.

Brush the outside of each fish with olive oil. Fill the cavity of each fish with 2 sprigs rosemary. Rub the garlic on the outsides of the fish. Season with salt and pepper, and grill the fish in the same indirect manner 8 to 10 minutes on each side.

Meanwhile, remove the leaves from the remaining 4 sprigs rosemary. Discard the stems, coarsely chop the leaves, and reserve.

Remove the fish to second platter and cool 5 or 6 minutes. Because the fish has already been cooked, it can be filleted easily by running a sharp knife along the dorsal fin and lifting the fillet away from the bones using two forks to tease it free gently. Place the first fillet on a serving plate, turn over the fish, and repeat the filleting process for the second side.

Serve 1 fish fillet to each person, accompanied with the grilled vegetables. Drizzle each serving with some of the remaining olive oil and sprinkle with the chopped rosemary.

*If you substitute fillets for whole fish, keep in mind that they can be tricky to grill and that they cook in half the time.

PEPPERED TUNA STEAK

SERVES 4

*T*his tuna was one of the first dishes I introduced on the '21' Club menu in 1989. Since then it has remained one of our most popular selections. It continues to be a crowd pleaser, and reflects our long history of featuring the bounty of the sea. A play on the classic beef Steak Au Poivre—with all of the full flavor and richness but without the cholesterol—Peppered Tuna is cooked in much the same fashion. Served rare and without a creamy sauce, it resembles sashimi in its luxurious deep-red interior, yet its peppery crust is a meat-eater's delight. The tuna steaks must be thick enough—at least 1 inch, preferably 2—so the interior stays rare and moist, while the exterior develops a crisp crust.

1/2 cup day-old white bread

4 tablespoons coarsely ground black pepper

1 1/2 pounds fresh tuna loin, cut into 4 equal portions, each 1 inch thick

Salt to taste

3 tablespoons pure olive oil

4 tablespoons finely chopped shallots

1/2 cup dry white wine

1/2 cup Fish Stock (page 331) *or* low-sodium canned chicken broth

Place the day-old bread in the bowl of a food processor fitted with a metal blade and process into fine crumbs. Combine the pepper and bread crumbs on a plate large enough for dredging the tuna steaks. Allow the tuna to come to room temperature just prior to cooking. This will ensure that the center of the steaks are warmed, not overcooked, and yet not icy cold. Lightly season the steaks with salt, then dredge them in the bread crumb mixture. Coat the tuna uniformly on all sides, pressing the coating in with your fingertips so that it adheres evenly.

Heat the oil in a heavy-bottomed skillet over medium heat until hot enough to brown a sprinkling of test crumbs. Add the fish steaks, being careful not to overcrowd them. Sear to form a crusty exterior on all sides, cooking approximately 3 minutes on each side, turning them to avoid burning. Remember that they will cook to medium rare in about 6 to 8 minutes. A gentle poke with your index finger at the center is a good way to judge doneness: The softer the interior feels, the rarer it is; the firmer, the more well done. When the steaks have cooked to your preference, remove them from the skillet with a slotted spatula and keep them warm—but not hot, or they will overcook.

Add the shallots to the skillet, return to the heat, and quickly sauté them until they begin to brown. Deglaze the pan with the wine, allowing it to reduce until nearly dry before adding the stock. Bring to a boil and reduce by half. The entire sauce-making process takes only a few moments. Pour the shallot sauce over the tuna steaks and serve quickly. Accompany with Tomato and Zucchini Gratin (page 255).

BROILED
RAINBOW TROUT WITH
PINE NUT STUFFING
AND SAGE BUTTER

SERVES 4

WINE NOTES:

Sauvignon Blanc and Riesling both work well to offset the richness of the nut and sage filling in this delicate trout recipe.

Sancerre, Reverdy, France. This herbacious Sauvignon Blanc is pleasantly "grassy"—like asparagus or hay—and has good, balanced acidity.

Lucas Riesling, New York. For generations, some of America's best Rieslings have come from New York State. This semidry 1993 New York Wine and Food Classic Gold Medal winner is deep, rich, and refined.

21' gets its trout from a delightful couple in upstate New York who raise them in artesian wells. The pure, clean taste of the trout goes unmasked in this dish.

SAGE BUTTER:

3 tablespoons chopped fresh sage

4 tablespoons unsalted butter, softened to room temperature

Juice of 1 lemon (about 2 tablespoons)

1/2 teaspoon salt

1/2 teaspoon freshly ground black pepper

1/2 teaspoon paprika

3 scallions, finely chopped

STUFFING:

1/2 cup dry bread crumbs

1/4 cup pine nuts

2 fresh jalapeño peppers, seeded and diced

1 clove garlic, finely chopped

1 tablespoon chili powder

Salt and freshly ground black pepper to taste

2 tablespoons vegetable oil

FISH:

4 butterflied rainbow trout, whole, skin on, bones removed (ask your fish dealer to do this for you)

Vegetable oil

Salt and freshly ground pepper to taste

Well in advance of cooking the fish, prepare the Sage Butter by placing all the ingredients in the bowl of a food processor fitted with a metal blade. Pulse to combine well. Using a rubber spatula, heap the mixture onto a sheet of waxed paper, and roll to form a sausage shape. Twist the ends to enclose the butter. Set on a plate and refrigerate at least 1 hour to harden enough so that it can be sliced. When the butter is firm enough to slice, remove the paper wrapping and cut it into $1/4$-inch rounds, which will be used at the final moment of cooking to season the fish. Keep refrigerated until ready to use.

Meanwhile, prepare the stuffing by combining the bread crumbs, pine nuts, jalapeños, garlic, chili powder, and salt and pepper in a bowl. Drizzle the 2 tablespoons vegetable oil into this mixture and blend together lightly with a fork.

Preheat the broiler. Brush both sides of the trout with vegetable oil, season with salt and pepper, and broil skin-side up to crisp the skin, a maximum of 2 minutes to 3 minutes. Remove the fish from the broiler. Place the fish, skin-side down, in a roasting pan that has been lightly rubbed with vegetable oil. Sprinkle the stuffing mixture over the fish. Place the fish in a 375° oven 6 to 7 minutes to finish cooking. When the fish have nearly finished baking, crumble several pieces of the reserved Sage Butter on each fillet, so that in the last moment of cooking, the butter will melt, seasoning the fish.

ABOVE:

'21' founder Jack Kriendler reportedly owned hundreds of outfits and changed clothes several times a day. Here, "the boys in the back room," part of '21's old inner-inner circle, included writer Louis Sobol, left, and sportscaster Ted Husing, right. (Courtesy of '21')

BELOW:

The amenities for '21's closest friends included a barber shop and a fitness room with steam cabinet, weights, and punching bag. (Courtesy of '21')

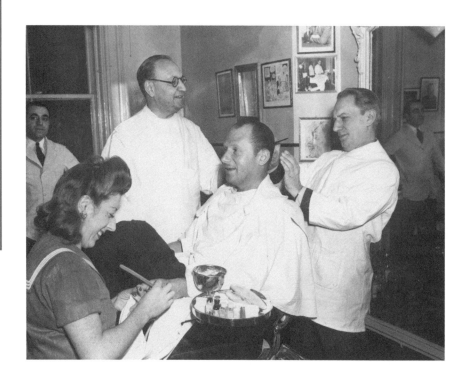

'21'

THE MAN WHO LIVED AND DIED AT '21'

*T*o say that '21' founder Jack Kriendler died at home is to say he died at '21,' for 21 West 52nd Street was literally, as well as figuratively, Jack's home. He and his wife, Luisa, kept an apartment on the third floor. The bedroom where Jack died from a sudden coronary thrombosis is now an executive office and part-time private dining room.

Across the hall, what was then Luisa's dressing room is now Pete Kriendler's office. Above Pete's manly clutter of lassos, Indian war clubs, a cartoon of Pete being cooked by cannibals while in search of Albert Schweitzer (Pete made the trip more than once, and lived to tell the tale), and autographed drawings of John Wayne and Jimmy Cagney, the cherubs and ribboned garlands that decorated Luisa's boudoir ceiling still smile down upon it all.

While Jack was dubbed "the Baron" by his friends, Luisa was a baroness in fact: the Baroness Luisa Dumont de Chassart of Belgium, whom Jack married (secretly, according to one source) in Miami Beach in 1940. When Jack died seven years later, more than 2,000 wreaths were sent to his funeral, including ones from then-Mayor William O'Dwyer and former postmaster general James A. Farley. (*The Herald Tribune* claimed "10,000 floral offerings surrounded the bier.") Over 1,000 mourners attended the services at Riverside Chapel, where honorary pallbearers included Supreme Court Justice Louis Valente and attendees included State Attorney General Nathaniel L. Goldstein, Superintendant of State Police John A. Gaffney, and County Judge Louis Goldstein—an interesting assembly for a man who made his name and fortune outside the law.

Farm-raised Striped Bass with Chili Peanut Sauce and Stir-fried Napa Cabbage

Serves 4

'21'

WINE NOTES:

A refreshing, uncomplicated white wine would pair well with the spicy peanut sauce in this dish.

Conde de Valdemar, M. Bujanda, White Rioja, Spain. Made from the Viura grape, this delicious, inexpensive aromatic wine is fruity and spicy.

Clos Floridène, Bordeaux Blanc, France. The Semillon grape predominates in this good, reasonably priced white Bordeaux.

With wild striped bass runs becoming increasingly sporadic, delicious, mild-flavored domestic striped bass is now being farmed from coast to coast. Leave the skin on for the crispiest, tastiest result.

MARINADE:

4 egg whites

$^1/_2$ cup dry (*not* cooking) sherry

$^1/_4$ cup cornstarch

1 tablespoon Oriental sesame oil

CHILI PEANUT SAUCE:

1 cup low-sodium soy sauce

3 tablespoons dry (*not* cooking) sherry

3 tablespoons peanut butter

1 tablespoon Oriental sesame oil

2 teaspoons crushed chili peppers or red pepper flakes

1 tablespoon garlic, peeled and chopped

1 tablespoon chopped fresh ginger

FISH:

1 pound striped bass fillets, cut into 1$^1/_2$ inch strips

$^1/_2$ cup sesame seeds

Vegetable oil for deep-fat frying

1 recipe Stir-fried Napa Cabbage (page 263)

Deep-fat fryer

Prepare the marinade by combining all the ingredients in a bowl. Mix well with a whisk. Marinate the fish strips, refrigerated, in this mixture at least 1 hour before cooking.

While the fish strips are marinating, prepare the Chili Peanut Sauce. Combine all the ingredients in a saucepan. Bring to a boil, then lower the heat and simmer 5 minutes. Allow to cool while preparing the fish.

After the fish strips have marinated, dredge them in the sesame seeds and allow to dry, refrigerated, 30 to 60 minutes before frying. Deep-fry in a 360° deep-fryer 6 to 7 minutes, until the seeds have toasted and the fish strips have become a crispy golden brown.

Serve on a bed of Stir-Fried Napa Cabbage with the Chili Peanut Sauce drizzled over the top.

WHITEFISH FILLETS WITH MORELS AND ASPARAGUS

SERVES 4

All across the Northern Hemisphere, spring is a time of delicious anticipation. In the Great Lakes region, where the winters are long and cold, morels and asparagus are signature delicacies that celebrate the coming bounty of summer. This authentically regional combination is the perfect complement to the sweet, mild flavor and delicate texture of whitefish from Lake Superior. Among the most delicious of wild mushrooms, morels may be difficult to come by, but they are worth the effort and expense. The Northwest has a bountiful harvest each spring that finds its way into gourmet food shops and better supermarkets across the country.

1/2 pound fresh morels or other wild mushrooms *or* 1 to 2 ounces dried morels or other wild mushrooms, washed and soaked in hot water 30 minutes

1 pound young, thin asparagus

4 tablespoons canola oil

3 tablespoons finely chopped shallots

1/2 cup Fish Stock (page 331)

1/4 cup dry white wine

4 (6-ounce) fillets of whitefish, skin on

Salt and freshly ground black pepper to taste

3 tablespoons chopped fresh thyme

3 tablespoons unsalted butter

Clean the morels carefully, washing them under cold water, then laying them out on paper towels to absorb the excess moisture and air dry. Trim the asparagus stems at the point where a knife slices through easily. If the skin seems at all tough or stringy, peel the stalks with a vegetable peeler.

In a sauté pan, heat 2 tablespoons canola oil over medium heat. Add the morels and sauté 3 to 4 minutes. Add the shallots and cook 3 minutes more. Add the fish stock and allow the morels to braise 2 to 3 minutes. Add the asparagus and white wine and continue to cook another 3 minutes. Remove from the heat and place on a warm platter and set aside.

Season the fish with salt and pepper. Heat the remaining canola oil in a second heavy skillet. Sauté the fillets $2^1/_2$ to 3 minutes on each side, and remove to the platter holding the asparagus.

Return the morels to the sauté pan to heat to the boiling point. Add the thyme and butter. Remove promptly from the heat and allow the butter (which adds a creamy texture to the dish) to melt. Spoon over the fish and serve promptly.

Pan-Roasted Halibut with Seared Tomatoes and Leeks

Serves 4

Wine Notes:

Hints of the sea in these two white wines marry well with the clean, mild flavor of the halibut.

Albariño Lagar de Cervera, Spain. Delicious in their fruitiness and high in appealing acid, Albariño grapes produce white wines that may have a little zestiness.

Vermentino Sella & Mosca, Italy. Made from the Vermentino grape, this ripe, soft, fruity Sardinian white is worth searching for. A wine that transports your taste buds to the warm Mediterranean.

Halibut is a large, deep-water ocean fish known for its delicate flavor, firm texture, and beautiful white color. This dish is a favorite of Maureen Cogan, owner of Art & Auction magazine and wife of '21' owner Marshall Cogan.

3 tablespoons pure olive oil

1¹/₂ pounds halibut, cut into 4 1¹/₂-inch-thick steaks

Salt and freshly ground black pepper to taste

1 cup canned plum tomatoes, crushed and drained (with juice reserved in another container)

3 large leeks, split, carefully washed, and chopped

2 tablespoons finely minced shallots

¹/₄ cup dry white vermouth

¹/₂ cup Fish Stock (page 331), Chicken Stock (page 332), or water

3 tablespoons chopped fresh tarragon

Preheat the oven to 350°. Meanwhile, on top of the stove, heat the olive oil in a large skillet. Season the fish with the salt and pepper, and sear the fish well in the oil, 2 to 3 minutes on each side. Remove the fish to an ovenproof platter and set aside. In the same pan, sear the tomatoes over medium heat, add the leeks, and cook together 3 minutes. Add the shallots, the reserved tomato juice, vermouth, and stock or water, and cook 10 minutes more over medium heat, or until the sauce reduces by half.

Pour the vegetable mixture over the fish and roast in the preheated oven for 8 minutes. Serve immediately, sprinkled with the chopped tarragon.

'21'

Bob Kriendler gives Marilyn Monroe a guided tour of '21' Club artifacts. Reprinted by permission of photographer Sam Shaw © from his and Leo Rosten's book: Marilyn Among Friends.

WHERE EAST MEETS WEST

*M*any of '21's early customers—especially the screen stars—would have been considered jet-setters if only there had been jets in those days. Nevertheless, they found numerous ways to keep in touch across the continent. Jack Kriendler, in a bid to sweep actress Arline Judge off her feet, would sing love songs to her in Hollywood, via telephone from '21's lobby, with a three-piece band to back him up.

A 1936 advertisement for "TWA; The Lindbergh Line" featured endorsements from Ginger Rogers, Douglas Fairbanks, Jr., Lupe Velez, Cary Grant, Ann Sothern, and Richard Dix, describing them as "the same delightful people you find dining at famed '21,' " and boasting overnight service from coast to coast (with stops in Albuquerque, Amarillo, Wichita, Kansas City, and Chicago).

Perhaps the largest single Hollywood invasion of '21' was hosted by the not-yet-reclusive Howard Hughes, who flew in twenty-five starlets on the maiden flight of his newest aircraft, the *Constellation*. Hughes took over the entire club for the night, entertaining a couple of hundred New Yorkers as well as his actress-imports.

One eventual Hollywood legend was actually on the '21' payroll. David Niven describes in his autobiography, *The Moon's a Balloon*, how a dubious Jack Kriendler had him "fingerprinted at FBI headquarters." Niven, who actually worked for '21' Brands, received a $40-a-week retainer against 10 percent of sales. According to Marilyn Kaytor, author of *"21": The Life and Times of New York's Favorite Club*, when he wasn't busy sitting in '21' with Barbara Hutton, he would grab a few bottles of Ballantine's and take them down the street to sell to Rose's Restaurant, then stand at their bar and drink up the profits of his sale.

By this super-effort Feg Murray has completely confounded Rudyard
Kipling. For he has clearly illustrated and demonstrated that the East
does meet the West, and where—at "21."

*Artist Feg Muray
portrayed several of the
speakeasy era's most
glamorous film stars in this
whimsical illustration for the
1936 edition of* The Iron
Gate *of Jack & Charlie's
"21." (Courtesy of '21')*

'21' TRADITIONAL BAY SCALLOPS WITH LEMON BUTTER

SERVES 4

*F*or hundreds of years, New Yorkers took the magnificent, sweet little bay scallops from Long Island for granted. But in recent years, because of changes in the ecosystem and overall warming of the bay, many of the Peconic Bay scallop beds have lost most of their productivity. While marine scientists believe the beds will return in time, we in New York have had to look elsewhere for true bay scallops. Fortunately, a comparably sweet, succulent bay scallop is found off Nantucket and Cape Cod, Massachusetts. This classic sauté method, which we have used at '21' for sixty-five years, is one of the simplest cooking techniques there is, but produces one of the most delicious dishes imaginable.

3 tablespoons vegetable oil

4 tablespoons unsalted butter

Salt and freshly ground pepper to taste

1 pound bay scallops

Juice of 1 large lemon (about 3 tablespoons)

$1/4$ cup chopped fresh flat-leaf parsley

Choose a sauté pan large enough to hold all of the scallops without overcrowding the pan. An overcrowded pan tends to cool too quickly, allowing the scallops to bleed their delicious juices and to steam rather than sauté.

Heat the vegetable oil and 1 tablespoon of the butter until nearly smoking. Season the scallops with salt and pepper and add them to the pan in one even layer. Do not move or shake the pan, but allow the scallops to brown well on one side before gently turning them with a spatula to cook the second side.

Remove the scallops from the pan to a warm serving platter. Return the pan to the heat, add the remaining butter, and cook until it begins to turn a light-brown color. When the butter has browned, stir in the lemon juice and parsley. Pour over the scallops and serve promptly.

GIANT BLUE PRAWNS
WITH GARLIC RISOTTO
SERVES 4

WINE NOTES:

Because the garlic has mellowed in the cooking process, the subtle flavor of the prawns is preserved, and leaves room for wines with definite personalities.

Jermann Vintage Tunina, Italy. A deeply flavored blend of Chardonnay, Sauvignon Blanc, Malvasia, Ribolla, and Picolit by a great wine maker.

Château Hureau, Loire, France. This inexpensive Chenin Blanc is aromatic, with fruit flavors reminiscent of green apples. Ultimately dry, but with a hint of sweetness and a good balance of acid.

Primarily a specialty item available in better markets, blue prawns are a wonderful delicacy resembling shrimp in outward appearance. The prawns have a different texture, more akin to crayfish, and their flavor is quite delicate. That's why we use paprika for this recipe, because it has a certain essence of chili peppers without a lot of heat. Depending on their size, 3 to 4 prawns per person should be more than adequate. The prawns can be cooked under a broiler, over a charcoal grill, or in a hot skillet while the Garlic Risotto is being finished. Blue prawns are also wonderful served with couscous or just quickly cooked and placed on a salad with a simple vinaigrette.

1 pound giant blue prawns (12 to 16 per pound), in their shells

Salt and freshly ground black pepper to taste

$1/4$ cup dry white wine

1 recipe Garlic Risotto (page 284)

DRY MARINADE:

3 tablespoons vegetable, olive, or canola oil

1 tablespoon Hungarian paprika

1 teaspoon ground cumin

2 shallots, very finely chopped

When cleaning the prawns, leave them intact: head on, tail connected to the body. Carefully remove the shell covering the tail meat, trying not to disturb the head, because within the head cavity are delicious morsels of roe. Using poultry shears, trim any antennae or sharp appendages to the head as well as the long legs. These tend to burn and make cooking difficult.

Combine the marinade ingredients, rub on the prawns, and marinate, refrigerated, 1 to 2 hours before cooking.

When ready to cook, season the prawns with salt and pepper. Prepare an outdoor grill or preheat the oven broiler. Grill or broil the prawns 4 minutes on each side until well charred and fully cooked. During the last 2 or 3 minutes of cooking, sprinkle ¼ cup white wine over and around the prawns to add flavor and to keep them moist. Serve the prawns on a bed of Garlic Risotto.

'21'

PITCHING THE YANKEES AT '21'

What do you do when you've just signed to buy the New York Yankees for $2.8 million (chump change today, but big bucks in 1945) and you've got maybe ten grand to your name and no backers in sight? In Larry MacPhail's case, you walk into '21' for a drink, strike up a conversation with old friend Dan Topping, home on leave from the Pacific, and hatch a plan.

Even between the two of them, they were still shy of the mark, so they decided to call Bing Crosby. Crosby knew baseball commissioner Judge Kenneshaw Mountain Landis would never approve of his participation because he owned the Del Mar racetrack, so he referred them to his pal Del Webb in Phoenix, who had once been a ball player himself. The deal was struck, another round of drinks undoubtedly was ordered, and Larry MacPhail left '21' with a smile on his face and a baseball team in his pocket.

Three years later, on October 12, 1948, the Yankees chose '21' as the place to unveil their controversial new manager to the press. As Red Patterson explained: "We hired the '21' Club. We were the Yankees. We went first class." But not even the polish of '21' was sufficient to smooth the way for Casey Stengel's stumbling tongue: First he got the name of his boss, Dan Topping, wrong; then, when asked what he thought about managing the great Joe DiMaggio (who was sitting right there), Stengel replied: "I can't tell you much about that, being as since I have not been in the American League so I ain't seen the gentleman play, except once in a very great while."

The biggest deal the Yankees ever cut at '21' was considerably less public. In 1983 contract negotiations between the Yankees, represented by a committee called KEG (Kuhn, Einhorn, & Giles), and NBC were held at one point in a file room at '21.' The result: baseball's first billion-dollar-plus deal for broadcasting rights; undoubtedly an occasion that merited a Jeroboam-size toast.

GRILLED SHRIMP ON SKEWERS

SERVES 4

This wonderful summertime dish begs to be cooked outdoors, preferably on a charcoal fire flavored with hickory or applewood chips.

24 large fresh shrimp, peeled and deveined, with tails left on

1 recipe Ginger-Pepper Marinade (page 343)

Salt and freshly ground black pepper to taste

1 recipe Wheat Berries with Onion and Curry (page 273)

Hot Chili Oil (page 360)

SPECIAL EQUIPMENT:

8 soaked bamboo or metal skewers, 6 inches or longer

Thread three shrimp on each of the skewers. Place the skewered shrimp in a dish large enough to hold the skewers and deep enough for the marinade. Pour the marinade over the shrimp and refrigerate 3 to 4 hours before cooking. Remember to turn the skewers periodically to fully flavor both sides.

Prepare an outdoor barbecue grill. Season the shrimp with salt and pepper, then place on the grill, directly over a hot fire (flavored with wood chips, if desired). Grill 3 minutes on each side. Remove promptly and serve with Wheat Berries with Onion and Curry and a drizzle of Chili Oil.

'21'

WINE NOTES:

The spicy marinade calls for a wine bold enough to hold its own.

Kunde, "Magnolia Lane," Sauvignon Blanc, California. A smattering of Viognier grapes gives this highly flavored Sauvignon Blanc exotic overtones.

Errazuriz Sauvignon Blanc, Chile. Sauvignon Blanc is Chile's most successful varietal. This one is herbacious, light, fresh, and clean. Very reasonably priced.

MOPSY

(Courtesy of '21')

CURRIED SHRIMP WITH ALMONDS

SERVES 4

*C*urried chicken and shrimp dishes have been mainstays of the '21' repertoire for decades. This recipe is based on a British curry sauce made with heavy cream—although the unsweetened Thai coconut milk adds a distinctly exotic touch.

1 pound raw shrimp in their shells, 5 to 6 per serving

Salt and freshly ground black pepper to taste

3 tablespoons Madras (hot) curry powder

2 tablespoons unsalted butter, melted

3 shallots, finely chopped

1/4 cup dry white wine

1 cup Chicken Stock (page 332)

1/2 teaspoon cayenne pepper (optional)

1/4 cup unsweetened coconut milk

1 cup fresh green peas

1/2 cup roughly chopped fresh tomato

1/2 cup heavy cream

1/2 cup slivered almonds, toasted 6 to 8 minutes in a 300° oven

1 recipe Saffron Basmati Rice (page 287)

Clean, peel, and devein the shrimp. Season with salt and pepper. Sprinkle the curry powder on the shrimp and coat well. In a skillet, heat the butter until bubbly. Add the shrimp to the pan, and sauté over medium heat until well browned on both sides, about 4 minutes. Add the shallots and cook until translucent, another 2 minutes. Add the white wine and reduce 2 minutes. With a slotted spoon, remove the shrimp to a warm platter. Add the Chicken Stock, cayenne (if using it), coconut milk, and vegetables to the skillet the shrimp were cooked in. Cook over medium heat 3 minutes. Add the heavy cream, being careful not to let it boil, and stir to incorporate. Remove from the heat, ladle over the shrimp, and sprinkle the toasted almond slivers on top. Serve with Saffron Basmati Rice.

SOFT-SHELL CRAB CLUB SANDWICH

SERVES 4

For a fleeting interval each summer, crabs molt their shells and become tender outside as well as in. Newcomers to this delicacy, daunted by the prospect of eating a crab shell and all, become serious devotees after a single bite. If you don't have access to fresh soft-shell crabs, frozen ones are the next best thing.

At '21', we use a brioche bun for this sandwich. But any good soft bun, croissant, or French bread would be wonderful. Clean and slice the vegetables and have everything ready to assemble before you begin the brief cooking process.

4 large soft-shell crabs

Salt and freshly ground black
    pepper to taste

2 tablespoons chili powder

2 tablespoons vegetable oil

4 soft buns, such as brioche,
    croissant, or other good-
    quality soft dinner buns

Several leaves of red-leaf lettuce

1 tomato, sliced

$1/2$ cup alfalfa sprouts

2 avocados, peeled, pitted, and cut
    in $1/4$-inch slices

$1/2$ cup Chili Mayonnaise
    (page 358)

Season the crabs with salt and pepper, and sprinkle both sides with the chili powder. Preheat a pan with the oil until nearly smoking. Add the crabs, belly-side down. Cook 5 minutes before turning. Lower the heat and cook another 5 minutes on the second side. Remove from the pan and pat dry with paper towels to remove any excess oil.

Build your sandwich with lettuce, tomato, sprouts, and avocado, topped off with the crab and Chili Mayonnaise. Perfect on a summer afternoon.

'21'

WINE NOTES:

Choose a simple, unassuming wine or—maybe even better with this dish— an interesting, little-known beer from any one of the growing number of microbreweries.

Aligoté Jayer-Gilles, France. This "other" white Burgundy, made from the Aligoté grape, is earthy, full-bodied, easy to quaff, and inexpensive.

Galestro Antinori, Italy. An inexpensive blend of Trebbiano and Malvasia grapes. Crisp and dry.

LOBSTER POT PIE
WITH TARRAGON
BISCUITS

SERVES 4

*T*he rich, luxurious flavor of fresh lobster side by side with homemade biscuits creates an experience that is simultaneously grand and unassuming.

TARRAGON BISCUITS
(YIELDS 36 1-INCH BISCUITS)

1 cup all-purpose unbleached flour

1/2 cup buttermilk

1 teaspoon baking powder

1/2 teaspoon salt

2 tablespoons chopped fresh tarragon

3 tablespoons unsalted butter, cut up and icy cold

4 (1-pound) live lobsters

2 tablespoons unsalted butter

3 carrots, peeled and finely diced (about 1/2 cup)

1 large Idaho potato, peeled and diced (about 3/4 cup)

2 ribs celery, diced (about 1/2 cup)

2 leeks, split, well washed, and diced (about 3/4 cup)

1 onion, peeled and diced (about 1/2 cup)

1/2 teaspoon each, salt and freshly ground pepper

1/2 cup dry (not cooking) sherry

1 cup Chicken Stock (page 332) or Fish Stock (page 331)

1 cup heavy cream

Preheat the oven to 350°. Prepare the biscuits before beginning to cook the lobster. In a bowl, combine all of the biscuit ingredients except the butter. When the ingredients are well mixed, add the butter and blend with a fork. Do not overmix. Allow the butter to stay chunky. (When your biscuit dough is lumpy, you know you've made it correctly.) Lay the dough out on a lightly floured board, shape into a rectangle and cut with a 1-inch-thick, round or square biscuit cutter. Place the biscuits on a nonstick baking pan and bake 14 minutes at 350°. (The ideal time to place the biscuits in the oven is just *after* you begin to cook the lobsters. They can be held unbaked, covered and refrigerated, for several hours, or overnight, before baking.)

Bring 2 cups of water to a boil in a lidded pot large enough to hold all four lobsters. Add the live lobsters, cover, and steam 12 to 14 minutes. Remove the lobsters from the pot and cool 5 minutes. Break the claws and tails away from the lobster body shells. Crack the claw and tail shells, remove the meat, cut the tail meat in half, and reserve.

Split the lobster bodies into two equal halves and sauté in the butter in a large skillet or wok over high heat. Add all of the vegetables and stir together with the lobster bodies, using a big wooden spoon. Add the salt and pepper, sherry, and Chicken or Fish Stock. Bring to a boil, cover, reduce to a simmer, and cook 10 minutes. After 10 minutes, remove all of the lobster bodies from the pot, trying to leave behind as much of the vegetable and liquid as you can. Place the lobster bodies—2 halves per person—on large individual platters.

Add the cream and reserved lobster meat to the vegetables and stock mixture in the pot. Heat 2 minutes, but do not boil the cream. Turn off when the cream is heated through. Spoon some of the vegetable sauce over each platter of lobster. Serve with warm Tarragon Biscuits on the side.

THE 1975 '21' BURGER

■

MICHAEL'S '21' BURGER

■

'21' TRADITIONAL STEAK DIANE

■

'21' TRADITIONAL RIB STEAK "BRIZZOLA"

■

ROASTED FILLET OF BEEF WITH
ROASTED SHALLOTS

■

BOURBON PEPPER STEAK

■

STANDING RIB OF BEEF

■

PAN-ROASTED VEAL CHOPS WITH
SAGE AND MUSHROOMS

■

BRAISED VEAL SHANKS WITH
CARROTS, PARSNIPS, AND TURNIPS

■

SAUTÉED CALVES' LIVER WITH
SMOTHERED ONIONS AND BACON

■

VEAL SWEETBREADS WITH CAPERS AND LEMON

■

RACK OF LAMB WITH MUSTARD SEED CRUST

■

BONELESS ROAST LEG OF LAMB WITH
FETA CHEESE, OLIVES, AND BABY EGGPLANT

■

CHILI-RUBBED PORK TENDERLOIN WITH
PEACH FRITTERS

MEATS

*To be free minded and cheerfully disposed at hours of meat and sleep
and of exercise is one of the best precepts of long lasting.*

—FRANCIS BACON

One of '21's great strengths as a restaurant has always been its ability
to procure the finest in provisions. Years ago, '21's meat lockers held
as many as 160 shells of beef at a time . . . enough for 1,000 portions.
Today the finest cuts of beef, lamb, and pork arrive pretrimmed, already aged to our precise specifications.

Much has been written about the declining per-capita consump-
tion of beef in America. While this is true overall, people are still eating plenty of beef in restaurants. Why? Probably because beef has
come to be considered a splurge—from both a monetary and a dietary
standpoint. Just the thing to order when you're painting the town red.

This is certainly the case at '21.' Even though they are among the
most expensive items on '21's menu, our Dry Aged Black Angus
Steaks are perennial best-sellers. One of the reasons an entrée like
Steak Brizzola, for instance, is so popular at '21' is because rib steak in
some ways embodies the best of a beef steak. It has a mouth-filling
moistness—the result of a high fat content. For the same reason, it has
a rich, "beefy" flavor and superb tenderness.

Shell steaks or sirloin steaks—sometimes called New York strip
steaks—are also known for their rich beef flavor but tend to have a
chewier texture overall. Filet mignon, on the other hand—a prized
cut of beef, especially in restaurants—is renowned for its tenderness

but not for its flavor. So while the filet mignon may have the reputation of being the most luxurious of steaks, true beef eaters tend to prefer strip sirloin or rib-eye steaks.

'21's all-time champion beef eater? One likely claimant would have been Bobby Lehman, son of New York governor Herbert Lehman, who drank as well as ate his beef. When Lehman ordered "beef tea" to drink with dinner, the captain would bring him a $60 filet mignon, cooked very rare, place it in one of '21's silver duck presses, and squeeze out the "tea."

The "longest-steady-diet" award would have gone to perennial patron Hubie Boscowitz, who enjoyed a nightcap of Steak Tartare with two raw egg yolks after the theater nearly every night, and remained cheerfully unrepentant until the day he died at age ninety-four.

Just as I seek out locally grown, organic produce for '21,' I am also constantly on the lookout for the leanest, healthiest meats to include on our menus. When veal is served, it is usually natural, free-range veal—meaning it came from calves raised with access to fresh air, sunshine, and room to move about. We also serve organic baby lamb from Vermont.

The fact that many people prepare and consume less meat today is all the more reason to make it the best when you do decide to splurge. Many specialty markets are beginning to feature drug-free, humanely raised meats. Ask your butcher whether the meat he or she is selling is free-range and organic. If the answer is no, let your interest be known.

THE MOST EXPENSIVE BURGER IN THE WORLD

*U*nquestionably the most talked-about, written-about hamburger in history, the '21' Burger inspires fierce partisanship. Currently $21.50 at lunch and $24.00 in the evening, the '21' Burger is still the least expensive entrée on the menu (except for omelettes).

President Jimmy Carter writes about a '21'-related incident he recalls from his presidential campaign:

During the summer of 1976 in Plains, all the significant news media were represented by reporters. There were literally hundreds of them, including some of the most famous TV anchors and newspaper columnists. Their favorite eating place was a double-wide mobile home just west of Americus, about nine miles from Plains. The restaurant was owned and operated by Mr. and Mrs. David West, who fascinated the reporters with good home-cooked, inexpensive meals. A big hamburger was 75 cents. Later, when the election was over, some of them took Mrs. West to New York, and asked her where she would like to eat. She chose the '21' Club, and later told us that she ordered a hamburger because she wanted to see what a $12 one looked like. She reported that it was excellent—but no better than hers. She figured the high rent and atmosphere were worth the difference.

The '21' Burger of today—a classic American open-face saloon burger—is significantly different from the '21' Burger of twenty years ago. For comparison, we've included the recipes for both.

At one time, '21's meat lockers held as many as 160 full shells of beef at a time—enough to feed a thousand people. (Courtesy of Walter Sanders, Life *magazine)*

THE 1975 '21' BURGER
SERVES 4

This older version of the '21' Burger—sautéed in butter and served with Brown Sauce (no bread or bun)—was really more like a Salisbury steak than a burger, even though it was shaped like a burger.

1 stalk celery, diced (about ¼ cup)

¼ cup Chicken Stock (page 332) or canned broth

2 pounds ground top sirloin

¼ teaspoon ground nutmeg

Dash Worcestershire Sauce

¼ cup fresh bread crumbs

Salt and freshly ground black pepper to taste

3 tablespoons unsalted butter (for cooking burgers)

BROWN SAUCE (OPTIONAL):

3 tablespoons cold, unsalted butter

3 tablespoons flour

1 cup Beef and Veal Stock (page 333)

Salt and freshly ground black pepper to taste

Preheat the oven to 350°. In a small saucepan, poach the celery in the Chicken Stock for 20 minutes. Drain, cool, and finely chop the celery. In a mixing bowl, combine the beef, nutmeg, Worcestershire Sauce, bread crumbs, and chopped celery by hand, using rapid motions, without overworking the mixture. Shape it into 4 round patties. Season the patties with salt and pepper, cover, and refrigerate until ready to cook.

To prepare the Brown Sauce, knead 3 tablespoons butter and flour together into a paste. Bring the Beef and Veal Stock to a boil, whisk the paste into the stock, and continue to cook 5 minutes, or until the sauce has thickened. Season with salt and pepper and reserve.

Heat the 3 tablespoons butter for cooking the burgers in a cast-iron skillet over medium heat until it begins to brown. Add the beef patties and brown them about 6 minutes on each side. Place the burgers, still in the cast-iron skillet, in the oven and continue to cook 6 to 8 minutes more for medium rare. Remove and serve with '21' Traditional Hash Brown Potatoes (page 237), '21' Traditional Creamed Spinach (page 252), and the optional Brown Sauce drizzled over the burger.

MICHAEL'S '21' BURGER

SERVES 4

This is a classic open-face bar burger, a carnivore's delight. Allow extra grilling time for this outsize knife-and-fork burger. The combination of two different beef cuts produces a flavorful juicy burger.

2 1/2 pounds fresh ground beef, equal parts top sirloin and top round (80 percent lean)

1/4 cup pure olive oil, plus additional to lightly coat the meat and grill

Salt and freshly ground black pepper to taste

1 tablespoon dried thyme

4 slices Italian peasant bread, 1/2-inch thick and 5 inches in diameter

2 ripe beefsteak tomatoes, cut into 1/2-inch-thick slices

1 red Bermuda onion, cut into 4 1/2-inch-thick slices

Handle the ground beef as briefly as possible—in other words, don't "knead" the meat—because overhandling changes its texture, moistness, and flavor. Using your bare hands, shape the meat firmly into 4 round, uniform patties about 1 1/2 inches thick. Brush both sides of the burgers lightly with olive oil and sprinkle with salt and pepper. Brush the grill lightly with olive oil and grill the burgers over a medium flame until done to your preference (about 5 to 6 minutes on each side for medium rare, 7 to 8 minutes on each side for medium, and 9 to 10 minutes on each side for well done).

Meanwhile, add the dried thyme to the 1/4 cup olive oil. Brush the bread, tomato, and onion slices with the thyme oil. Salt and pepper the tomato and onion slices. Place the bread, onion, and tomato on the grill, and grill lightly on both sides.

'21'

CHEF'S TIP:

Resist the temptation to press the burgers with a spatula while they are on the grill. I always tell my new grill cooks, "Press pants, not burgers." Pressing on a burger makes a big show, with flames flying, but it also makes a dried-out burger because you press out all its juiciness.

Place the grilled bread on a warm plate, top with the onion, tomato, and finished burger. Serve with French Fries (page 240) and '21' Serious Steak Sauce (available in gourmet food stores or by mail from the '21' Club).

That's a lot of "spinach"!

'21'

Both Popeye's originator, Segar (see cartoon on page 253), and Segar's successor, B. Zaboly, were good friends of '21's. Zaboly's poke at the high price of dining at '21' reflects a recurring theme in the cartoons donated by numerous artists for both the 1936 and 1950 editions of '21's privately published Iron Gate.
(Courtesy of '21')

'21' TRADITIONAL
STEAK DIANE

At '21,' Steak Diane is traditionally prepared tableside by the captains or maître d' Walter Weiss. The beef, sizzling in a large copper pan with brandy flaming and sauce bubbling, makes a wonderful show reminiscent of the days when Humphrey Bogart and friends would bound in at midnight following the newest opening on Broadway. Today, because many of us eat beef less frequently, we tend to want something special when we do. Steak Diane fills the bill perfectly. Showy but simple to prepare, the quick cooking keeps the meat juicy, while the savory sauce is appropriately wicked for a self indulgence.

2 tablespoons unsalted butter

4 (6-ounce) shell steaks, butterflied and pounded with a meat tenderizer to $1/4$-inch thick

Salt and freshly ground black pepper to taste

3 tablespoons chopped shallots

2 ounces fine brandy

$1/4$ cup white wine

1 teaspoon hot prepared English mustard

$3/4$ cup Beef and Veal Stock (page 333)

4 tablespoons heavy cream

3 tablespoons chopped fresh chives

Since each pounded, flattened steak should have a large circumference, it will be necessary to cook the steaks one or two at a time, setting each aside on a warm platter as you finish those that remain.

Preheat the oven to 350°. On top of the stove, heat a large, heavy skillet over medium heat. Add $1/2$ tablespoon butter to the hot pan and heat until it begins to foam. Season the beef with salt and pepper. Add the first steak and sear, cooking no more than 1 to 2 minutes before turning it over and allowing another minute on the second side. Remove the steak from the pan to a warm ovenproof platter. Repeat with the remaining butter and the remaining steaks. After the fourth steak has been cooked and removed from the pan, add the shallots and cook 2 minutes, until translucent. Lower the heat, move the pan away from the stove, and cautiously add the brandy. Being careful not to flame the brandy, return the pan to the stove, and over low heat, allow it to cook off. Add the white wine to the pan, raise the heat, and bring quickly to the boil. Stir in the mustard. Allow this to cook 1 minute before adding the Beef and Veal Stock. Cook 1 minute more. Add the cream. Bring just to the boil. Remove from the heat and stir in the chives.

Place the ovenproof platter of steaks in the oven 1 to 2 minutes to reheat them very quickly before placing them on individual dishes and topping with some of the Diane Sauce. Serve with Chive Mashed Potatoes (page 248).

'21' TRADITIONAL RIB STEAK "BRIZZOLA"

SERVES 4 TO 8*

I think this is the perfect grilled steak. It's been served at '21' for so long that the origin of the name is shrouded in mystery. It is simply a top-quality 16- to 18-ounce rib steak, a "real" steak for the real meat eaters out there. At '21' we cook Steak Brizzola on a high-temperature restaurant grill. At home, outdoor grilling is the best way to simulate this technique since the outdoor grill tends to be hotter than a home oven broiler. The humidity is also too high in the closed chamber of an oven broiler, preventing the formation of a crisp outer crust as the steak cooks. If you must use an oven broiler, keep the door ajar to help give the excess moisture a chance to escape. This steak could be pan-fried with equally fine results.

4 (16- to 18-ounce) rib steaks

2 tablespoons pure olive oil

2 tablespoons chopped fresh garlic

Salt and freshly ground black pepper to taste

Brush the steaks with olive oil. Spread a little of the chopped garlic on both sides of all the steaks. Season with salt and pepper to taste.

Over a hot barbecue grill, or in a broiler that has been preheated at least 20 minutes, cook the steaks on both sides to the desired doneness. Generally, a steak of this size, cooked over a barbecue grill, will be medium-rare within about 12 minutes (6 minutes on each side).

Serve with '21' Traditional Hash Brown Potatoes (page 237).

*While '21' serves one full steak per person, one steak could be sliced and shared by two.

Roasted Fillet of Beef with Roasted Shallots

SERVES 8 TO 10

*T*his is a great party dish because it is prepared easily and can be served as part of a buffet as well as for a more formal sit-down dinner.

1 (5- to 6-pound) beef tenderloin, trimmed and defatted, but left whole

¼ cup pure olive oil

Salt and freshly ground black pepper to taste

1 recipe Roasted Shallots (page 260)

Preheat the oven to 425°. Place an empty, heavy-bottomed roasting pan into the oven for 10 minutes. While it is heating, season the fillet with salt and pepper to taste. After 10 minutes, remove the roasting pan from the oven, add the olive oil to the pan, tilt to coat the bottom, and then add the seasoned fillet. Place in the oven 10 minutes. Then turn the fillet over and return to the oven to sear the second side an additional 10 minutes. Reduce the oven temperature to 375°, and cook until the meat reaches an internal temperature of 145° for medium rare (approximately 15 to 20 minutes more).

While the fillet is cooking, prepare the Roasted Shallot recipe.

When the tenderloin has finished roasting, remove it from the oven and allow to rest 15 to 20 minutes. Slice the tenderloin into ½-inch-thick slices and arrange on a platter. Spoon the shallots over the top, and serve with Roasted Potatoes with Garlic and Thyme (page 247) and Rosemary-Seared Spinach with Olive Oil and Garlic (page 251).

WINE NOTES:

The concept here is simple—permit food and wine to shine equally—so each enriches and complements the taste of the other.

Joseph Phelps "Insignia," Napa, California. A complex yet subtle fusion of three powerful grapes: Cabernet Sauvignon, Merlot, and Cabernet Franc.

Penfolds Bin 389, Australia. This great Australian Cabernet-Shiraz blend is all ripe-berry flavors, but also pleasingly dry.

Bourbon
Pepper Steak
Serves 4

4 (8-ounce) New York cut strip
  steaks, trimmed of all
  visible fat

4 tablespoons cracked black
  peppercorns (more if desired)

Salt to taste

1 tablespoon pure olive oil

1/4 cup good Kentucky bourbon

1/2 cup red wine

1/2 cup Beef and Veal Stock
  (page 333)

1 tablespoon unsalted butter

Coat the steaks with the cracked pepper and season with salt. Place
the olive oil in a cast-iron skillet and heat 1 minute before adding the
steaks. Cook over medium heat 3 minutes on each side for medium
rare. Remove the steaks to warm serving plates. Drain the excess fat
from the pan and carefully add the bourbon, away from the heat. Reduce the heat to low and reduce the bourbon until the pan is nearly
dry. Add the red wine, raise the heat to medium, and reduce by half.
Add the Beef and Veal Stock, bring to a boil, cook 6 minutes, and
"finish" by swirling the butter into the sauce. Remove from the heat
and divide the sauce among the steaks. Serve with Matchstick Potatoes (page 240) and Creamed Spinach (page 252).

Wine Notes:

*This assertively seasoned
steak calls for an equally
spicy, equally American
wine.*

*Ridge "Lytton Springs"
Zinfandel, California. This
has just the hint of bramble,
briar, Western spiciness, and
oak to fill the bill.*

*Kenwood "Jack London"
Zinfandel, California. A
dark wine with a plumlike
quality that is perfectly suited
to this American dish.*

Chef's Tip:

*A coffee grinder works well
for cracking peppercorns.*

STANDING RIB OF BEEF

SERVES 6 TO 8

WINE NOTES:

A special-occasion roast like this calls for a wine with enough character to withstand the massive flavor of aged Western beef, body to mellow the richness, and intensity to carry you from bite to bite.

Niebaum-Coppola "Rubicon," California. This Cabernet-Merlot blend matures to a distinctive smoky taste.

La Rioja Alta "Gran Reserva," Spain. Aged for at least five years, this stunning deeply colored, full-flavored, and highly scented red wine made from the Tempranillo grape is very reasonably priced.

A standing rib of beef, also called prime rib or rib roast, is definitely a special-event recipe. For six to eight people, a five-rib roast is plenty. Ask your butcher for a roast cut from the sixth through twelfth ribs. This section is the best, the most tender and flavorful. Some people cut the eye of the rib away from the bone, then tie it back to the bone section to roast (which makes it easier to carve after cooking), but I prefer to leave the meat attached to the bones and roast them as one. This ensures good flavor and minimizes shrinkage during cooking.

1 oven-ready rib roast, approximately $4^1/_2$ to $5^1/_2$ pounds

3 tablespoons pure olive oil

$^1/_4$ cup cracked black peppercorns

3 teaspoons coarse kosher-style salt

2 tablespoons chopped fresh garlic

3 tablespoons dried thyme

Preheat the oven to 425°. Brush the meat with the olive oil. Combine all of the seasonings in a small bowl. Rub the seasoning paste uniformly over the meat. Place the meat, bone-side-down, in a roasting pan and roast 20 minutes at 425°.

At the end of 20 minutes, reduce the oven temperature to 350° and continue cooking $1^1/_4$ hours for medium rare. Remove from the oven and allow the roast to stand 20 minutes before carving.

Transfer the roast to a large cutting board, bone-side down. Insert a sharp knife between the meat and the rib bones, separating the meat from the ribs in one large piece. Carve the meat into $^1/_2$-inch-thick slices, and serve with Stuffed Poblano Peppers (page 258).

The ribs, with their attached crispy meat, are wonderful separated into individual ribs, brushed with spicy Dijon mustard, and returned to the oven 6 to 7 minutes to make a crispy mustard coating.

PAN-ROASTED VEAL CHOPS WITH SAGE AND MUSHROOMS

SERVES 4

This roasting and braising technique will yield a moist veal chop and a delicious natural pan-juice sauce.

4 center-cut $\frac{1}{2}$-inch-thick rib veal chops

Salt and freshly ground black pepper to taste

3 tablespoons pure olive oil

1 cup parboiled pearl onions (frozen are fine)

12 ounces fresh, cleaned, sliced mushrooms such as cremini, Portobello, shiitake, oyster, or any combination

$\frac{1}{4}$ cup dry white wine

1 cup Beef and Veal Stock (page 333)

3 tablespoons chopped fresh sage leaves

2 ounces prosciutto ham, thinly sliced and julienned

Season the veal chops with the salt and pepper. Heat the oil in a large, deep skillet over medium heat. Add the veal chops, and brown 3 to 4 minutes on each side, until nicely browned. Remove from the pan. In the same pan, sauté the onions in the pan juices 3 to 4 minutes, or until they're browned. Add the mushrooms to the onions and sauté until the mushrooms begin to wilt. Add the white wine and reduce until the wine evaporates. Add the veal stock, sage, and prosciutto, and bring to a boil. Return the veal chops to the pan and cover, leaving the lid slightly ajar. Reduce the heat to low and cook an additional 10 minutes. Serve the chops on individual plates, with some of the sauce spooned over each, and accompanied by Roasted Garlic (page 261) and Roasted Tomato and Goat Cheese Salad (page 109).

'21'

WINE NOTES:

This simply prepared dish calls for a hearty, dry red to withstand the bold herb flavor.

Clos du Val Merlot, Stag's Leap District, California. A rich, concentrated wine with lush Merlot fruit. A few years in the bottle is a big help.

Cousiño Macul, Maipo "Antiguas Reservas," Chile. A big bang for your buck, this very dry Cabernet—produced from vines as old as ninety years—has an attractive herb and black currant character.

BRAISED VEAL SHANKS WITH CARROTS, PARSNIPS, AND TURNIPS

SERVES 4

WINE NOTES:

Full-flavored wines for a full-flavored dish based on the Italian classic, osso buco.

Chianti Classico, Badia a Coltibuono, Italy. A well-made example of what Tuscan wine can be—and a bargain to boot.

Ravenswood "Sonoma County Old Vine" Zinfandel, California. A rustic wine that is solid and reliable.

Veal shanks—called osso buco in Italian restaurants—are a full-flavored juicy cut. The shank bone, surrounded by succulent meat, requires careful braising to render the meat as tender as it can be.

4 veal shanks, with the bone in the center surrounded by meat, cut into 8- to 10-ounce portions

Salt and freshly ground black pepper to taste

3 tablespoons pure olive oil

1 cup diced carrots

1 cup diced parsnips

1/2 cup diced turnips

4 cloves garlic, left whole, peeled

2 tablespoons tomato paste

1 cup dry white wine

1 cup Chicken Stock (page 332) or Beef and Veal Stock (page 333)

GARNISH:

Chopped fresh thyme

Preheat the oven to 350°. Season the veal with salt and pepper. Heat the olive oil in a large, heavy skillet and sear the veal shanks over high heat on all sides until well browned, about 6 minutes. Remove the browned veal shanks from the skillet and place them in an oven-proof casserole. To the skillet, add the diced vegetables and the whole garlic cloves, and sauté them 3 to 4 minutes.

When the vegetables have begun to cook and wilt, add the tomato paste and combine thoroughly. Add the white wine and the Chicken or Beef and Veal Stock and bring to a boil. Pour the boiling vegetable-liquid mixture over the veal shanks in the casserole and braise covered in the oven 1 hour 45 minutes. The veal should be served fork-tender, with the meat just beginning to separate from the bone.

Serve with Mushroom Risotto (page 284) or Toasted Polenta (page 274), and garnish each veal shank with a sprinkling of fresh chopped thyme.

THE "RULES" OF '21'

'21's "front desk," an eighteenth-century Danish mahogany secretary, is manned by Harry Lavin (right) and Mark Shekhar Naini. Between them, they are responsible for directing several hundred guests a day to the barroom, lounge, or one of '21's seven banquet rooms. (Photo: Christopher Baker)

For a place that was founded for the express purpose of flouting the law of the land, '21' has been a stickler for its own rules over the years. Long a holdout against admitting women in pants, '21' is—to this day—off-limits to men without jacket and tie.

There are stories, apocryphal perhaps, of celebrities who found ways around the rules. Groucho Marx, it is said, wore his tie on his T-shirt; Sammy Davis, Jr., wore his around his head. Both Prince Bernhardt of the Netherlands and Richard Burton often arrived in turtleneck sweaters. They would pick up a tie (usually black) at the front desk and proceed to the dining room. But more often, the tieless didn't make it past the door. Charles Koppelman, chairman of EMI Records, tells of bringing Barbra Streisand and a tieless John Peters to '21' about twenty years ago, only to be told to go away.

Katharine Hepburn was reportedly the only early exception to the no-women-in-pants rule, a rule that came under serious fire in the '70s. Maître d' Walter Weiss reports the club surrendered after one guest, being told that pants were not allowed on women at '21,' went into the ladies' room and removed them, returning in just her minilength top.

Before Marshall Cogan bought the restaurant, the "rules" of admittance could be arbitrary indeed. "In those days if you wore a blue suit with brown shoes, forget it, they wouldn't let you in," confirms Weiss. Status was no guarantee of admittance either. In 1984 the *New York Post* reported an incident in which three ambassadors were turned away because one of their luncheon partners, a New York hotelier, had reputedly "stolen" two of '21's top employees.

"People were very intimidated coming here," continues Weiss. "Not like today with an open door. It's a different era since 1987. I like this era much better. It's more democratic. There's not so much of a hassle."

WE CAN'T ADMIT HIM—OUR RULES CLEARLY STATE
LADIES DON'T HAVE TO WEAR **ANYTHING,** BUT
GENTLEMEN **MUST** WEAR A TIE.

(Courtesy of '21')

SAUTÉED CALVES' LIVER WITH SMOTHERED ONIONS AND BACON

SERVES 4

This is a classic '21' lunch dish, and was a favorite of Joan Crawford. Although Americans are generally standoffish about organ meats (euphemistically referred to as "variety meats"), the two most popular in this country have always been veal sweetbreads and calves' liver. While somewhat out of fashion, these delicacies are a special treat to all who recognize their considerable gustatory virtues.

2 tablespoons vegetable oil

1 pound of calves' liver in 8 equal slices, cut as thinly as possible

Salt and freshly ground black pepper to taste

2 red onions, peeled and very thinly sliced

1 tablespoon granulated sugar

¼ cup balsamic vinegar

½ cup Beef and Veal Stock (page 333)

8 to 12 slices cooked bacon

Heat the vegetable oil in a sauté pan or skillet until hot. Season the calves' liver with the salt and pepper, and add to the hot pan, searing well 2 to 3 minutes on each side for medium rare. If all of the liver doesn't fit into the pan at one time, cook it in two batches and remove the cooked liver to a warm platter.

Add the onions to the same skillet and sauté until they begin to crisp and brown. Add the sugar and continue cooking another 2 minutes.

Do not allow the sugar to burn. Add the vinegar and stock, bring to a boil, then reduce the heat to low and simmer an additional 2 or 3 minutes.

Serve the liver on a bed of the smothered onions and top each serving with 2 or 3 slices cooked bacon.

WHO'S GOING
TO TAKE ME
TO "21"?

JAMES MONTGOMERY FLAGG

'21'

When James Montgomery Flagg wasn't designing patriotic posters such as his famed UNCLE SAM WANTS YOU!, he sometimes sought inspiration on the beach and at '21.'
(Courtesy of '21')

VEAL SWEETBREADS WITH CAPERS AND LEMON

SERVES 4

*S*weetbreads, the thymus gland of the calf, should be special-ordered from your butcher. Insist on fresh, clean sweetbreads that have a sweet aroma. Sweetbreads may be cooked in one stage, but I prefer the results of two-stage cooking. The first stage—blanching (or parboiling)—can be done a day or two ahead of time. The second stage—sautéing or broiling the sweetbreads—should be done just moments before serving.

1 recipe Court Bouillon (page 335), substituting ¼ cup whole milk for the vinegar

1½ pounds fresh veal sweetbreads (4 pieces, approximately 6 ounces each), cleaned of any visible connective tissue or blood

Salt and freshly ground black pepper to taste

3 tablespoons unsalted butter

2 tablespoons capers

Juice of 2 lemons (about ¼ cup)

¼ cup white wine

½ cup Chicken Stock (page 332)

3 tablespoons chopped fresh flat-leaf parsley

1 tablespoon chopped fresh thyme

Bring the Court Bouillon to a boil, reduce the heat, and simmer 20 minutes. Add the veal sweetbreads and simmer 15 minutes. Remove the pot from the stove and allow the sweetbreads to cool in the liquid an additional 30 minutes. If the sweetbreads are to be used another day, store them, refrigerated, in the Court Bouillon until ready to use.

When you are ready to continue cooking, remove the sweetbreads from the Court Bouillon. Remove any remaining visible connective tissue, and slice the sweetbreads in half, lengthwise, so that you have 8 equal portions. Season with salt and pepper.

Heat 1 tablespoon of the butter in a heavy skillet until it begins to brown and bubble. Add the sweetbreads and cook 3 minutes on each side. The blanched sweetbreads are very fragile at this point. Turn them gently, using a spatula. When the sweetbreads have cooked a total of 6 minutes, add the capers to the pan, and swirl with the sweetbreads. Add the lemon juice and cook 1 minute more. Add the white wine and chicken stock, and allow the sweetbreads and capers to braise in the sauce an additional 3 minutes before adding the chopped parsley, thyme, and remaining 2 tablespoons butter. Serve immediately.

RACK OF LAMB WITH MUSTARD SEED CRUST

SERVES 4

MUSTARD SEED CRUST:

¹/₂ stick (4 tablespoons) unsalted butter	1 tablespoon mustard seeds
1 egg yolk	¹/₃ cup spicy Dijon mustard
¹/₂ cup fresh bread crumbs	1 teaspoon salt
1 tablespoon dried rosemary	1 teaspoon cracked black peppercorns
2 racks of lamb, 8 ribs each (this allows 4 chops per person)	1 teaspoon cracked black peppercorns
1 teaspoon salt	2 tablespoons pure olive oil

Combine the ingredients for the Mustard Seed Crust in the bowl of a food processor fitted with a metal blade and pulse until thoroughly mixed. Line a loaf tin with plastic wrap. Using a spatula, spoon the Mustard Seed Crust mixture into the pan, smooth the surface, and place in the refrigerator. Chill until solid. This can be done well in advance of cooking the lamb, or even frozen for use at a later date.

Preheat the oven to 350°. Season the lamb with the salt and pepper. Heat the olive oil in a heavy skillet over medium heat 2 minutes. Place the lamb racks, meat-side down, in the skillet, and brown 2 to 3 minutes, to a crispy brown coating. Turn over. Cook 1 minute more on the bone side. Remove from the skillet and place in a roasting pan. Place the racks in the oven and cook 8 to 10 minutes for medium rare.

While the lamb is roasting, remove the mustard crust by lifting the plastic wrap out of the loaf. You should now have a rectangular slab of seasoned mustard crust. Cut it lengthwise into ½-inch slices. Set them aside until the lamb has cooked 8 to 10 minutes. Remove the lamb from the oven and lay the slabs of seasoned mustard crust on the meat side of the lamb. Return to the oven 2 minutes more to allow the mustard crust to brown slightly.

Remove and let cool 1 to 2 minutes before slicing into individual chops or four-rib servings. Serve with Roasted Shallot-Potato Cake (page 244) and Roasted Eggplant Firecracker Rolls (page 266).

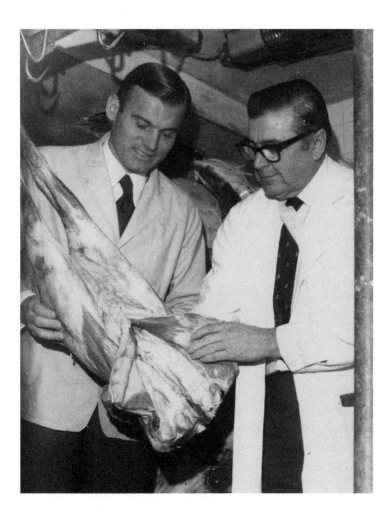

TIME OUT AT 21: Between the 1968 and 1969 football season, renowned New York Giant place kicker Pete Gogolak took time out for a six-month apprenticeship at '21,' learning the restaurant business from the cellar up. Here Chief Steward Ed Quigley explains what to look for when selecting lamb. Although Gogolak never became a restaurateur himself (he played professional football for another decade, and is now with R. R. Donnelly, the largest printing firm in America), he feels he learned a lot about marketing and sales from the experience and is proud to have a son who recently graduated from his alma mater, Cornell's Hotel School. (Courtesy of '21')

BONELESS ROAST LEG OF LAMB WITH FETA CHEESE, OLIVES, AND BABY EGGPLANT

SERVES 6 TO 8

This flavorful lamb cut, filled with a savory stuffing, also makes an impressive presentation when sliced. Ask your butcher to bone and butterfly a leg of lamb for you so that it can be opened out in one relatively flat, seamless piece.

1 (7- to 8-pound) leg of lamb, butterflied, bones removed

1 cup fresh bread crumbs

1/4 cup chopped fresh flat-leaf parsley

3 large cloves garlic, chopped

1/2 pound Greek feta cheese, crumbled

1/2 pound Kalamata or other Mediterranean-style ripe black olives, pitted and coarsely chopped

2 tablespoons dried rosemary, crushed

2 tablespoons pure olive oil

Juice of 1 lemon (about 2 tablespoons)

Salt and freshly ground black pepper to taste

8 to 10 small baby eggplants, washed

SPECIAL EQUIPMENT:
Toothpicks, skewers, or butcher's twine to close the leg of lamb

Preheat the oven to 375°. Lay the butterflied leg of lamb flat on a work surface, fat-side down. Pound briefly to flatten. Combine the bread crumbs, parsley, garlic, feta cheese, olives, rosemary, olive oil, and lemon juice in a bowl and blend well to make a coarse stuffing for the lamb. Spread the stuffing evenly along the center of the inside of the leg of lamb. Fold the lamb toward the center, one side and then the other, to enclose the stuffing and form a roll. Tie the roll in several places with butcher's twine so that it does not open during cooking.

Season the outside of the lamb with the salt and pepper and place, seam-side down in a roasting pan. Place in the oven and roast 45 minutes, then add the whole baby eggplants to the pan. Continue roasting the lamb and eggplants another 35 to 40 minutes for medium rare.

Remove the lamb and eggplants from the oven and allow the roast to cool 20 minutes before slicing. Serve 2 to 3 slices of lamb per person, with Roasted Potatoes with Garlic and Thyme (page 247) and 1 roasted eggplant. Split the eggplant down the middle to serve. They should be eaten by scooping out the creamy eggplant interior, leaving the shells behind.

CHILI-RUBBED PORK TENDERLOIN WITH PEACH FRITTERS

SERVES 4

A pleasant change from ribs or chops, the tenderloin (filet mignon) of pork is the leanest, most tender and delectable cut available. The Chili Marinade keeps the pork from drying out during cooking.

2 pounds whole pork tenderloin

Vegetable oil to fill a deep-fryer or
    deep skillet to an appropriate
    level

CHILI MARINADE:

2 tablespoons Chili Paste (page
    357)

1/2 cup fresh orange juice

Juice of 1 lemon (about
    2 tablespoons)

3 tablespoons honey

2 tablespoons ketchup

1 teaspoon ground cumin

3 tablespoons mango chutney

PEACH FRITTERS:

1 cup unbleached white flour

1 teaspoon baking soda

2 large eggs

1 tablespoon honey

4 ounces dark beer

1/2 cup whole milk

6 ripe peaches, peeled, stones
    removed, and sliced into
    eighths

Flour, for dredging

SPECIAL EQUIPMENT:

Deep-fryer

Combine all the marinade ingredients in a container large enough to accommodate the pork tenderloin strips. Add the pork tenderloin, turning to cover it completely with the marinade, and marinate in the refrigerator overnight, or at least several hours before cooking.

About 30 minutes before beginning to cook the pork, combine the flour, baking soda, eggs, honey, beer, and milk to make the fritter batter. Be careful not to overmix, and allow the flour to stay lumpy. Allow the batter to rest 30 minutes.

The pork is particularly delicious marinated overnight and grilled on an outdoor barbecue grill. In a pinch, it can be broiled in a hot oven broiler or roasted in a 375° oven. In any case, each tenderloin is small, so they should cook in no more than 15 to 20 minutes.

If grilling outdoors, prepare a barbecue with white-hot coals. Remove the pork from the marinade, letting the excess drain back into the container. Season each tenderloin lightly with salt and pepper. Brush the grill with cooking oil. Lay the pork on the grill and cook, turning frequently to avoid burning. Before removing it from the grill, broiler, or oven, use a meat thermometer to check that the pork has reached an internal temperature of 165°.

While the pork is cooking, heat the vegetable oil to between 320° and 340° in a deep-fryer or a heavy, steep-sided skillet. If using a skillet, the oil should be handled with care.

Dredge the peach sections in flour, and drop each floured piece into the fritter batter. Using tongs, carefully place the battered peach slices into the frying oil.

Fry only a few fritters at a time, so that they don't stick to each other or cause the temperature of the oil to drop below 320°. At the other extreme, the oil should not be hotter than 340° to prevent burning the coating before the peaches have cooked. As each fritter becomes golden brown and crispy, drain it on paper towels, then remove it to a platter and keep warm while the rest are cooking. When the tenderloin is done, cut it into ¹/₂-inch-thick slices and serve together with the peach fritters and Chili Onion Rings (page 257).

POUSSIN WITH RED WINE SAUCE

■

'21' TRADITIONAL CHICKEN HASH

■

THYME-ROASTED CHICKEN

■

ROASTED CORNISH HEN WITH HONEY MUSTARD GLAZE

■

ROAST GUINEA HEN

■

SLOW-ROASTED LONG ISLAND DUCKLING

■

DUCK BREAST WITH BALSAMIC VINEGAR GLAZE

■

PAN-ROASTED QUAIL WITH PORT SAUCE

■

GRILLED QUAIL SALAD

■

QUAIL WITH ROASTED FIGS

■

WILD PARTRIDGE WITH SAGE AND PROSCIUTTO

■

ROASTED SQUAB WITH CORN-AND-CHILI SAUCE

■

ROASTED SCOTTISH PHEASANT WITH APRICOTS AND DATES

■

GRILLED YOUNG PHEASANT

■

WILD TURKEY WITH GINGER CHESTNUT STUFFING

■

GRILLED RABBIT LOIN WITH
FRESH THYME AND FRAGRANT OLIVE OIL

■

BRAISED RABBIT WITH PEARL ONIONS, SMOKEHOUSE
BACON, AND HOMINY GRITS

■

VENISON CHOPS

■

RACK OF VENISON WITH
APPLE AND SZECHUAN PEPPERCORN SAUCE

■

QUICK-COOKING RED VENISON CHILI

POULTRY AND GAME

What is sauce for the goose may be sauce for the gander
but is not necessarily sauce for the chicken, the duck,
the turkey or the guinea hen.

—ALICE B. TOKLAS

Although the *Food Lover's Companion* defines poultry as "any domesticated bird used as food," that definition now encompasses numerous birds once found only in the wild. Today pheasant, quail, partridge, and squab are as likely to be farmed as chickens and turkeys. Unfortunately, Americans rarely venture beyond the latter two (and even turkey generally is reserved for special occasions). More's the pity. All poultry and wild game birds have excellent nutritional value. Not only are they sources of complete protein, they are also rich in calcium, iron, and phosphorus.

Of the many delicious and varied alternatives to "the big two," Cornish hen is probably the most widely available. If you want to try the recipe on page 199 for the tender, succulent young spring chicken the French call *poussin*, you'll probably have to look to a specialty butcher or one of the mail-order sources we've listed in the "Resources" (page 381). Guinea hen is equally worth seeking out for its full flavor and moist, tender meat.

Duck is growing steadily in popularity. And the varieties available are more than keeping pace: In addition to the traditional mild-flavored "Long Island" (Pekin) duck, specialty butchers usually can supply domestically raised mallards, Muscovies, and moulards (a hybrid cross of Pekin and Muscovy, celebrated for its foie gras and breast meat).

'21's menus have always catered to the well-traveled palates of sophisticated patrons accustomed to dining on the likes of Scottish grouse, Russian boar, and Swedish elk. '21's menu for Saturday, November 6, 1982, included Bob-White Quail, Venison Steak, Mallard Duck, Partridge, and Baby Pheasant. The dining room captains were all trained in the use of special silver presses that transformed Muscovy ducks into '21's famed Pressed Duck. There was even a Hunt Room, decorated with game trophies brought back by big-game hunters such as Frank Buck and Robert Ruark.

With the proliferation of game ranches both here and abroad, game is no longer so difficult to obtain that it can be enjoyed only in fine restaurants, prepared by a brigade of professional chefs. Sophisticated distribution networks can now put fresh or frozen game on your table within a day or two, no matter where you live.

By law, all the game birds and meats sold in the United States are inspected under government permit and are subject to the same standards that ensure the safety and quality of domestic beef, chicken, and pork. The game birds purchased for '21' are raised in conditions similar to those on high-quality poultry farms producing free-range chickens or turkeys.

Even when deer and elk are raised free-range in the United States, they are harvested under close Department of Agriculture regulation and supervision. The so-called gamey flavors associated with wild game ineptly processed by amateurs need not be a concern for anyone purchasing legal game in this country. Nor do the following recipes require complicated procedures. They've all been tested by cooks of varying skill, who found them both practical and delicious.

So go ahead and take the plunge. You, and whomever you share the results with, will be glad you did. If your local markets don't carry some of the game you'd like to try, ask if they can order it for you, or see the "Resources" (page 381) for additional suggestions. Many of the recipes for game birds also can be prepared using chicken or Cornish hens, although, of course, the results will be different from those if you used quail or squab or pheasant.

POUSSIN WITH RED WINE SAUCE

SERVES 4

*P*oussin, *or young spring chicken, is available from specialty butchers and mail-order sources listed in the "Resources" (page 381). Its mild and delicate flavor is a real change of pace from ordinary chicken.*

3 tablespoons pure olive oil

4 small spring chickens, 12 to 16 ounces each, split in half down the back

Salt and freshly ground black pepper to taste

1 cup pearl onions, peeled (frozen are fine)

1/2 cup diced carrots

1/2 cup diced turnips

2 tablespoons dried thyme

3 cloves garlic, crushed

1 cup dry red wine

1/2 cup canned plum tomatoes, drained and crushed

2 cups Chicken Stock (page 332)

1/4 cup crumbled crisp-fried bacon

Preheat the oven to 350°. Heat the olive oil in a large, deep skillet. Season the chicken halves with the salt and pepper, and brown well on both sides before removing and placing in an ovenproof casserole.

To the skillet in which you cooked the chicken, add the onions, carrots, turnips, thyme, and garlic, and sauté until the vegetables begin to wilt. Add the red wine, plum tomatoes, and Chicken Stock to the vegetables, and cook 10 minutes over medium heat. Pour the vegetable mixture over the chicken in the ovenproof casserole and bake 1¼ hours.

When the chicken has finished baking, add the cooked, crumbled bacon to the casserole, and serve with Chive Mashed Potatoes (page 248).

'21'

WINE NOTES:

These higher-acid reds echo the acidity of the tomato and wine sauce. Uncomplicated, neither would overpower baby chicken.

Marqués de Cáceres "Reserva," Spain. Like all Spanish "Reservas," this flavorful, beautifully scented Rioja is aged a minimum of three years prior to release.

Dal Forno Romano Valpolicella Superióre, Italy. A top producer of this soft and elegant red from the region near Verona.

Comfort Food for Presidents, Princes, and Prima Donnas

*M*aître d' Walter Weiss recalls that when he was a young waiter at '21' just after World War II, Chicken Hash was the most popular dish they served. Especially on Monday nights—opera night. After the performance, men in white tie and ladies in designer gowns would gather at '21' for Chicken Hash and scrambled eggs at midnight.

Special names were given to each of the various ways Chicken Hash was served. Chicken Hash '21' is the name for Chicken Hash served with wild rice. Chicken Hash St. Germaine is served with a puree of peas and grilled cheese on top. Chicken Hash Beyers—served with both wild rice and puree of peas—is named for William Paley's daughter, Mrs. Hilary Beyers, who always ordered it that way.

(© KFS)

'21' TRADITIONAL
CHICKEN HASH

SERVES 4

*O*ne of the all-time great comfort foods, Chicken Hash has been a staple at '21' throughout the restaurant's history. '21's recipe has evolved over the years, from finely chopped chicken in a rich, heavy béchamel sauce to today's larger chunks of chicken in a lighter, velouté-style cream sauce.

1½ pounds skinless and boneless chicken breasts

Salt and freshly ground black pepper to taste

3 cups Chicken Stock (page 332)

1 stick (8 tablespoons) unsalted butter, softened

½ cup unbleached white flour

¼ cup dry (*not* cooking) sherry

¼ cup heavy cream

1 recipe Wild Rice (page 286) omitting the pecans

1 recipe Rosemary-Seared Spinach with Olive Oil and Garlic (page 251)

Season the chicken breasts with salt and pepper. Bring the Chicken Stock to a boil. Add the chicken breasts. Lower the heat to a simmer, and poach the chicken breasts 20 minutes, or until fully cooked. Remove the chicken from the poaching liquid, and cool completely before cutting into 1-inch cubes. Reserve the liquid.

Combine the softened butter with the flour, kneading them together into a paste. Return the reserved Chicken Stock to a boil and, using a wire whisk, carefully add the flour/butter combination in 1-tablespoon increments.

Cook 5 minutes, then add the sherry and cream. Adjust the seasoning with salt and pepper, and cook at a low simmer 10 minutes more. Add the diced chicken to the cream sauce, and cook an additional 5 minutes before serving with Wild Rice and Rosemary-Seared Spinach with Olive Oil and Garlic.

'21'

WINE NOTES:

Pair this '21' classic with a good white "quaffer": a simple Chardonnay to offset the creaminess of this rich dish.

St.-Véran J.J. Vincent, France. A Chardonnay-based white with fine body and character. Should be enjoyed in its youth.

Calera "Table White," California. A simple, easy-drinking, inexpensive Chardonnay.

THYME-ROASTED CHICKEN

SERVES 4 TO 6

While we use smaller chickens for individual orders at '21,' a large flavorful roaster makes chicken an "event."

1 (5- to 6-pound) roasting chicken

3 tablespoons pure olive oil

Salt and freshly ground black pepper to taste

1/2 cup dried bread crumbs

1/4 cup fresh chopped thyme *or* 3 tablespoons dried thyme

4 cloves garlic, peeled and finely minced

1 cup Chicken Stock (page 332) *or* low-salt canned chicken broth

1/4 cup dry white wine

Preheat the oven to 425°. Rub the chicken with 1 tablespoon of the olive oil, and season inside and out with the salt and pepper. Place the chicken breast-side up in a roasting pan and roast 30 minutes. Meanwhile, in a small bowl, combine the bread crumbs with the thyme, garlic, and remaining olive oil. Set aside. After the first 30 minutes of roasting, reduce the oven temperature to 350° and continue roasting 45 minutes more.

Combine the Chicken Stock or broth, the white wine, and in a saucepan, bring to a boil, simmer 5 minutes, then remove from the heat and set aside. After the 45 minutes additional roasting time, remove excess grease from the roasting pan. Sprinkle the chicken with the seasoned bread crumbs and roast another 30 minutes, or until the juices run clear when a thigh joint is pierced and the bread crumbs are browned.

Note: If the bread crumbs are already brown but the juices have not begun to run clear, tent the chicken with aluminum foil to keep the crumbs from burning.

Remove when done and allow to rest on a platter 15 to 20 minutes before carving.

While the chicken is resting, place the roasting pan on top of the stove, remove any chicken fat with a spoon, and, over medium heat, deglaze the pan drippings with the chicken broth. Use a spoon to scrape up all the crusty bits (which contain the most concentrated flavor) and bring to a boil. Remove from the heat and strain the liquid into a gravy boat to pass at the table. Serve with Maple-glazed Root Vegetables (page 269) (which can share the oven with the chicken) and Roasted Shallot-Potato Cake (page 244).

WINE NOTES:

The bouquet and herbaceous notes in both these wines complement the herbs and spices that enliven this dish.

'Coudoulet' de Beaucastel, France. This "second" wine of the great Châteauneuf-du-Pape producer is a terrific blend of Syrah, Mourvedre, and Grenache grapes.

Robert Mondavi Zinfandel, California. An unusual and exotic Zinfandel, peppery and spicy.

ROASTED CORNISH HEN WITH HONEY MUSTARD GLAZE

SERVES 4

The interplay of sweet, hot, and sour flavors turns an otherwise-common bird into something almost exotic.

4 1-pound Cornish game hens

Salt and freshly ground black pepper to taste

4 bay leaves

2 tablespoons dried thyme

2 dried chili pepper pods *or* ¹/₂ teaspoon crushed chili pepper flakes

4 cloves garlic, crushed

2 tablespoons pure olive oil

¹/₂ cup honey

¹/₂ cup spicy brown mustard *or* Pomeroy mustard with seeds

3 tablespoons balsamic vinegar

1 teaspoon dried cumin

1 tablespoon crushed juniper berries

2 tablespoons chopped cilantro leaves

Preheat the oven to 375°. Season the Cornish hens inside and out with the salt and pepper. Place equal portions of the bay leaves, dried thyme, chili peppers, and garlic inside of the cavity of each of the hens. Brush the hens with the oil, and place, breast-side down, in a roasting pan. Roast 20 minutes before turning the hens onto their backs. Continue roasting another 20 minutes.

Meanwhile, combine the honey, mustard, vinegar, cumin, juniper berries, and cilantro leaves in a bowl, and brush over the hens at the end of the second 20-minute roasting time. Cook an additional 10 minutes to brown the glaze. Serve immediately, with Apple Sage Stuffing (page 290).

ROAST GUINEA HEN

SERVES 4

*C*alled pintade *or* pintadeau *in French, guinea fowl—which are native to Africa—have been domesticated for centuries. (The Romans called them Numidian or Carthaginian hens.) The delicate flavor of young guinea fowl is reminiscent of pheasant.*

MARINADE:

$^1/_2$ cup cider vinegar

$^1/_2$ cup dry white wine

2 tablespoons dried thyme

1 tablespoon dried rosemary

1 tablespoon dried oregano

3 cloves garlic, finely chopped

2 tablespoons honey

1 teaspoon salt

1 teaspoon cracked black peppercorns

3 bay leaves

1 (3$^1/_2$ to 4 pound) guinea hen

2 tablespoons pure olive oil

Combine all of the marinade ingredients in a bowl. Place the guinea hen in a large, deep bowl, pour the marinade over and inside the hen, cover the bowl, and marinate, refrigerated, 1 to 2 days, turning occasionally to ensure that all parts of the bird are covered.

Preheat the oven to 375°. Remove the hen from the marinade. Reserve the marinade. Put the hen in a roasting pan and brush with the olive oil. Turn the hen breast-side down in the pan and roast 20 minutes. Then turn the hen onto its back, decrease the oven temperature to 325°, and roast another 1$^1/_4$ hours.

While the hen is roasting, place the reserved marinade in a saucepan, bring to a boil, and reduce to approximately $^1/_4$ cup. When the hen has 15 minutes left to cook, pour the reduced marinade over it and then finish cooking it.

Remove the hen from the oven and let it rest 10 to 15 minutes before dividing into serving portions. Serve with Cornbread and Smoky Bacon Stuffing (page 293).

'21'

WINE NOTES:

This full-flavored bird needs a wine ripe with the warm fruits of summer.

Edmunds St. John Syrah, California. A great Rhône-inspired California creation. This is a small property that produces some fine wines.

Beringer "Knight's Valley" Cabernet Sauvignon, California. Concentrated flavors make this fresh, lively wine particularly enjoyable with this dish.

SLOW-ROASTED LONG ISLAND DUCKLING

SERVES 4

WINE NOTES

These two assertive Pinot Noirs have the structure to offset duck's rich flavor.

Morey-St.-Denis "Premier Cru," Vielles Vignes, H. Lignier, France. This full-flavored Côte de Nuits Pinot Noir is bold, without overwhelming.

Ponzi Pinot Noir, Oregon. One of America's top Pinots. Because of its long, cool growing season, Oregon is a region to watch for Pinot Noir.

Duck—both wild and domestic—has been popular at '21' for as long as anyone can remember. Long Island duck, ever-popular at '21,' is actually a Pekin duck descendant, a very mild-flavored domestic breed that produces dark and flavorful meat. One of '21's most spectacular presentations was reserved for wild Muscovy ducks. These were roasted rare and brought to the dining room by a maître d' or captain, who would carve the tenderest cuts of meat, then place the bones and the tougher meat in one of '21's silver duck presses, squeeze the juices from the meat, and prepare a sauce at tableside to be ladled over the Duck à la Press.

2 ducklings, weighing approximately 5 to 6 pounds each	3 tablespoons dried thyme
	1/2 cup honey
Salt and freshly ground black pepper to taste	1/2 cup cider vinegar
	1 recipe Pineapple Chutney (page 354)
Several bay leaves	

Preheat the oven to 375°. Season the ducks inside and out with the salt and pepper. Place several bay leaves and half the thyme inside each duck. Pierce the skin of the duck repeatedly, front and back, with the tines of a fork. This will allow the fat to drain away, leaving a crisp, golden skin. Place the ducks, breast-side down, in a roasting pan, and roast until they have begun to brown nicely (about 25 minutes). Turn the ducks onto their backs and reduce the oven temperature to 325°. Combine the honey and vinegar in a saucepan, simmer over low heat 5 minutes, and remove. Brush the ducks with some of the cider vinegar-honey mixture, being careful to avoid splattering. Continue to roast the ducks for another 1$\frac{1}{2}$ hours, brushing them with honey-cider vinegar every 15 minutes. This will help keep the meat moist and produce a crisp, golden skin while rendering most of the fat. After the ducks are fully cooked, remove from the oven, place breast-side down on a platter or a cutting board with sides, and let them rest 15 minutes before splitting into serving portions. Serve with Pineapple Chutney (page 354).

DUCK BREAST WITH BALSAMIC VINEGAR GLAZE

SERVES 4

*B*reast of Long Island duckling, which usually is served rare to medium rare, is a quick, simple alternative to the traditional whole roasted duck.

1 cup balsamic vinegar

2 tablespoons honey

1/4 cup dried currants

1/4 teaspoon cayenne pepper

4 whole duck breasts, approximately 6 to 8 ounces each

Salt and freshly ground black pepper to taste

3 tablespoons pine nuts, toasted 4 minutes in a 250° oven

Combine the balsamic vinegar, honey, currants, and cayenne in a small pot. Bring to a boil, reduce to a simmer, and reduce by half to form a thick, syrupy glaze. Remove from the heat and set aside.

With the point of a knife, score the skin side of the duck breasts in a crosshatch pattern, being careful not to pierce the flesh.

Season the duck breasts with the salt and pepper. Heat a sauté pan over medium heat 2 minutes before adding the breasts, skin-side down. Cook over medium to low heat approximately 6 to 8 minutes to render the fat.

Carefully remove the excess fat from the sauté pan, then turn the breasts over and sauté the flesh side 3 to 4 minutes before removing the duck breasts from the pan.

WINE NOTES:

The contrast of sweet and sour in this dish calls for red wines with intense fruit flavors to penetrate the richness of the glaze.

Dolcetto d'Alba, A. Conterno, Italy. The young, fruity, and acidic tones in this modest red would work very well with this recipe's contrasting themes.

Chalk Hill Cabernet Sauvignon, California. This wine's hard edge cuts through the glaze, while the richness of the duck, in turn, mellows the wine.

The breasts should now be medium rare. Slice lengthwise or crosswise and arrange several slices on each plate. Reheat the Balsamic Vinegar Glaze and drizzle some over each of the duck breasts. Sprinkle with toasted pine nuts and serve with Ginger Chestnut Stuffing (page 291).

PAN-ROASTED QUAIL WITH PORT SAUCE

SERVES 4 AS AN ENTRÉE OR 8 AS A FIRST COURSE

*T*his is one of '21's most popular dishes. Rich and succulent, the full flavors are deeply satisfying. Quail can be purchased already boned, or your butcher may provide this service on request. Of course, if you don't mind nibbling on bones, just purchase the quail whole. To remove the breast and backbones yourself, use poultry shears to expose the bones, then remove gently by hand. Leave the tiny leg and wing bones in place.

8 quail, preferably fresh, with breast and backbones removed (If unavailable, substitute 4 whole chicken breasts)

2 tablespoons pure olive oil

MARINADE:

1/2 cup dry red wine

1/4 cup good-quality port (preferably not too sweet)

1/4 cup pure olive oil

2 tablespoons balsamic vinegar

2 tablespoons maple syrup

2 tablespoons low-salt soy sauce

2 bay leaves

1 teaspoon coarsely ground black pepper

2 cloves garlic, crushed

Several sprigs of fresh thyme *or* 1/4 teaspoon dried thyme

1/2 teaspoon juniper berries

PORT SAUCE:

2 pounds poultry bones, necks, and wing tips (quail, chicken, duck, or any combination)

2 carrots, roughly chopped (about 1/2 cup)

1 onion, diced (about 1/2 cup)

3 ribs celery, roughly chopped (about 3/4 cup)

1 bay leaf

1/2 teaspoon dried thyme

1 clove garlic, crushed with the flat
    of a knife blade

3 quarts water

$^1/_2$ cup Beef and Veal Stock (page
    333) *or* canned low-salt beef
    broth

1 cup good-quality port

FINAL ENRICHMENT:

2 tablespoons good-quality port

2 tablespoons unsalted butter

Using a wire whisk, combine the marinade ingredients in a stainless-steel bowl. Add the quail and rub thoroughly with the marinade, inside and out. (Don't be afraid to use your hands.) Cover the bowl and refrigerate several hours or overnight.

Preheat the oven to 375°. The Port Sauce with which the quail will be served may be made while the quail is marinating or as much as 2 days in advance. Combine the bones, vegetables, and seasonings in a roasting pan and roast 2 hours, turning occasionally, until everything is well browned. Transfer the bones and vegetables to a heavy-bottomed stock pot and cover with the water. Bring to a boil, add the stock or broth, lower the heat to a simmer, and cook $1^1/_2$ hours. Strain this rich stock into another saucepan, add the port, and simmer again to reduce the liquid to $1^1/_2$ cups. At this point, the sauce may be cooled and refrigerated up to 2 days. Rewarm the sauce during the quail's preparation and add the final enrichment of port and butter just prior to serving. This will both enhance the final flavor and give the sauce a silken sheen.

To cook the quail, lower the oven to 350°. Heat 2 tablespoons olive oil in a cast-iron or other heavy-bottomed, ovenproof skillet over medium heat. Drain the quail of excess marinade and pan roast, uncovered, until mahogany in color (about 3 minutes on each side). Place the ovenproof skillet and quail in the oven 9 minutes. Serve immediately with the Port Sauce and Couscous with Fragrant Spices (page 276).

GRILLED QUAIL SALAD

SERVES 4

WINE NOTES:

Either of these aromatic reds would complement this light, disarmingly simple dish.

Morgon "Jean Descombes," Georges Duboeuf, France. One of the biggest, earthiest, and most concentrated of the ten "Cru" Beaujolais. Serve slightly chilled for a fresh accent.

Bonny Doon "Cigare Volant," California. This is a true California "Rhône-style" blend. Certainly fuller-bodied than the Morgon, but not at all heavy.

Quail has gained broad acceptance on menus from coast to coast. With distinct and subtle flavor, moistness that can withstand the grill, and a light and flavorful presentation, this dish might become one of your "house specials."

8 boneless quail

MARINADE:

^{1}/2 cup orange juice

1 lemon, cut into quarters

2 bay leaves

1 teaspoon dried thyme

1 teaspoon crushed juniper berries

2 tablespoons molasses

2 whole chili pepper pods *or* ^{1}/2 teaspoon crushed chili peppers

2 cloves garlic, peeled and crushed

SALAD DRESSING:

1 tablespoon Dijon mustard

3 tablespoons tarragon vinegar

^{1}/2 cup extra-virgin olive oil

2 oranges, peeled and segmented

1 mango, peeled, pitted, and sliced

^{1}/2 cup shelled pumpkin seeds, toasted 2 minutes in a 250° oven

2 cups mesclun, or your own mix of tender salad greens

Combine the marinade ingredients, squeezing the lemon quarters to release their juices, and marinate the quail for several hours, or overnight, covered, in the refrigerator.

To make the salad dressing, combine the mustard and vinegar, then whisk in the olive oil very slowly to create an emulsion. Add the fruit and toasted pumpkin seeds, and macerate in the refrigerator several hours before serving.

Remove the quail from the marinade and grill over an outdoor barbecue 4 to 5 minutes on each side, or cook over medium heat in a cast-iron skillet 10 to 12 minutes, turning frequently to avoid burning. Remove from the heat and let the quail rest for several minutes before serving. Discard the marinade.

Toss the salad greens with the dressing. Divide among 4 plates and top each with 2 quail. Serve with Pineapple Chutney (page 354) and Waffle Potato Chips (page 241).

'21'

Michael Lomonaco helps prepare quail for a Wine Cellar Dinner. (Photo: Christopher Baker)

WINE NOTES:

The marinade and figs in the recipe are right at home with red wines whose primary fruity components mimic these ingredients.

Montepulciano d'Abruzzo, F. Guelfi, Italy. A robust wine with an intense aroma. Inexpensive.

Sullivan Merlot, California. This smaller California property's organic, low-yielding fruit is rich and dark in style, with a mouthful of flavor.

QUAIL WITH ROASTED FIGS

SERVES 4

*T*his recipe would work equally well with squab or rabbit.

8 whole quail

Marinade from Quail Salad recipe (page 212)

16 large fresh figs (substitute dried if fresh are unavailable)

3 tablespoons pure olive oil

$^1/_2$ cup dry white wine

4 tablespoons granulated sugar

$^1/_2$ cup sherry vinegar

Salt and freshly ground black pepper

Marinate the quail in the marinade several hours or overnight in a covered container in the refrigerator.

If fresh figs are unavailable, which is highly likely considering their short season, dried figs are a wonderful way to complete this dish year-round. Refresh the dried figs by covering them with boiling water and allowing them to steep, as you would tea, 15 minutes until they have softened. Drain the water. Dry the excess moisture from the figs with paper towels, and cut the figs in half.

Preheat the oven to 350°. Remove the quail from the refrigerator, discard the marinade, and sprinkle the quail with salt and pepper. On top of the stove, heat the olive oil in a skillet until hot, and sauté the quail, 3 minutes on each side, before removing to an ovenproof platter.

To the sauté pan, add the figs and sauté briefly over high heat, then add the white wine, sugar, and vinegar, and cook 5 minutes, until the liquid is reduced by half. Pour the fig mixture over the quail. Roast the quail 6 to 8 minutes, or until the breasts are firm and the quail is cooked. Serve immediately with Soft Herbed Polenta (page 274).

Life

★ June 12 1931

10¢

"A Mr. Peebles phoning from New York, Mr. President. He wants to know
if you can push the button and open a place at 21 West 52nd Street?"

WILD PARTRIDGE WITH SAGE AND PROSCIUTTO

SERVES 4

WINE NOTES:

The delicate flavor of the bird, the herbs, and the saltiness of the prosciutto need wines like these, chosen for their long finishes.

Rosso di Montalcino, Poggio Antico, Italy. The flavor of this long-finish wine lingers until you're ready to enjoy the next bite of this delicate dish.

Nuits-St.-Georges, Jaffelin, France. This big Côte de Nuits from Burgundy does a superb job of tying all the flavors of this dish together.

*W*ild Scottish partridge, a delicious, delicate bird, is available in limited supply in the fall and early winter from specialty butcher shops or by mail order from specialty meat companies. (See "Resources," page 381.) Harvested in regulated numbers, the partridge are processed under strict EEC inspection and flown to the United States within forty-eight hours. Domestic farm-raised partridge are more readily available and yield fine results. This dish employs two cooking techniques, but the results justify the few extra minutes spent in preparation.

4 Scottish partridge, about 12–16 ounces each

Salt and freshly ground black pepper to taste

2 tablespoons vegetable oil

8 large fresh whole sage leaves

4 slices thinly cut prosciutto

3 tablespoons unsalted butter

2 tablespoons chopped shallots

2 tablespoons crushed dried thyme

1/4 cup Madeira wine

1 cup Chicken Stock (page 332)

Preheat the oven to 375°. Season the partridge with the salt and pepper. Heat the vegetable oil in a heavy skillet, add the partridge, and brown—first the breast side, then the back side—2 to 3 minutes. Remove the partridge from the pan and cool.

Once the partridge are cool enough to handle, place 2 sage leaves on the breast of each. Wrap each partridge with 1 slice of prosciutto, using a toothpick to seal the seam by piercing the back skin. Place the partridge in a roasting pan and roast 20 minutes, or until the juices run clear when a joint is pierced with a fork.

While the partridge are roasting, heat 1 tablespoon of the butter in a saucepan and sauté the shallots and thyme 2 minutes. Add the wine and cook until it has all but evaporated. Add the stock and cook 10 minutes to reduce by half.

When the partridge are done, remove from the oven, transfer to a platter, and keep warm. Pour the contents of the saucepan into the roasting pan to deglaze the juices, then pour the sauce back into the saucepan and return to a boil. Stir in the remaining butter, allowing it just to melt before pouring the sauce over the partridge and serving with Roasted Shallots (page 260).

'21'

J. W. Wryn's painting "Wild Game for Wild Men," which portrays Native Americans hunting buffalo, is part of '21's extensive collection of Western paintings, sculpture, and memorabilia. (Courtesy of '21')

ROASTED SQUAB WITH CORN-AND-CHILI SAUCE

SERVES 4

*T*his dish is particularly good in the summer or early autumn, when fresh local corn is available. Squab should be served medium rare to avoid drying the meat. The sauce can be made while the squab are roasting, or it may be made in advance and reheated.

4 squabs, 12–16 ounces each, dressed

Salt and freshly ground black pepper to taste

2 tablespoons crushed juniper berries

1/4 cup pure olive oil

CORN-AND-CHILI SAUCE:

4 ounces slab bacon cut into 1/2-inch cubes

1 onion, peeled and diced (about 1/2 cup)

3 ears fresh corn

3 tablespoons Chili Paste (page 357)

2 tablespoons maple syrup

2 tablespoons red wine vinegar

1 cup dry red wine

1 tablespoon ground cumin

1 large ripe tomato, seeded and diced

1 cup Chicken Stock (page 332)

Preheat the oven to 425° for 20 minutes. Season the squabs inside and out with the salt and pepper. Place the juniper berries into the cavities and brush the squabs with olive oil. Place breast-side down in a roasting pan and roast in the hot oven 20 minutes for rare.

Meanwhile, in a heavy-bottomed saucepan, over low heat, cook the cubed bacon until fully browned. Remove the bacon bits, leaving the

WINE NOTES:

This full-flavored dish needs wines that can withstand the spiciness of the sauce as well as the gaminess of the squab.

Cabernet Sauvignon Don Melchor, Concha y Toro, Chile. This powerful wine is almost Bordeaux-like, with the fruity flavors and tannic structure needed for this dish.

Rosenblum Zinfandel, Napa Valley, Hendry Vineyard, California. A firm wine with enough spice and fruity blackberry tastes and aromas to hold its own beside this bold entrée.

bacon fat in the saucepan. Add the diced onion to the bacon fat and slowly sauté until translucent.

While the onion is cooking, cut the corn from the cob, and set the kernels aside. Cut or break the cobs to a size that will fit the saucepan, and add them to the cooking onions. The cobs will contribute a wonderful flavor to the finished sauce.

Add the chili paste to the onion/corn cob mixture and cook 2 to 3 minutes. Add the maple syrup, vinegar, and red wine, and reduce by half. Add the remaining ingredients, except the reserved corn kernels. Cook another 15 minutes, then remove the corn cobs and add the kernels. Cook 2 minutes longer, then remove from the heat and pour over the roasted squabs to serve.

CHEF'S TIP:

To seed tomatoes, cut them into a top and bottom half. Hold half the tomato cut-side down over the trash and squeeze the tomato gently. The seeds will drop right out.

ROASTED SCOTTISH PHEASANT WITH APRICOTS AND DATES

SERVES 4

*T*he king of game birds, perhaps because of their brilliant plumage. At '21,' wild Scottish pheasants are served in season (November through January). The rest of the year, we serve free-range farm-raised pheasant. See "Resources" (page 381) for sources of wild and farm-raised mature and young pheasant.

See "Resources" (page 381)

1/2 cup dried apricots

1/2 cup pitted dates

2 tablespoons granulated sugar

1/4 cup orange liqueur

Juice of 2 limes (about 1/4 cup)

1/2 cup dry white wine

2 pheasants, 2 1/2 to 3 pounds each

Salt and freshly ground black pepper to taste

2 bay leaves

2 teaspoons dried thyme

Vegetable oil, for brushing birds

Rehydrate the apricots by covering them with boiling water and steeping them 10 minutes before draining and slicing into quarters. Roughly chop the dates, mix them with the apricots, and set aside. In a saucepan, combine the sugar with all of the liquid ingredients. Bring to a boil and simmer 5 minutes, then set aside.

Remove the legs of the pheasants (which are very sinuey) and reserve or freeze for making Game Stock (page 334). Season the pheasants, inside and out, with the salt and pepper. Place 1 bay leaf and 1 teaspoon dried thyme inside each bird, and close the body cavity with a skewer or toothpicks so that the bird holds its shape. Trussing them with butcher twine is best.

Preheat the oven to 375°. Brush the pheasants with vegetable oil, place them breast-side down in a roasting pan, and roast 20 minutes.

making Game Stock (page 334)

WINE NOTES:

The king of game calls for a sophisticated wine that will allow the tastes of the pheasant and fruit to be the stars.

Châteauneuf-du-Pape, Brunel, France. This Châteauneuf-du-Pape is clearly high-toned, not as deep and dark as some.

El Molino Pinot Noir, California. The Pinot Noirs from California can be generally riper than those from Burgundy. This exceptional California producer makes stunning Chardonnay as well.

At the end of 20 minutes, pour off any excess fat from the pan. Turn the pheasants breast-side up, add the apricots, dates, and the liquid to the roasting pan, and roast another 25 minutes. Check the oven every few minutes to see that the liquid has not all evaporated. If it has, add ½ cup water.

At the end of the cooking time, allow the pheasants to rest 10 minutes before splitting them down the back. Place half a pheasant on each plate, pour some of the apricot and date sauce over the top, and serve with Ginger Chestnut Stuffing (page 291).

At '21,' game birds used to be presented with great panoply, often encrusted in pastry. The quail dish pictured is not unlike the pheasant dish served to Winston Churchill in 1948. (Courtesy of '21')

'21'

*I*n 1948, while Winston Churchill was being entertained at a private party at '21,' it was the responsibility of young waiter Walter Weiss to present the Pheasants Souvaroff, an elaborate dish cooked in a big copper casserole with truffle sauce and foie gras, all encased in a pastry crust. "The idea was to open it up in front of the honored guest, releasing all the steam and aroma. But it was too hot. I burned myself and dropped all four pheasants at Churchill's feet. If I could die, this would be the perfect moment. But Churchill laughed. We scooped up the mess, retreated to the kitchen, and started over with different pheasants."

GRILLED YOUNG PHEASANT

SERVES 4

These small young birds offer an individual portion without carving. Pheasant legs contain a large number of tendons; you may prefer to remove the legs before serving and reserve them for making Game Stock (page 334).

4 young pheasants, 14–18 ounces each, butterflied

Salt and freshly ground black pepper to taste

2 tablespoons curry powder

1 teaspoon ground cumin

1/8 teaspoon ground nutmeg

1/2 teaspoon ground cinnamon

3 tablespoons pure olive oil

Season the pheasants with the salt and pepper. Combine the remaining spices, and rub the mixture all over the outside and inside of the pheasants. Marinate, refrigerated, in this dry spice mix 1 hour before cooking. Brush with olive oil. Over an outdoor barbecue grill, or in a hot cast-iron skillet over medium heat, cook the young pheasants 6 minutes on each side, or until crisp and golden brown. Test their doneness by piercing at the joint of the leg to make sure the juices run clear. Serve with Tuscan White Beans with Olive Oil (page 256).

WILD TURKEY WITH GINGER CHESTNUT STUFFING

SERVES 6 TO 8

Wild turkey, even when farm-raised, is as different from the hybridized "supermarket" turkey as French baguettes are from sandwich white. Wild turkeys have darker, moister breast meat. They also tend to be smaller overall. Although raised in a domesticated, agricultural setting, farm-raised wild turkeys are usually grown in free-range conditions.

1 (10-pound) farm-raised wild turkey

Salt and freshly ground black
    pepper to taste

Several bay leaves

1 unpeeled head of garlic,
    split in half

2 cups hot water

3 tablespoons melted unsalted
    butter

1 recipe Ginger Chestnut Stuffing
    (page 291), cooked separately

Preheat the oven to 425°. Season the turkey inside and out with the salt and pepper. Place several bay leaves and the garlic inside the body cavity. Place the turkey breast-side down on a rack in a roasting pan. Pour the water into the bottom of the pan and roast 30 minutes. Turn breast-side up, brush the melted butter on the breast, reduce the heat to 350°, and roast 1 to 1½ hours more, or until the juices run clear when the thigh joint is pierced with a fork and the internal temperature in the thickest part of the meat reaches 165°. If the water evaporates before the turkey has finished roasting, add more hot water, to keep the turkey moist. Allow it to stand 20 minutes before carving. Serve with Ginger Chestnut Stuffing (page 291).

CHEF'S TIP:

Farm-raised wild turkeys average between 8 and 12 pounds. Allow 1 to 1¼ pounds per person. Thus, a 10-pound turkey would serve about 6 to 8 people. As with all poultry, I recommend cooking the stuffing separately, rather than in the bird, to ensure that the bird cooks evenly and the stuffing is thoroughly cooked without drying out the bird.

WINE NOTES:

Red wine is not always considered a partner for turkey. These wines bring new personality to any turkey, but especially to the darker "wild" type.

Mommessin Brouilly, France. This Beaujolais delivers a fruitiness that is welcome with this American bird. Very easy to drink when served cool.

Caymus Zinfandel, Napa Valley, California. Made in a Bordeaux "claret" style, with some taste of new oak.

GRILLED RABBIT LOIN WITH FRESH THYME AND FRAGRANT OLIVE OIL

SERVES 4

A staple of European and Mediterranean cuisines, rabbit is not as commonly eaten in the United States, although in the last several years it has become more popular on restaurant menus and in our supermarkets. The saddle or loins of the rabbit are the most succulent and tender portions, and are best cooked quickly over high heat. If outdoor grilling is out of the question, quickly pan roast them instead.
The following two recipes make buying whole rabbits feasible; use the loins in this recipe and the legs and shoulders in the classic rabbit stew that follows.

4 rabbit loins (saddles), weighing approximately 2 to 2½ pounds each

3 tablespoons pure olive oil

Salt and freshly ground black pepper to taste

MARINADE:

1 tablespoon finely minced garlic (about 2 cloves)

3 large shallots, finely chopped (about ¼ cup)

2 tablespoons fresh chopped rosemary *or* 1 tablespoon dried

Juice of 2 lemons (about ⅓ cup)

½ cup dry white wine

¼ cup extra-virgin olive oil   3 tablespoons fresh chopped thyme

Combine the marinade ingredients in a covered container large enough to accommodate the rabbit loins. Add the loins to the marinade, turning to make sure they are thoroughly coated, and marinate, refrigerated several hours or overnight.

Before grilling on a charcoal fire or pan roasting in a heavy (preferably cast iron) pan over high heat, brush the loins with the 3 tablespoons olive oil and season with the salt and pepper. Cook 7 to 8 minutes on each side for a pleasant pink, medium-rare to medium degree of doneness. The rabbit will be moist and not dried out. To test for doneness, pierce with a knife at the bone. The juices should run clear. Serve the cooked loins on a warm platter, garnished with a drizzle of extra-virgin olive oil and a sprinkle of the fresh thyme. Accompany with Toasted Polenta (page 274).

BRAISED RABBIT WITH PEARL ONIONS, SMOKEHOUSE BACON, AND HOMINY GRITS

SERVES 4

'21'

WINE NOTES:

The ideal match for braised rabbit is a red wine with both character and humility—an authentic country wine.

Chianti Classico Riserva, Antinori, Italy. An elegant wine that harmoniously balances the many flavors of this country cottage dish.

Flora Springs Trilogy, Napa Valley, California. Made from a blend of Cabernet, Merlot, and Cabernet Franc, this stylish wine gives a woodsy aroma to this dish.

1/4 pound slab bacon cut into 1/4-inch cubes

1 cup pearl onions, peeled

Legs and shoulders of 4 rabbits *or* 2 whole rabbits, 2 to 2 1/2 pounds each

Salt and freshly ground black pepper to taste

1 cup 1/4-inch diced carrots

1/2 cup dry white wine

1/2 cup canned crushed tomatoes, drained

1 1/2 cups Chicken Stock (page 332)

2 tablespoons fresh tarragon

HOMINY GRITS:

1 cup coarse hominy

3 cups water

1 1/2 tablespoons unsalted butter

1 teaspoon salt

1/2 teaspoon coarsely ground black pepper

Heat a Dutch oven or large deep skillet over medium heat. Add the bacon cubes and cook until evenly browned. Remove the bacon and reserve on paper towels, leaving the bacon fat in the skillet. Sauté the pearl onions in the fat over moderate heat about 3 minutes, until they begin to caramelize. Being careful not to let them burn, reduce the heat and continue to sauté another 4 to 5 minutes, or until the onions begin to soften. Remove the onions and reserve.

Season the rabbit with the salt and pepper and sauté in the same skillet over medium-high heat until crispy and brown on both sides, about 6 minutes total. If necessary, sauté the rabbit in two batches. Remove the rabbit from the pan and pour off any excess fat. Return the onions to the pan, add the carrots, and sauté for a couple of minutes to color the carrots lightly. Add the wine and let it reduce for a few seconds. Add the tomatoes; stir and cook together 1 or 2 minutes at low heat until the liquid is reduced by half.

Add the stock, return the rabbit to the pan, and bring to a boil. Reduce the heat to a simmer, cover the pan, and braise the rabbit for about 45 minutes. Halfway through the cooking time, turn and move the pieces around in the pan so all pieces will cook evenly. The rabbit is done when it is fork-tender and the meat is beginning to fall off the bone.

While the rabbit is cooking, combine the grits ingredients in a saucepan. Bring to a boil, reduce to a low simmer, and cook, uncovered, 30 to 35 minutes, stirring occasionally, until the grits are fully cooked and have absorbed all of the liquid. Remove from the heat, cover the pot to keep warm, and set aside until ready to serve. Should the grits thicken up too much, add a few spoonfuls of hot water.

When the rabbit is done, return the bacon to the pan, add the tarragon, and cook 5 minutes more before serving on a bed of hominy grits.

VENISON CHOPS

SERVES 4

'21'

WINE NOTES:

This distinctive-flavored yet delicate meat provides the opportunity for an extra-special wine.

Château La Conseillante, Pomerol, France. A stunning wine. A mature vintage would be ideal, even though expensive.

Caymus Cabernet Sauvignon, California. One of California's best Cabernets. Consistently well made, even in lesser years.

Farm-raised venison is available year-round. This domesticated variety of red deer is delicious, without any off flavors, and extremely low in fat. It cooks quickly, simply, and can be served in a variety of ways. Avoid marinating farm-raised venison in any heavy vinegar-laden marinades, which tend to mask the true, sweet mild flavor of the meat. Venison racks (somewhat similar to rack of lamb) have 8 to 9 chops per rack, so 1 rack should yield enough to serve 4 people 2 chops apiece.

3 tablespoons pure olive oil

1 clove garlic, peeled and finely minced

1 teaspoon ground cumin

1 tablespoon chili powder

1 rack farm-raised venison, sliced into chops

Salt and freshly ground black pepper to taste

Combine 2 tablespoons of the olive oil with the garlic, cumin, and chili powder, and coat the venison chops uniformly with this seasoning mixture. Heat the remaining 1 tablespoon olive oil in a large heavy skillet over medium heat until hot. Season the venison chops with the salt and pepper, and lay them in a single layer in the pan. Depending on the size of your skillet, you may need to do this in two batches. Cook 3 minutes on each side for medium-rare chops. The venison will cook very quickly because of its naturally lean texture.

Serve immediately, with Stuffed Poblano Peppers (page 258) and Cranberry-Orange Relish (page 353).

Rack of Venison with Apple and Szechuan Peppercorn Sauce

Serves 4

3 tablespoons vegetable oil

1 whole 9-rib rack farm-raised venison

Salt and freshly ground black pepper to taste

2 tablespoons unsalted butter

4 tart apples (such as Granny Smith), cored and sliced into eighths

1/4 cup granulated sugar

1/2 cup red wine vinegar

2 tablespoons Szechuan peppercorns, toasted and crushed*

1/4 cup Game Stock (page 334) or Chicken Stock (page 332)

Heat the oil in a skillet over medium heat until hot. Season the venison with the salt and pepper and sear 2 to 3 minutes on all sides. Remove the venison from the skillet to a roasting pan and pour off and discard the oil from the skillet.

Preheat the oven to 350°. Over medium-high heat, add 2 tablespoons butter to the skillet. When the foaming of the butter subsides, add the apples and the sugar and sauté until they begin to caramelize about 3 to 4 minutes. Add the vinegar and cook another 1 to 2 minutes to reduce the vinegar by half before adding the Szechuan peppercorns and stock. Return to a boil and cook 1 minute more. Ladle the apples and peppercorns over the venison and place in the oven 10 to 12 minutes, until the venison reaches an internal temperature of 125° to 130° for medium rare. Remove from the oven and let rest 5 minutes before slicing into chops. Serve 2 chops per person, with some of the apple-peppercorn sauce ladled over each serving.

*Szechuan peppercorns are available in specialty food shops. Rather than being fiery like chili peppers, they have a mild, exotic mustiness. Toast them 2 to 3 minutes in a dry hot skillet to release their pungent aroma.

QUICK-COOKING RED VENISON CHILI

SERVES 8

WINE NOTES:

The flavors of cumin, chili, wine, and tomatoes need a sturdy and dependable wine that will carry its own weight throughout the meal.

Saintsbury Pinot Noir Carneros, California. A jammy, fruity wine with enough personality to withstand the chili assault.

Taurino Salice Salentino Riserva, Apulia, Italy. A great value from Dr. Cosimo Taurino, this wine is deep, darkly rich, and a delicious pairing for rustic food.

The "heat" of this chili depends on the "fire" of the individual chilis you use. Some say the smaller the chili, the hotter it is, but there are quite a few chilis smaller than habañeros yet none is more scalding. So be cautious and remember: Chili is easy to make hotter if you want, but it's tough to cool down if you've overdone it.

2 pounds venison shoulder or other suitable stew meat

4 ounces good-quality smokehouse-style slab bacon

½ cup finely chopped white onion

2 tablespoons chopped garlic

3 tablespoons Chili Paste (page 357)

1 tablespoon ground cumin

½ cup crushed plum tomatoes

1 teaspoon sea salt

½ cup zinfandel or other full-bodied dry red wine

1 cup Game Stock (page 334) or ½ cup each Chicken Stock (page 332) and Beef and Veal Stock (page 333)

Trim out and discard any sinews or connective tissue in the venison that would toughen during cooking. Cut the meat into 1-inch square chunks. Cut the bacon into ½-inch-thick slices. In a heavy-bottomed casserole, over medium heat, cook the bacon until crisp. Remove the bacon and reserve. Pour off all but 1 tablespoon of the bacon drippings. Sauté the onion and garlic in the remaining drippings until they are soft and translucent but not browned. Add the venison and brown well on all sides. Add the Chili Paste, cumin, tomatoes, and salt. Cook 2 minutes to release the flavors, then add the wine. Reduce the liquid until the pan is dry, then add the stock. To prevent the meat from toughening and to retain the natural moisture and flavor of the venison, simmer it in the stock no more than 10 minutes. Add the diced bacon in the final 5 minutes of simmering, to extract its smoky flavor and add its distinctive texture to the finished dish.

Serve with Stuffed Poblano Peppers (page 258), Polenta Corn Cakes (page 68), Wild Rice with Spicy Pecans (page 286), and/or Roasted Corn and Tomatillo Salsa (page 356).

'21'

Jerry Berns, younger brother of '21' founder Charlie Berns, explains the history of '21' to coauthor Donna Forsman. They are seated beneath three of the numerous Remington paintings that line the walls of '21's lounge.
(Photo: Christopher Baker)

THE REMINGTONS OF '21'

The soldier, the cowboy and rancher, the Indian, the horse and the cattle of the plains, will live in his pictures, I verily believe, for all time.

—THEODORE ROOSEVELT,
IN HIS EULOGY FOR FREDERIC REMINGTON

*L*ook to your right as you enter '21.' Between the men's and ladies' rooms, and just above the colorful screen of stock quotes, is a stark black-and-white image of the American West. Head in that direction and you'll find yourself in '21's lounge—a veritable gallery of Frederic Remington *grisailles* (paintings in shades of black and white). Because many of these originals were intended for reproduction in popular journals of the late 1800s—such as *Harper's Weekly*—they were painted with a palette limited to black, gray, and white. '21's collection of Remington *grisailles* is believed to be the largest in private hands.

No artist captured the spirit of the American West more spontaneously than Frederic Remington. Between 1881 and 1909, he traveled extensively throughout the West, sketching as he went. These sketches formed the foundation for a body of work that immortalized the lifestyles of Plains Indians and cowboys alike.

Jack Kriendler began collecting Remingtons in 1929. The collection has left the premises only once, for an exhibition at the Windsor Cinerama Theater in Houston in 1963 in conjunction with the opening of the movie *How the West Was Won.*

According to Marshall Cogan, '21's Remingtons definitely played a role in his decision to buy the restaurant. Both Marshall and his wife, Maureen, are lifelong lovers and collectors of art. After the purchase of '21,' Maureen, a member of the board of directors of the Brooklyn and Israel museums, and owner of *Art & Auction* magazine, called in an expert to authenticate the works. Five of the Remingtons proved to be fakes and were promptly disposed of. The Remington bronzes in the collection were all determined to be posthumous castings, of no extraordinary value. The best of the rest grace '21's lounge and a private dining room named for the West's most famous artist.

ABOVE:

The Romantic Adventure of Old Sun's Wife." This black-and-white wash drawing portrays the resistance of a Blackfoot maiden to her capture by a Gros Ventres chief. Remington met the revered heroine in Canada many years after the event portrayed. The drawing was offered to the '21' Club by a man who found it among a stack of Remingtons in a drawer. (Courtesy of '21')

BELOW:

*Painted to illustrate one of a series of short stories Remington himself wrote for Harper's Monthly, 'Order No. Six' portrays the story's central character and narrator, Sundown LeFlare, a French-Indian scout battling through a blizzard to deliver a sealed order from Fort Keough to Fort Buford. When overcome by hunger, cold, and exhaustion, the vision of an Indian girl with a pot of steaming meat sustains him through the completion of his mission. (Courtesy of '21')

'21' TRADITIONAL HASH BROWN POTATOES

■

'21' TRADITIONAL POMMES SOUFFLÉES

■

FRENCH FRIES

■

MATCHSTICK POTATOES

■

HOMEMADE WAFFLE POTATO CHIPS

■

ROASTED SHALLOT-POTATO CAKE

■

ROASTED POTATOES WITH GARLIC AND THYME

■

MASHED POTATOES, WITH OR WITHOUT CHIVES

■

SWEET POTATO AND PARSNIP CASSEROLE

■

ROSEMARY-SEARED SPINACH WITH OLIVE OIL AND GARLIC

■

'21' TRADITIONAL CREAMED SPINACH

■

BRAISED KALE WITH GARLIC AND RED WINE

■

TOMATO AND ZUCCHINI GRATIN

■

TUSCAN WHITE BEANS WITH OLIVE OIL

■

CHILI ONION RINGS

■

STUFFED POBLANO PEPPERS

■

ROASTED SHALLOTS

■

ROASTED GARLIC

■

STIR-FRIED NAPA CABBAGE

■

CURRIED VEGETABLE FRITTERS

■

ROASTED EGGPLANT FIRECRACKER ROLLS

■

BRAISED EXOTIC MUSHROOMS

■

MAPLE-GLAZED ROOT VEGETABLES

VEGETABLES

*If a seasonal item is freshly picked or dug or gathered and has
great flavor, I am apt to make an entire luncheon of that one thing,
savoring each bite with pure sensual enjoyment.*

—JAMES BEARD

Vegetables have gained a new measure of well-deserved respect in recent years. Rather than being relegated to the role of side dish, afterthought, or gratuitous garnish, vegetables have grabbed the spotlight at center plate. As a bounty of "new" Asian and Latin American vegetables and cooking methods have become more and more widely available and understood, underseasoned steamed vegetables are no longer an adequate response to a diner's request for a vegetarian entrée. At '21,' at least, we respond with a highly flavored assortment of vegetables, prepared in a nearly endless variety of ways.

All of the dishes we serve at '21' have accompaniments that have been well thought out and are specifically chosen to highlight and complement some aspect of the main component, be it meat, fish, fowl, or game. In this chapter and the next—which features grains, pastas, and stuffings—you will find any number of dishes that would make fine meals in themselves. Going farther, each recipe in the meat, poultry, fish, and game chapters suggests vegetable and grain dishes that work particularly well with that specific dish.

'21' uses a tremendous variety of fresh seasonal vegetables. We always have on hand a farmer's market variety: root vegetables; new peas; heirloom tomatoes and potatoes; summer and winter squash. We search out locally grown, organic produce whenever possible. We talk to farmers about crops, seeds, new varieties, and safe use of pesticides. We believe being involved is not only important but absolutely necessary. We hope you do, too.

This is not to say that we've turned our back on '21's meat-and-potatoes heritage. Indeed, the kickoff recipe in this chapter is a '21' classic, Pommes Soufflés, the most elegant of fried potatoes. And we haven't left out the homey favorites like hash browns and *real* mashed potatoes that have been comfort foods to so many generations of Americans. But we hope you'll also give some of the more "exotic" recipes, such as Stuffed Poblano Peppers, a try as well. There's a place for each and all in the planning of well-balanced menus.

'21' TRADITIONAL
HASH BROWN POTATOES

SERVES 4

*H*ash browns are deceptively simple. There are as many variations on this recipe as there are great regional cooks. Long a favorite, this version dates back to speakeasy days.

3 cups peeled, $^1/_2$-inch-dice Idaho potatoes (about 2 pounds)

2 large onions, peeled and cut in $^1/_2$-inch dice

$^1/_4$ cup vegetable oil

5 tablespoons unsalted butter

Salt and freshly ground black pepper to taste

Parboil the potatoes approximately 5 to 6 minutes in salted water. Drain and cool to room temperature.

Meanwhile, sauté the diced onions in the oil plus 1 tablespoon of the butter until richly browned and caramel colored. This step ensures that all of the onion's sweetness is developed. Cool the onions, then mix with the potatoes.

Preheat the oven to 350°. Melt half the remaining butter in a 10-inch nonstick sauté pan over medium heat, and add half the diced potato/onion mixture. Take care to pack the mixture tightly in one neat layer to sauté and brown.

Using the back of a spoon, form the potato and onion mixture into a rounded cake. When the potatoes and onions begin to adhere and brown, flip them over using a large spatula or the back of a plate. Brown the second side, then transfer the hash-browned potatoes to a cookie sheet and reserve while you cook the second half of the potato/onion mixture. Add the second batch to the cookie sheet and bake 10 minutes. Remove from the oven, season with the salt and pepper, and serve.

'21' TRADITIONAL POMMES SOUFFLÉES

SERVES 6

*P*ommes Soufflées, or soufflé potatoes, are one of those classics like Chicken Kiev and Baked Alaska that elicit oooohs, aaaaahs, and "How'd-they-do-thats?" when served. But these puffy oval potato chips, filled with air as a result of the two-stage cooking process, are more than just a culinary novelty. They are delicious, unusual, and texturally appealing because of their airy crunch. But they also are extremely difficult to make. You'll need a deep-fryer, an accurate thermometer, and a lot of practice to perfect your technique before trying this on guests.

6 large Idaho potatoes, washed and peeled (about 3 pounds)

Vegetable oil to fill fryer to correct frying level (can be filtered, strained, and used again)

Salt to taste

SPECIAL EQUIPMENT:

Large deep-fat fryer *or* large, heavy-bottomed pot and a frying thermometer

French mandolin or Japanese slicer

After peeling the raw potatoes, pare them into uniform oval shapes as close to the same size as possible. Slice each potato lengthwise into $1/8$-inch-thick slices, using a French mandolin or Japanese slicer. Wash the slices in cold water twice to remove excess starch. Remove them from the water, and pat them dry with paper towels.

The potatoes will require two separate deep-fat fryings to become Pommes Soufflées. The first stage can be completed hours, or even days or weeks, ahead of time. For the first stage of cooking, heat the vegetable oil to about 240° in an electric deep-fryer or a deep-fry pot on your stove. Accurate temperatures are crucial for the success of this dish.

Drop 4 or 5 potato slices into the hot oil, being careful of splash-back. Using a slotted spoon, swish the oil so that the potatoes move about freely. The potatoes will cook and begin to puff slightly in about 6 to 8 minutes, even though they will not have browned.

When they are slightly puffed, remove the slices from the oil and lay them on paper towels to drain and pat dry to remove excess oil. Continue to cook the rest of the potato slices in the same way. Once the potato slices have drained and cooled, they can be refrigerated or frozen until a few moments before you want to serve them.

The final frying will result in the puffy, crisp exterior that characterizes Pommes Soufflées. Again, heat the vegetable oil in a deep-fryer, this time to 350° to 360°. When the oil is hot, drop the potatoes in one by one, allowing no more than 5 or 6 in the deep-fryer at a time, so as not to reduce the oil temperature. Be careful of splattering oil. As before, gently swish the potatoes so they move about freely in the oil.

In about 3 minutes, the potatoes will begin to brown, puff, and crisp. When they are deep golden brown and crisply puffed,* remove them with a slotted spoon, place them on paper towels to absorb excess oil, and salt lightly. Continue cooking the rest of the potatoes in the same fashion, keeping the previously cooked batches warm in a 200° oven.

*Not all potatoes will puff in the final frying so do not be discouraged. Be patient, be careful, and enjoy the sight of those potatoes you've produced successfully.

FRENCH FRIES

To make french fries, use the large blade on your mandolin or vegetable slicer. Heat the vegetable oil in a deep-fryer to at least 240° but no more than 260°. (For successful french fries, I strongly recommend using a thermostatically controlled electric deep-fat fryer rather than attempting stovetop frying.) Add to the hot oil a handful of potatoes at a time, so that you don't decrease the temperature of the oil dramatically or crowd the pot. Cook approximately 3 to 4 minutes. Remove and shake off excess oil. Place on paper towels to drain. At this point, the blanched potatoes are ready for their final frying, or they can be cooled and refrigerated several hours. For the final frying, increase the heat of the fryer to 350° to 360°, add the blanched potatoes a handful at a time, and deep-fry until golden brown and crisp. Remove to paper towels to drain, and salt lightly while still hot. Serve immediately.

MATCHSTICK POTATOES

Unlike Pommes Soufflés and the classic french fries described in the last recipe, matchstick fries are thin enough to cook in a single frying. Use the julienne attachment on your mandolin or vegetable slicer to cut the "matchsticks." Heat the vegetable oil in a deep-fryer to at least 310° but no more than 320°. Add only a handful of potatoes at a time, so that you don't decrease the temperature of the oil dramatically or crowd the pot. Each small batch should take approximately 2 to 3 minutes to cook. Remove and shake off excess oil. Place on paper towels to drain, and salt lightly while still hot.

Homemade Waffle Potato Chips

Yield: 2 to 3 dozen potato chips

*T*his great side dish is easy to make with a mandolin or vegetable slicer equipped with a krinkle-cut blade. The trick to cutting waffle potato chips is to rotate the potato a quarter turn between each slice. These may be a bit tricky and labor-intensive to make, but the result is nothing like store-bought. They're not intended to consume by the bowlful; rather, they're a delightful dinner-party accompaniment to roast game.

4 Idaho potatoes, peeled (about 2 pounds)

Salt to taste

Corn oil to fill fryer to correct frying level (can be filtered, strained, and used again)

Special Equipment:

Mandolin or slicer with krinkle-cut blade

Large deep-fat fryer *or* large, heavy-bottomed pot and a frying thermometer

Insert the ridged waffle-cut blade into your mandolin or vegetable slicer, set at $\frac{1}{8}$-inch slices. Make one slice, then rotate the potato a quarter turn before making the second slice. Return the potato to its original position for the third slice, and repeat the sequence until all of the potatoes have been sliced.

Heat the oil in a deep-fryer to at least 300° but no more than 310°. The fries must cook slowly to achieve a crisp, golden-brown, not-burned potato. Add only a few slices of potato at a time, so that you don't decrease the temperature of the oil dramatically or crowd the pot. Each small batch should take approximately 6 to 7 minutes to cook. Remove to paper towels, and salt lightly while still hot.

THE CHANGING FACE OF
"STRIPTY-SECOND STREET"

*J*ack and Charlie's '21' has outlived them all: the handsome brownstone mansions that lined the block in the '20s; the rowdy "speaks" that moved in when fortunes crashed; the comedy clubs, strip joints, and jive dives that earned the block nicknames like "Swing Street" in the '40s and "Stripty-second Street" in the '50s.

Neighbors from the old days included Club 18, a comedy club across the street, which paid '21' a backhanded compliment each night when a waiter would interrupt the evening's show by barging past owner/emcee Jack White with a garbage can on his shoulder. "Where are you going?" White would ask. "It's very urgent," the waiter would explain. "It's the menu for '21.' " Another well-known club a couple of doors west of '21' was Leon & Eddie's, famous for its sign claiming: "Through these portals the most beautiful girls in the world pass out."

One day Jack Kriendler and Robert Benchley made it their mission to determine just how many speakeasies there were on the block (by visiting each one). Although the two had forgotten the original purpose of their jaunt by the time they knocked on the last door, Benchley had been taking notes; they documented thirty-eight speakeasies in that one block.

Having moved once (from 49th to 52nd Street) to accommodate the construction of Rockefeller Center, '21' balked at moving again. When told that its property was all that stood in the way of Rockefeller Center's expansion all the way from 48th Street clear up to 54th Street, Jack Kriendler refused to budge. As Jerry Berns tells it: "Jack—being a nice, practical Jewish boy—replied: 'If you're going to build all those office buildings, you'll need a good place to eat.' "

Two unexpected results of Jack's stubbornness have been nurturing New Yorkers (and the world) ever since. The property immediately behind '21' was donated by the Rockefellers to the city and became the 53rd Street branch of the New York Public Library. Across the street and down the block from the library, the Museum of Modern Art also stands on land donated by the Rockefellers—both part of the tracts they wanted to connect to Rockefeller Center, via '21.'

Today '21' is the only brownstone left on either side of the block, dwarfed to the east by the Tischman Building at 666 Fifth Avenue, to the south by Time-Warner, to the west by the Museum of Broadcasting and, beyond that, CBS.

ROASTED
SHALLOT-POTATO CAKE

SERVES 4 TO 6

he rich caramelized shallots and fresh thyme make this dish anything but ordinary. The result: a dish that is at once luxurious but also homey "comfort" food.

1 cup peeled and thinly sliced shallots (about 10 large shallots)

3 tablespoons pure olive oil

2 pounds (about 3 large) Idaho potatoes, peeled

Salt and freshly ground black pepper to taste

3 tablespoons chopped fresh thyme

3 tablespoons unsalted butter

In a heavy skillet over low heat, sauté the sliced shallots in the olive oil until caramelized and dark golden brown, about 10 to 12 minutes. While the shallots brown, julienne the potatoes with the fine julienne blade of a food processor. If you do not have a julienne blade, substitute a shredding blade or cut them by hand.

Preheat the oven to 325°. Season the cooked shallots with salt and pepper, add the thyme, and set aside. Melt the butter over medium-high heat in an ovenproof, 10-inch nonstick skillet. Add half the julienned potatoes and flatten with the back of a spatula. Remove the shallots with a slotted spoon, leaving the oil behind, and spread the shallots over the potatoes in the skillet, then top the shallots with the remaining potatoes, again smoothing them down with the back of a spatula. Cook over high heat a couple of minutes to evaporate any moisture and begin the browning process.

Reduce the heat to low and continue to brown the mixture another 5 to 7 minutes. Then place the skillet in the oven and bake 15 minutes. The top will be wilted but still white, while the bottom should be nicely browned, a dark rich color. Carefully flip over the potato cake onto a sheet pan without sides or onto the back of a sheet pan. Remove the skillet and then gently slide the flipped potato cake back into the skillet to brown the second side. Bake an additional 20 minutes, then remove from the oven. Slide the Roasted Shallot-Potato Cake onto a serving platter, and season with salt and pepper. Serve with Thyme-roasted Chicken (page 202).

YELLOW PEPPER GAZPACHO WITH SEARED SHRIMP AND HOT CHILI OIL

BROILED RAINBOW TROUT, PINENUT STUFFING, SAGE BUTTER,
AND GRILLED CORN ON THE COB

SEA BASS POACHED WITH LEMON GRASS AND CHILI-COCONUT BROTH,
SERVED WITH SAFFRON BASMATI RICE AND CRISP GINGER

GRILLED RABBIT LOIN WITH FRESH THYME AND OLIVE OIL,
SERVED WITH TUSCAN WHITE BEANS AND TOASTED POLENTA

Venison Chops with Stuffed Poblano Peppers and Dry-roasted Chestnuts

**CHILI-RUBBED PORK TENDERLOIN
WITH CHILI ONION RINGS AND PEACH FRITTERS**

OYSTERS ON THE HALF SHELL, RAW AND ROASTED WITH COUNTRY BACON

BONELESS ROAST LEG OF LAMB WITH FETA CHEESE, OLIVES,
BABY EGGPLANT, AND PEAR TOMATOES

ROASTED POTATOES
WITH GARLIC
AND THYME

SERVES 4 TO 6

2 pounds small potatoes: Red Bliss, small whites, Yukon Golds, Yellow Finns, or Fingerling potatoes

¼ cup pure olive oil

3 tablespoons unsalted butter

3 cloves garlic, peeled and finely minced

2 tablespoons chopped fresh thyme

2 tablespoons chopped fresh flat-leaf parsley

Salt and freshly ground black pepper to taste

Preheat the oven to 350°. Leaving their skins on, scrub the potatoes with a brush to remove any dirt or blemishes. Dry the potatoes with paper towels or a cloth. Cut the potatoes in half or in quarters, depending on their size. Pour the olive oil into a roasting pan or large cast-iron skillet and heat in the oven 10 minutes before adding the potatoes.

Roast the potatoes 45 minutes, until crisp. Shake the pan several times during cooking, so that the potatoes roll around to brown evenly. Remove from the oven. Drain the potatoes on paper towels or a cloth to absorb the excess oil, then place in a serving dish.

In a sauté pan, melt the butter, then add the garlic and sauté until light golden brown. Add the chopped herbs to the garlic butter, stir together quickly, and remove from the heat. Pour the garlic-herb butter over the potatoes, season with the salt and pepper, and serve.

CHEF'S TIP:

The key to crisp-roasted potatoes is to use a baking pan large enough to hold all the potatoes comfortably in a single layer. Crowding them together will produce steamed rather than crisp potatoes.

MASHED POTATOES, WITH OR WITHOUT CHIVES

SERVES 4 TO 6

*O*nce upon a time, everyone knew how to make mashed potatoes. In the meantime, so many of us grew up on boxed substitutes, it's worth restating the right way to make the real thing. I prefer to use Yukon Gold or Yellow Finn potatoes for their buttery color, sweet, vibrant potato flavor and wonderful texture for mashing.

3 pounds Yukon Gold or Yellow
    Finn potatoes, peeled and cut
    into 1$^1/_2$- to 2-inch chunks

4 quarts cold water

1 cup heavy cream

$^1/_2$ stick (4 tablespoons) unsalted
    butter

1 teaspoon salt

$^1/_2$ teaspoon freshly ground white
    pepper

$^1/_4$ cup chopped fresh chives
    (optional)

SPECIAL EQUIPMENT:

Potato ricer

Put the cut potatoes into a pot filled with the cold water, bring to a boil, and cook about 20 minutes, or until a fork or a knife pierce the potato chunks easily.

While the potatoes are cooking, put the cream, butter, salt, and pepper into a saucepan. Heat the cream until the butter melts, but do not allow the mixture to boil. Keep the mixture warm until you are ready to add it to the potatoes.

When the potatoes are fully cooked, drain in a colander 5 minutes to remove all excess moisture. It is important to rice the potatoes while they are still hot, because cold potatoes will become rubbery and starchy. Fill the ricer no more than half full. Squeeze the hot potatoes through the ricer and into a stainless-steel bowl, being careful that the potatoes do not squeeze out the top of the ricer, which would cause lumps in the mashed potatoes. When all of the potatoes have been riced, stir in the hot cream and butter mixture, using a wooden spoon to incorporate the seasoning, cream, and butter fully into the potatoes. If you like, add the chopped chives. Serve promptly. If the mashed potatoes must be held a few minutes, keep them warm in a double boiler or in a bowl wrapped with plastic wrap and placed over hot water.

'21'

CHEF'S TIP:

A potato ricer is a necessity for making proper mashed potatoes. This simple gadget is available in most kitchenwear stores and will produce a great-textured product. A food mill makes an acceptable substitute.

SWEET POTATO AND
PARSNIP CASSEROLE

SERVES 6 TO 8

A nice winter complement to roast chicken and other poultry dishes.

1¹/₂ pounds sweet potatoes or yams, peeled

1 pound parsnips, peeled

2 tablespoons unsalted butter

1 cup heavy cream

¹/₂ cup Chicken Stock (page 332)

¹/₄ teaspoon ground nutmeg

¹/₂ teaspoon ground cinnamon

¹/₂ teaspoon salt

¹/₄ teaspoon freshly ground black pepper

Preheat the oven to 350°. Cut the sweet potatoes and then the parsnips into paper-thin slices using a food processor fitted with the thinnest vegetable-slicing blade. If necessary, cut the potatoes in half or quarters lengthwise so they fit into the feeder tube.

Use 1 tablespoon of the butter to coat the inside of a 2-quart oven-proof casserole (a 6- × 10-inch Pyrex pan works well). Combine the cream, stock, nutmeg, cinnamon, salt, and pepper. Place one-third of the sweet potatoes in a thin layer across the bottom of the casserole. Layer half the parsnips on top of the sweet potatoes. Repeat this sequence until all the sweet potatoes and parsnips have been used. Pour the cream mixture over the top. It should reach about three-quarters of the way up the vegetables. Butter a piece of aluminum foil with the remaining butter and wrap the foil tightly over the casserole.

Bake the casserole 1 hour. Remove the foil and continue to cook another 15 minutes, until the vegetables are tender when pierced with a knife and the top is browned. Allow to cool slightly before serving. Serve warm.

ROSEMARY-SEARED SPINACH WITH OLIVE OIL AND GARLIC

SERVES 4

3 tablespoons pure olive oil

2 large cloves garlic, peeled and finely minced

1 pound fresh spinach leaves, thoroughly washed, with stems removed

2 tablespoons finely chopped fresh rosemary

Salt and freshly ground black pepper to taste

Heat the olive oil in a large skillet over medium heat. Add the garlic. Before the garlic begins to brown, add the spinach leaves. Sear the spinach quickly on one side, then add the rosemary and salt and pepper. Toss or turn with tongs or a spatula to cook the rest of the spinach until just wilted but still bright green. (The whole cooking process takes no more than 5 or 6 minutes.) Turn out onto a hot platter and serve immediately.

'21' TRADITIONAL
CREAMED SPINACH

SERVES 4

*S*pinach à la Jack, a favorite at '21' for many years, was essentially the following recipe garnished with crumbled bacon.

½ cup heavy cream

2 tablespoons unsalted butter

½ teaspoon salt

Freshly ground black pepper to
    taste

¼ teaspoon freshly ground nutmeg

1 pound fresh spinach leaves,
    thoroughly washed, with
    stems removed

Heat the cream and butter together. Add the salt, pepper, and nutmeg and set aside. Steam the spinach leaves in a vegetable steamer or a covered pot with ½-inch boiling water in the bottom until the spinach has wilted—about 3 to 4 minutes at most. Empty the hot spinach into a colander and, with the back of a spoon, try to push out the excess water to drain the spinach as much as possible.

Put the still-warm spinach into the bowl of a food processor fitted with a metal blade. Pulse three or four times to begin chopping the spinach. Then, while still pulsing, add the hot cream in a steady stream. Reheat briefly and serve the hot creamed spinach in small dishes with a pinch of freshly ground nutmeg on top.

(Courtesy of '21')

BRAISED KALE WITH GARLIC AND RED WINE

SERVES 4 TO 6

*K*ale *is a delicious member of the cabbage family with a delicate, easy-to-digest leaf rich in vitamins and minerals.*

1 large head kale, stem end removed

$^{1}/_{4}$ cup pure olive oil

4 cloves garlic, peeled and finely chopped

Salt and freshly ground black pepper to taste

$^{1}/_{2}$ pound sliced chorizo or other spicy sausage (optional)

$^{1}/_{2}$ cup Chicken Stock (page 332)

$^{1}/_{2}$ cup dry red wine

Roughly chop the kale leaves into 1-inch pieces, then wash and drain thoroughly. In a large skillet, heat the olive oil 2 minutes. Add the garlic and lightly brown, then immediately add the kale. Turn the kale leaves to coat evenly with the olive oil and to prevent the garlic from burning on the bottom of the pan. Season with the salt and pepper.

At the same time, in a separate pan over medium heat, brown the sausage slices, if desired, on both sides 5 to 6 minutes.

Continue to sauté the kale leaves 3 to 4 minutes. Reduce the heat to medium and add the Chicken Stock and sausage slices. Cover the pan, and cook the kale in the stock 5 minutes more. Remove the cover, add the red wine, and continue to braise the kale in the red wine and stock until nearly all of the liquid has evaporated. The entire cooking process will take 12 to 15 minutes, at which time the kale should be tender and the liquid cooked off.

TOMATO AND ZUCCHINI GRATIN

SERVES 6 TO 8

3 pounds ripe plum tomatoes

3 pounds firm zucchini

1/2 cup dry bread crumbs

1/4 cup freshly grated Parmesan
cheese

2 tablespoons chopped fresh
flat-leaf parsley

1 tablespoon chopped fresh thyme

1 tablespoon chopped fresh oregano

Salt and freshly ground black
pepper to taste

1/4 cup pure olive oil

Preheat the oven to 375°. Slice the tomatoes and zucchini into
1/4-inch-thick round slices as uniformly as you can. On a cookie sheet
or ovenproof platter, overlap the tomato and zucchini in a decorative
pattern, like red and green shingles on a gingerbread house. Blend all
the dry ingredients together, then scatter them evenly over the tomatoes and zucchini. Sprinkle the olive oil on top and bake until golden
and crusty, about 20 minutes. Present the platter or, using a cake
server or metal spatula, slide several overlapping pieces onto each
diner's plate.

Tuscan White Beans
with Olive Oil
Serves 4 to 6

Serve this warm or at room temperature as a side dish. It's perfect with fish such as the Pan-roasted Red Snapper (page 136) or the Grilled Shrimp (page 160), as a salad or as a meatless luncheon dish.

1 pound dried Great Northern, navy, pea, or other white beans

2 quarts Chicken Stock (page 332)

1 teaspoon salt

1/3 cup extra-virgin olive oil

2 tablespoons chopped garlic

1/4 cup chopped fresh flat-leaf parsley

2 tablespoons chopped fresh thyme

1/2 teaspoon dried red pepper flakes

1/4 cup fresh lemon juice

Salt and freshly ground black pepper to taste

Sort the beans to make sure they are free of stones or other debris. Rinse, then cover with cold water, refrigerate, and soak overnight. The next day, drain the beans, place them in a large pot, and cover with the stock. Bring to a boil, then lower the heat and simmer the beans 1 1/2 to 2 hours, or until they are tender. Add 1 teaspoon salt in the final 15 minutes of cooking. (The addition of salt earlier in the cooking process will result in tough beans.)

Remove the beans with a slotted spoon and transfer to a large mixing bowl. Add all the remaining ingredients except the salt and pepper and toss together with the warm beans.

Adjust the salt and add freshly ground pepper to taste. Serve warm or chilled.

CHILI ONION RINGS

While this recipe requires the use of a deep-fryer or a pot set up for deep-frying, the results are well worth it. This is a light, crispy onion ring without a heavy batter. It's equally terrific as a nibble or with grilled meats or chicken.

4 large Spanish onions, peeled

2 cups unbleached white flour

5 tablespoons chili powder

Vegetable oil to deep-fry

Salt to taste

SPECIAL EQUIPMENT:

Deep-fat fryer

Using a very sharp knife, slice the onions into thin rings no more than $1/8$- to $1/4$-inch thick. Separate the slices into individual rings and pat dry with paper towels to remove excess moisture.

Combine the flour and chili powder, using a sifter for the best, most even combination. Preheat a deep-fat fryer to 350°. At the very last moment before frying, dip the onion rings in the flour mixture to coat evenly. (Shaking them together in a paper or plastic bag works well.) Be sure to shake off all the excess flour through a mesh strainer before frying.

Cook the onions until they're golden brown, but be careful not to overcook them because they will continue to cook slightly even after they are removed from the heat. If they've been left in the deep-fryer too long, they will burn. Drain on paper towels, sprinkle with salt, and serve immediately.

STUFFED POBLANO
PEPPERS

SERVES 4 TO 6

*F*resh and dark green, or ripened to a brownish-red, poblano
peppers are mildly spicy chili peppers. When mature and dried they
turn a dark brown, almost black color, and may be familiar as
decorative ristras tied on string. Fresh, these 4- to-5-inch chilis can be
used in many of the same ways you would use a sweet bell pepper,
although they have some heat. They are particularly delicious stuffed
with a mild goat cheese mixture. A number of mild, creamy goat
cheeses, both imported and American, are available in specialty
cheese shops and better supermarkets.

4 to 6 large poblano chili peppers
($^{3}/_{4}$ to 1 pound)

1 (8-ounce) package mild, creamy
fresh goat cheese such as
Montrachet (softened at room
temperature and cut into
pieces)

$^{1}/_{4}$ cup zante currants (tiny raisins)

2 tablespoons pine nuts

1 teaspoon ground cumin

$^{1}/_{4}$ cup chopped fresh cilantro
leaves

$^{1}/_{2}$ teaspoon salt, plus additional
to taste

$^{1}/_{2}$ teaspoon freshly ground black
pepper, plus additional to
taste

2 tablespoons pure olive oil

Preheat the oven to 350°. Wash the peppers. Place in a single layer
under a hot broiler 3 minutes on each side to blacken the skin. Remove to a paper bag, close the bag, and allow the peppers to "sweat,"
which will loosen their skins while they cool. When cool, remove
from the bag and peel away the blackened skin with your fingers. Remove the stem end with a sharp knife and reserve. Without cutting
the peppers open, use the sharp knife to remove the ribs and as many

of the seeds as possible from inside the pepper. Rinse under running water and pat the peppers dry with a paper towel. Set aside. Wash your hands carefully with some milk to neutralize any volatile oils you will have picked up from the peppers.

In a stainless-steel bowl, combine the cheese, currants, pine nuts, cumin, cilantro, and ½ teaspoon each of the salt and pepper. Stir to blend thoroughly. Divide the filling evenly among the peppers. Reseal the end of the pepper with the reserved stem end.

Place the peppers in an oven-proof baking dish. Drizzle with 2 tablespoons olive oil. Season the outsides of the peppers with salt and pepper, then bake 20 minutes. The peppers can be served immediately after baking, or reserved and served at room temperature as part of a salad or with a grilled dish.

'21'

Actress Mary Martin and Jerry Berns reminisce together while browsing through the pages of The Iron Gate, *published in 1950 to commemorate the death of Jack Kriendler and raise money for the Heart Association.*
(Courtesy of '21')

ROASTED SHALLOTS

SERVES 4

Shallots roasted whole become beautifully caramelized and take on a rich, sweet flavor and a soft and buttery texture. These are wonderful on mashed potatoes or creamed spinach, and make a terrific topping for roast chicken.

12 to 16 large shallots
(about $^3/_4$ pound)

2 tablespoons unsalted butter

3 tablespoons granulated sugar

$^1/_2$ teaspoon salt

Freshly ground black pepper
to taste

$^1/_2$ cup Chicken Stock (page 332)

Preheat the oven to 350°. Peel the shallots, being careful to leave them whole rather than split into cloves. Melt 1 tablespoon of the butter in a sauté pan over medium heat until it begins to bubble. Add the shallots and brown on all sides until nicely caramelized to a rich, golden brown color, about 6 minutes.

Place the shallots in a baking dish, sprinkle with the sugar, dot with the remaining butter, add the salt, pepper, and stock, and roast in the oven for 35 minutes. Check after 15 minutes to be sure the liquid has not all evaporated. If it has, add $^1/_4$ cup water to keep the pan moist until the shallots have cooked completely.

After 30 to 35 minutes, the liquid will have evaporated and the shallots will be a rich dark-golden-brown color and soft when pierced with a knife.

ROASTED GARLIC

SERVES 2

To a true garlic lover, roasted garlic is pure Nirvana. The creamy texture of the garlic after it has been roasted is wonderful spread on toasted country bread with a drizzle of olive oil. Or the cloves can be removed with a tiny spoon and served with grilled roasted fish or chicken and vegetables.

2 large bulbs garlic

2 tablespoons extra-virgin olive oil

Salt and freshly ground black pepper to taste

In this recipe, we do not peel the garlic bulb but rather roast it in its papery covering. With a very sharp knife, remove just enough of the root end of the garlic bulb to flatten it enough to sit upright. From the more tapered, flower end of the bulb, slice ¼ to ½ inch off the top to reveal the garlic cloves within, but do not remove too much of the cloves' flesh.

Preheat the oven to 350°. Place the garlic bulbs upright in a baking dish, and drizzle 1 to 2 tablespoons olive oil over the top of the exposed cloves.

Season with a touch of salt and pepper, cover with aluminum foil, and roast 30 to 35 minutes, until the garlic cloves take on a rich golden color and the papery covering has begun to brown but has not blackened.

Remove from the oven and cool several minutes before serving. The garlic also can be served at room temperature and used in place of butter on the dinner table.

"IT'S A DOG'S LIFE"

The expression "It's a dog's life" takes on quite a different meaning at '21.' In the old days, while their owners dined on Oysters Rockefeller and Dover sole in the barroom, privileged pets might feast on filet mignon in the lounge. It is said Salvador Dali even brought his cheetah to '21' on occasion, although it's unclear where the cheetah was parked while Dali dined.

Dogs are no longer as much in evidence as they were when the lounge was equipped with brass rings to leash them to (see the accompanying photograph from the *Life* magazine 1946 story on '21,') but at least one customer, Princess Cecile Thurstonberg, still brings her dachshund Albert, who waits in the ladies' room while the princess dines.

At least one pampered patron got away with bringing her pet to the table. Thirties' film star Arline Judge and Jack Kriendler were close friends. Among the seven men she married during her lifetime were at least two '21' Club regulars: Yankee owner Dan Topping and his brother Bob. (Photo: Standard Flashlight Co., Inc.)

The caption accompanying this photograph in a 1946 Life magazine story entitled "Life Goes to '21'" explains that: "Dogs are allowed in '21' but they must be parked in lounge. At most other fashionable restaurants they would be put in checkroom." Pictured from left are Duke, best friend of sculptor June Harrah Lord; Schmoolie Boy, whose owner was '21's attorney, Julius Hallheimer; and Balzac, who belonged to '21' regular Melba Deane. (Courtesy of Life magazine)

STIR-FRIED NAPA CABBAGE

SERVES 4

A sweet-sour complement to the Striped Bass with Chili Peanut Sauce (page 148), this side dish is also delicious with Sautéed Calves' Liver (page 186).

3 tablespoons vegetable oil

10 to 12 fresh shiitake mushrooms, julienned (about 1½ cups)

1 small head Napa Cabbage, shredded (about 2 cups)

3 tablespoons granulated sugar

3 tablespoons red wine vinegar

2 tablespoons low-sodium soy sauce

Salt and freshly ground black pepper to taste

Heat the oil in a large skillet or wok over medium heat. Add the mushrooms and cook 3 to 4 minutes, until tender. Add the cabbage and stir-fry briefly, shaking the pan and tossing the vegetables with a slotted spoon. Add the sugar, vinegar, soy sauce, and salt and pepper, and cook, tossing, about 3 minutes more, removing from the heat before the cabbage loses its crispness and color.

CURRIED VEGETABLE
FRITTERS

SERVES 4 TO 6

*D*elicious with Poached Sea Bass (page 138) or Grilled Shrimp on Skewers (page 160), these also make wonderful hors d'oeuvres.

1 large Idaho potato, peeled and cut in $1/2$-inch dice

1 large onion, peeled and diced

2 carrots, peeled and diced (about $1/2$ cup)

3 stalks celery, diced (about $1/2$ cup)

3 tablespoons canola oil

1 tablespoon chopped garlic

2 tablespoons curry powder

1 tablespoon tomato paste

FRITTER BATTER:

1 cup unbleached white flour

$1/2$ cup club soda

$1/4$ cup whole milk

2 large eggs

$1/2$ teaspoon baking soda

$1/2$ teaspoon salt

Several grinds of fresh black pepper

Corn oil to fill fryer to correct frying level

SPECIAL EQUIPMENT:

Deep-fat fryer

Sauté the diced vegetables in the olive oil until the vegetables are browned on all sides and cooked through. Add the chopped garlic to the vegetable mixture and cook 1 minute more before adding the curry powder. Stir 1 to 2 minutes to coat the vegetables evenly with the curry powder, then add the tomato paste. Cook 2 minutes more, then remove from the heat and allow to cool in a clean bowl.

Preheat the oven to 325°. Combine the batter ingredients, then let the batter rest 20 minutes, refrigerated. Meanwhile, heat the oil in a deep-fryer to approximately 325°. Combine the vegetables with the fritter batter. Using a large tablespoon or a dessert spoon, spoon portions of the vegetables and batter into the fryer, allowing them to make free-form shaped cakes.

The cakes will brown in 2 to 3 minutes. Flip them over with a slotted spatula or spoon, to brown the other side. After removing the fritters from the fryer, drain them on paper towels to remove excess oil. Before serving, bake the fritters on an ovenproof platter in a 325° oven 4 minutes. This will cook the inside of the fritters and give them a nice crisp finish.

THE UBIQUITY OF CURRY

To a chef or to anyone who loves food, one of the fascinating things about curry is its universality. From Taipei, to Thailand, to Timbuktu, to Tunbridge Wells, to Trinidad and Tegucigalpa, half the cultures in the world enjoy curry on a regular basis. Curry is one of the most misunderstood of spices because it is actually a blend of as many as fifteen or twenty different ingredients. And every regional variation is different. Indian-style curry powder blends, which are probably the most familiar in America, typically contain turmeric (the primary source of curry's rich, orangey-yellow color), coriander, ginger, nutmeg, cloves, fenugreek, cumin, pepper, allspice, anise, mustard, cinnamon, garlic, dill, fennel, mace, and more. Always look for a good brand, preferably imported from India. It may cost a dollar or so more a can, but it's worth it because you'll be buying pure spices rather than the fillers that are put in cheap curry powders. We also use Thai curry pastes at '21.' These all-purpose seasoning blends are available in red, green, and yellow versions—with varying degrees of hotness.

ROASTED EGGPLANT
FIRECRACKER ROLLS

SERVES 4 TO 6

*$\mathcal{T}$hese are a perfect accompaniment to roasted or grilled lamb.
They also make festive hors d'oeuvres.*

2 pounds fresh, whole eggplant

5 tablespoons pure olive oil

1 small onion, peeled and finely
    diced (about 1/2 cup)

2 cloves garlic, peeled and finely
    chopped

1 tablespoon ground cumin

Salt and freshly ground black
    pepper to taste

1/4 cup chopped fresh cilantro
    leaves

1/4 cup dry bread crumbs

1 package phyllo dough, defrosted
    according to package
    directions

4 tablespoons unsalted butter,
    melted

Preheat oven to 350°. Cut the eggplants in half lengthwise. Brush the exposed flesh with 2 tablespoons of the olive oil. Lay the eggplant halves cut-side down on a cookie sheet and roast for about 35 minutes, until the flesh side of the eggplant is nicely browned and the eggplant has softened and fully cooked. Remove from the oven and cool.

When cool, use a large spoon to scoop the pulp away from the skin. Discard the skin. Heat the remaining 3 tablespoons of olive oil in a large skillet and sauté the onion until translucent. Add the garlic and continue to cook 1 minute more. Do not allow the garlic to brown.

Add the eggplant pulp to this mixture and cook another 6 to 7 minutes, until all the flavors have mingled and the eggplant has begun to brown. Add the cumin, salt and pepper, cilantro, and bread crumbs, and mix well. Set aside to cool.

Preheat the oven to 375°. Using 3 phyllo pastry leaves at a time, brush each leaf very lightly with melted butter and layer the sheets together. Cut the stack in half. Place 3 tablespoons of the eggplant mixture in a long thin strip in the center of each stack, so the phyllo can be rolled around it to form a cigar or firecracker shape. Roll the phyllo tightly, crimping the ends shut to seal in the filling. Repeat until all of the eggplant has been used. This will yield approximately 10 to 12 eggplant firecrackers. At this point, they can be held up to 2 days, covered and refrigerated.

To cook the firecrackers, lay them on a nonstick baking pan, and bake until lightly browned, about 10 to 12 minutes. Serve hot.

BRAISED EXOTIC MUSHROOMS

SERVES 4 TO 6

Any combination of available wild or exotic mushrooms is delightful prepared this way. Dried, reconstituted versions of these mushrooms can be substituted for fresh if necessary.

2 pounds assorted mushrooms, such as morels, chanterelles, shiitake, or oyster

4 tablespoons unsalted butter, melted

4 large shallots, peeled and finely chopped

1 cup of Chicken Stock (page 332) *or* the reserved juice from soaking dried mushrooms

¼ cup Madeira wine

3 tablespoons chopped fresh thyme

3 tablespoons chopped chives

Salt and freshly ground black pepper to taste

Remove any hard fibrous stems from the mushrooms. Wash morels carefully. Brush the remaining mushrooms with a damp cloth or mushroom brush to remove excess dirt. Slice the mushrooms into bite-size pieces.

Heat the butter in a large skillet over high heat until hot. Add the chopped shallots and sauté until translucent. Add the mushrooms to the shallot/butter mixture. Sauté until the mushrooms begin to wilt, about 7 to 8 minutes. Add the Chicken Stock or reserved mushroom-soaking liquid. Bring to a boil, then reduce to a simmer and allow the liquid to cook off in the uncovered sauté pan.

By the time the liquid has cooked off, the mushrooms should be tender. Add the wine and allow to cook off. Season with the herbs, and salt and pepper, and serve immediately.

CHEF'S TIP:

If substituting dried mushrooms for fresh, use 4 to 6 ounces dried for each pound of fresh mushrooms. Rinse the dried mushrooms with cold water to remove any dirt and then soak them in hot water for 30 minutes. Drain the mushrooms, but reserve the soaking water, which is full of mushroom flavor, to use in place of the Chicken Stock called for in this recipe.

'21'

MAPLE-GLAZED ROOT VEGETABLES

SERVES 4 TO 6

A cozy winter accompaniment to roasted poultry and game.

½ stick (4 tablespoons) unsalted butter

2 medium yellow onions, diced (about 1 cup)

3 leeks, split, carefully washed, and chopped

6 carrots, peeled and sliced into ¼-inch rounds

1 large or 2 medium rutabagas (sometimes called waxy turnips), peeled and diced

3 or 4 parsnips, peeled and cut into ¼-inch round slices

½ cup maple syrup

1 cup Chicken Stock (page 332) *or* canned, low-sodium chicken broth

½ teaspoon each, salt and freshly ground black pepper

1 tablespoon crushed cardamom seeds

Preheat the oven to 350°. Heat 1 tablespoon of the butter in a sauté pan until it begins to brown. Add the onions and leeks and sauté 10 to 12 minutes, until they begin to caramelize. Remove from the heat and allow to cool. Combine the remaining ingredients except the butter in an ovenproof casserole. Dot the top with the remaining butter. Cover with aluminum foil and bake 45 minutes. Uncover, return to the oven an additional 15 minutes, and bake until nicely glazed. Cool slightly before serving.

WHEAT BERRIES WITH ONION AND CURRY

■

SOFT OR TOASTED HERBED POLENTA

■

COUSCOUS WITH FRAGRANT SPICES

■

COUSCOUS WITH ROASTED TOMATO

■

PASTA WITH SPICY TOMATO, OLIVE, AND BASIL SAUCE

■

PASTA WITH SUN-DRIED TOMATOES AND MUSHROOMS

■

BASIC RISOTTO AND SEVERAL VARIATIONS

■

WILD RICE WITH SPICY PECANS

■

SAFFRON BASMATI RICE

■

APPLE SAGE STUFFING

■

GINGER CHESTNUT STUFFING

■

NEW ENGLAND OYSTER STUFFING

■

CORNBREAD AND SMOKY BACON STUFFING

GRAINS, PASTA, AND STUFFINGS

*The earliest known writing, alphabets, and arithmetical systems,
dating from about 3000 B.C., are devoted to grain transactions.
The culture of the fields made possible the culture of the mind.*

—HAROLD MCGEE

In homes all across America, as night follows day, "What should we serve with it?" follows "What should we have for dinner tonight?" At '21,' we serve some sort of pasta, rice, or grain-based dish as part of practically every meal. This approach to menu planning not only rounds out the meal, it also makes it much more interesting.

Delicious alternatives to potatoes are always a pleasant surprise for the diner. Homemade stuffings are more than worth the effort, if just for the praise you'll receive. The ways to cook and flavor rices and risotto are limited only by your imagination and verve. Popular rediscovered grains such as wheat berries, buckwheat (kasha), and quinoa are finding their way to more people's markets, and onto their tables.

To most Americans of thirty years ago, rice was rice, and not thought about very much. Today a gamut of choices are readily available: arborio, the basis for classic Italian risotto; basmati and jasmine, fragrant offerings of the Orient; and a growing number of newcomers to the marketplace, such as Wehani®, and Black Japonica™.

Pastas have taken hold even more firmly. Where once pasta meant spaghetti and meatballs or macaroni and cheese, it's now hero food for harried too-much-to-do'ers, along with everyone looking for a healthier way to eat. In the old days pasta was never served at '21' (except perhaps a little macaroni in the minestrone), even though I'm not '21's first chef of Italian extraction. Now that's changed. Current menus feature everything from Shellfish Ravioli (page 54), to Polenta (page 274), to Couscous (page 276).

Grains are, I believe, inherently more interesting and varied than potatoes (no matter how many ways you slice them). Grains offer richer tastes, more variety of texture. The richness of a grain can change the overall impact of the dish itself. The wealth of grains available can both enrich the variety of your culinary repertoire and give your menu planning solid nutritional footing. Explore. Enjoy!

WHEAT BERRIES WITH ONION AND CURRY

SERVES 4

*W*heat berries are the whole berries from the wheat plant, before they are ground into flour or cracked to make bulgur wheat for such dishes as tabouli. Because they are unprocessed, wheat berries contain the whole bran, which both makes them very nutritious and gives them a chewy texture even after they are cooked. Wheat berries can be found in health food and other stores that carry whole unprocessed grains. Their nutty flavor is just right with game. This same recipe can be used to prepare bulgur wheat or tabouli.

$^1/_2$ cup wheat berries

2 cups cold water (for soaking) plus 2 cups cold water (or chicken broth for a richer flavor) for cooking

1 teaspoon salt, plus additional to taste

$^1/_2$ teaspoon freshly ground black pepper, plus additional to taste

1 onion, peeled and finely chopped

2 tablespoons unsalted butter

2 tablespoons curry powder

$^1/_4$ cup water

2 tablespoons coconut milk

Cover the berries with the cold water and soak them overnight. (This will increase their volume threefold.) Drain and place in a lidded pot. Add 2 cups cold water or chicken broth, 1 teaspoon salt, and $^1/_2$ teaspoon pepper. Cover and bring to a boil. Reduce to a simmer and cook 1 to $1^1/_4$ hours, until the berries are tender and have absorbed all the liquid. They will, however, still retain some crunch.

Sauté the onion in the butter until translucent. Add the curry powder and cook over low heat, stirring, to toast the curry powder and coat the onion evenly, about 1 to 2 minutes. Add the cooked wheat berries and combine well. Stir in $^1/_4$ cup water. Put a lid on the pot, and steam over medium heat 10 minutes. Stir in the coconut milk, adjust the seasonings, and serve immediately.

SOFT OR TOASTED
HERBED POLENTA
SERVES 6

*P*olenta and risotto are to northern Italy what pasta is to southern Italy. You'll also find polenta in the parts of Austria, France, and Switzerland that border Italy. Imported polenta meal is very finely ground. I prefer to use our less-refined American cornmeal for its rustic character and appealing texture.

2 cups whole milk

1 cup cold water

$^1/_2$ teaspoon salt

1 cup cornmeal

$^1/_2$ stick (4 tablespoons) unsalted
    butter (optional)

$^1/_4$ cup plus 2 tablespoons freshly
    grated Parmesan cheese

$^1/_4$ cup chopped fresh herbs, such as
    thyme, oregano, parsley, and
    chives

Combine the milk, water, salt, and cornmeal in a 2- or 3-quart heavy-bottomed saucepan. Stir with a fork to eliminate any lumps. Heat just to a boil (but without scorching). Reduce the heat to low and simmer the polenta 25 minutes, stirring occasionally with a wooden spoon. If, near the end of the cooking, the polenta is becoming too thick and heavy to stir, add 1 or more tablespoons cold water to loosen the mixture enough to be able to stir it and to maintain a creamy consistency.

Remove from the heat. Immediately add the butter, $^1/_4$ cup of the Parmesan, and the chopped herbs, and stir quickly to incorporate. The polenta can now be served soft, similar to a porridge, to accompany meat or game. Or pour the still-hot polenta into a buttered cake pan and smooth evenly with a spatula.

Cool thoroughly until firm before cutting into serving portions. If prepared ahead of time, the polenta can be covered and refrigerated, uncut, for several hours or overnight.

To complete the polenta, turn it out of the pan and cut into the desired serving size and shape. Place the pieces on a sheet pan, sprinkle with the remaining Parmesan cheese, and place in a preheated 375° oven 10 minutes, to heat through. If the top has not browned sufficiently, toast under the broiler briefly before serving.

Serve toasted polenta as an appetizer (see Polenta Corn Cakes with Wild Mushroom Pan Roast, page 68) or as a side dish with poultry, game, or meat.

COUSCOUS WITH
FRAGRANT SPICES

SERVES 4

*R*ather than being a whole grain, like wheat berries or rice,
couscous is actually a tiny pasta made from semolina flour.
A staple in the Middle East, couscous has been well known
in Europe much longer than in the United States. There is a
special pot—a couscousière—designed specifically for steaming
couscous. With the advent of preblanched or parcooked packaged
couscous, it is extremely quick and simple to make, without need of
special pots.

1 cup "quick" couscous

1 shallot, peeled and finely minced

1 carrot, peeled and finely shredded

1 celery stalk, finely shredded

2 tablespoons pure olive oil

1 tablespoon chopped fresh flat-leaf
parsley

1 tablespoon fresh thyme

1 tablespoon ground cumin

$1/2$ tablespoon ground cinnamon

$1/4$ teaspoon ground nutmeg

Pinch ground cloves

Salt and freshly ground black
pepper to taste

$1/4$ cup pine nuts, toasted 2 minutes
in a 350° oven

Steam the couscous according to package directions. Sauté the shallot, carrot, and celery in the olive oil over medium heat 7 minutes,
until they begin to wilt. Season the cooked couscous with the herbs,
spices, and salt and pepper. Stir in the sautéed vegetable mixture.
Combine all ingredients well. Keep warm until served. Sprinkle with
pine nuts.

COUSCOUS WITH ROASTED TOMATO

SERVES 4

The tomatoes can be roasted a day or two in advance and stored, refrigerated and covered, until the brief final cooking and mixing of the couscous.

4 beefsteak tomatoes, halved and seeded

3 tablespoons extra-virgin olive oil

1 cup "quick" couscous, steamed according to package directions

2 tablespoons chopped or julienned fresh basil

2 tablespoons pitted and finely chopped kalamata olives

Salt and freshly ground black pepper to taste

VINAIGRETTE (OPTIONAL):

3 tablespoons olive oil

2 tablespoons balsamic vinegar

Preheat the oven to 200°. Cut the tomatoes in half, remove the seeds, and place them, cut-side down, on a baker's rack set in a roasting pan in the oven. After 15 minutes, the skins can be easily plucked off the tomatoes, using your fingers, a pair of tongs, or a fork.

Drizzle the peeled tomato halves with the olive oil and return them to the oven another 1 $^1/_2$ hours, until the tomatoes are roasted to a dark red. The excess moisture will have evaporated, and the remaining tomatoes will have a delicious concentrated flavor and aroma.

Cut the roasted tomato halves into quarters, and combine with the steamed couscous. Add the olives and basil and adjust the seasoning. Serve hot, or toss with a vinaigrette of 3 tablespoons olive oil and 2 tablespoons balsamic vinegar and serve as a cold salad.

CHEF'S TIP:

To seed tomatoes, cut them into a top and bottom half. Hold half the tomato cut-side down over the trash, and squeeze the tomato gently. The seeds and some pulp will drop right out.

'21' AND THE LITERARY LIONS

*J*ohn Steinbeck called '21' a "home about forty dollars away from home." Robert Ruark described it as "nothing but a country store, trading heavily on cracker-barrel philosophy." John O'Hara said simply: " '21' is my Club." Robert Benchley held court so regularly at table 3 that a bronze plaque marking the spot reads: "Robert Benchley, His Corner." Ernest Hemingway experienced one of his best moments and one of his worst moments—within a few hours of each other—at '21.' (See "Flirting with Danger," page 39.)

The late Bob Kriendler collected—and donated to his alma mater, Rutgers— literally hundreds of signed copies of books written by '21's friends and regulars, many of whom devoted pages and even whole chapters to describing real or imagined events at the Club. In chapter 9 of Ian Fleming's 1956 James Bond adventure *Diamonds Are Forever*, Tiffany Case introduces Agent 007 to '21', saying: "You know what they say about this place? 'All you can eat for three hundred bucks.' " In Judith Krantz's *Mistral's Daughter*, Lolly Longbridge organizes a 1931 scavenger hunt that begins with: "one debutante of this season, only beautiful ones count," and ends with "one waiter's jacket from Jack and Charlie's."

Today writers of every genre, from Gay Talese and Norman Mailer, to Helen Gurley Brown and James Bradey, continue to consult the muse at 21 West 52nd Street, to rub shoulders and come away refreshed enough to write again another day.

ABOVE:

'21' has long been a popular setting for book-launching parties, such as this luncheon hosted by Metro-Goldwyn-Mayer in 1977 for Mary Hemingway's How It Was. *Mrs. Hemingway is flanked in the photograph by '21' captains Frank Squitterie, left, and Ermido Zambon, right.*
(Courtesy of '21')

BELOW:

The 1946 Life *magazine pictured story entitled "Life Goes to '21'" included this view of Nobel Prize–winning novelist Sinclair Lewis, having lunch with his literary agent, Marcella Powers.*
(Courtesy of Life *magazine)*

Pasta with Spicy Tomato, Olive, and Basil Sauce

Serves 4

This is a delightful summer luncheon or supper dish to make with fresh plum tomatoes, fresh basil, and pasta. You'll find the sauce equally welcome in the winter, made from canned plum tomatoes and tossed with fresh or good-quality, imported dried pasta. But summer or winter, use only European-style olives. California olives are just too bland.

2 tablespoons salt

6 to 8 quarts water

1 pound imported dried penne, bowtie, or other-shaped pasta

Sauce:

2 pounds fresh plum tomatoes *or* 2 (14-ounce) cans plum tomatoes, drained and crushed

1 (2-ounce) can olive oil–packed flat anchovy fillets

1/4 cup pure olive oil

2 tablespoons peeled and chopped garlic

1/2 cup pitted and coarsely chopped Niçoise or kalamata olives

1/4 cup dry white wine

1 teaspoon salt

1 teaspoon freshly ground black pepper

1/2 to 1 teaspoon dried red pepper flakes

2 tablespoons julienned fresh basil leaves

If using fresh tomatoes, they must be peeled first. Dip them briefly in boiling water to loosen the skins. Peel, cut in half, remove and discard the seeds. Dice the tomatoes and have ready beside the stove.

Drain the anchovy fillets, rinse off the excess salt under cold water, pat dry, and chop roughly. Heat the olive oil in a saucepan over medium heat. When hot, add the chopped anchovy fillets and the chopped garlic and sauté, stirring, until the anchovies actually begin to dissolve and melt away. Before the garlic begins to brown, add the diced tomato and cook 8 to 10 minutes longer, until soft and pulpy. Add all the remaining sauce ingredients except for the basil leaves, and simmer 10 minutes more.

Meanwhile, bring the water to a boil in a large pot and add the salt. Cook the pasta according to package directions, timing it so the pasta will be completed at about the same time as the sauce. Just before you drain the pasta, add the basil to the tomato sauce and continue cooking just 1 minute longer. Remove the sauce from the heat and toss in a bowl with the drained pasta.

Serve immediately *without cheese*, which would overpower the fresh tomato, basil, and anchovy flavors. The sauce also can be made ahead of time and reheated.

'21'

CHEF'S TIP:

To pit ripe olives easily, lay them on a wooden board and, with the palm of your hand, press on each olive to break the skin. Squeeze the olives between your fingers to remove the pits.

PASTA WITH SUN-DRIED TOMATOES AND MUSHROOMS

SERVES 4

6 to 8 quarts water

2 tablespoons salt

1/4 cup fresh basil leaves

1 pound dried pasta, such as fettucine

3 tablespoons pine nuts

1/2 pound assorted mushrooms, such as shiitake, oyster, and cremini, cleaned and sliced

1/2 cup sun-dried tomatoes, soaked in 1 cup hot water 30 minutes, then drained and julienned

1/4 cup extra-virgin olive oil

1 tablespoon chopped garlic

1/4 teaspoon red pepper flakes

1/4 cup freshly grated Parmesan cheese

Salt and freshly ground black pepper to taste

Preheat the oven to 350°. Bring the water to a rolling boil in a large pot and add the salt. Meanwhile, stack the basil leaves and slice into julienne strips using a very sharp knife so that you don't bruise the basil and cause it to blacken. Set aside. Add the pasta to the boiling water. Place the pine nuts on a cookie sheet and bake until slightly browned. Sauté the mushrooms and tomatoes in the olive oil. Remove from the heat and add the basil, garlic, red pepper, half the pine nuts and cheese, and salt and pepper to taste.

When the pasta is *al dente*, drain and toss with the mushroom/tomato/herb mixture. Divide among 4 plates and garnish each serving with the remaining pine nuts and cheese.

Chef's-eye view of the dining room. Waiters, captains, and glasses on the service bar are reflected in the glass of the doors that separate kitchen from barroom at '21.' Ironically, tables closest to these constantly swinging doors are among the most coveted in the restaurant. A plaque above the second round table from the door identifies it as President Nixon's table, although many others, including Frank Sinatra, lay claim to it as well.
(Photo: Christopher Baker)

BASIC RISOTTO AND
SEVERAL VARIATIONS

SERVES 4

*I*n the same way that Americans love pasta, risotto is rapidly gaining
popularity in the United States. Risotto is more than simply a technique
for cooking rice; to be authentic, it must be made from a particular
variety of rice, called arborio, which is indigenous to northern Italy.
Arborio rice is rounder than the longer-grained varieties we are
accustomed to in America. It also has the virtue of developing a creamy
texture when cooked, without becoming sticky or glutenous. Arborio rice
is available in gourmet food shops and often in large supermarkets.

1 cup arborio rice	2^1/$_2$ cups Chicken Stock (page 332)
2 tablespoons pure olive oil	2 tablespoons unsalted butter
1 large onion, peeled and finely diced	^{1}/$_4$ cup freshly grated Parmesan cheese
^{1}/$_2$ cup dry white wine	2 tablespoons heavy cream

Pick through the rice to remove any stones or foreign matter, but do
not wash it before cooking.

Using a large skillet with a heavy bottom, heat the olive oil over low
heat and sauté or "sweat" the onions until translucent, being careful
not to allow them to color or brown at all.

Add the arborio rice, stir to coat with the olive oil, and sauté with the
onions to toast each grain of rice, about 7 minutes. This toasting
process adds the chewy, *al dente* quality that attracts so many people
to risotto.

Once the rice is lightly toasted, add the white wine slowly, stirring
with a wooden spoon. (A wooden spoon is always preferable when

making risotto, as a metal spoon tends to cut or injure the grains of rice. Constant stirring should be avoided for the same reason.)

Preheat the Chicken Stock just to the boiling point, then have it ready at stoveside. After the rice has absorbed the white wine and the skillet is nearly dry, add 1 cup stock, stirring occasionally, and cook over very low heat until the stock is absorbed. Continue adding the stock, 1 cup at a time, until all the stock has been absorbed.

(Adding the liquid in stages, instead of all at once, allows the grains of rice to expand more fully, adding to the risotto's creamy texture.) Once the rice has been added to the pan, the entire cooking process will take about 17 to 20 minutes.

After all of the liquid has been added and the rice is chewy yet fully cooked, with a creamy texture, add the butter, Parmesan, and heavy cream. Stir to combine all the ingredients and serve immediately.

CHEF'S TIP:

Substituting any other type of rice for the arborio will not yield an appropriate result. While risotto takes no longer to cook than other rice dishes, it does require a bit more patience and attention.

VARIATIONS ON A THEME:
Add any of the following to the basic risotto recipe.

- Sautéed shrimp
- Mixed seafood (such as salmon, shrimp, and scallops) sautéed in olive oil and herbs
- Diced fresh vegetables, steamed or sautéed in olive oil (asparagus and carrots make a wonderful combination)
- Fresh green peas in season
- Sautéed mushrooms and herbs
- Roasted Garlic (page 261)

WILD RICE WITH SPICY PECANS

SERVES 4

*O*ne of North America's great contributions to the world of cooking is the indigenous wild rice still harvested in the Great Lake regions of our Midwest and adjoining provinces of Canada. Domesticated "wild rice" is now grown in other regions of the United States as well, and is equally rich and flavorful, with a nutty character and texture.

2 cups water

2 bay leaves

Salt and freshly ground black
    pepper to taste

1 cup wild rice

$^{1}/_{2}$ cup pecan pieces

1 tablespoon unsalted butter

$^{1}/_{2}$ teaspoon cayenne pepper

$^{1}/_{2}$ teaspoon ground cumin

$^{1}/_{2}$ teaspoon salt

Combine the water, bay leaves, and salt and pepper to taste in a pot with a snug-fitting lid. Bring to a boil. Add the rice, reduce to a simmer, and cook 40 to 45 minutes.

Combine the remaining ingredients in a sauté pan and sauté over low heat until the nuts have toasted lightly. Remove from the heat and combine with the cooked wild rice. Serve with game, poultry, roasted lake trout, or whitefish.

CHEF'S TIP:

Wild rice takes longer to cook than white rice—about 45 minutes. It can be cooked in advance and reheated, recooked with additional ingredients, or added to a cold salad.

SAFFRON
BASMATI RICE
SERVES 4

Basmati rice, native to India, is delightfully fragrant and flavorful. Because it is slightly shorter-grained than our typical domestic rice, it cooks more quickly. Basmati rice is now being grown in the United States and has become more widely available in supermarkets, sometimes under brand names such as Texmati.

$1^1/2$ cups basmati rice

$1/2$ teaspoon saffron threads

1 tablespoon unsalted butter

1 bay leaf

1 teaspoon salt

Several grinds white pepper

$2^3/4$ cups cold water

Examine the rice for foreign objects but do not wash. Combine all ingredients except the rice in a heavy-bottomed pot with a close-fitting lid. Bring to a boil. Add the rice, cover, and cook over the lowest possible heat 17 to 20 minutes, or in a preheated 350° oven 16 minutes.

'21'

CATERING TO CREATURES OF HABIT

'21' has always catered to its regular customers' special likes and dislikes. Retired businessman Jack Hausman, for example, has a single pretzel each day before lunch. Industrialist Jeff Silverman starts his lunch each day with an appetizer the busboys make from cottage cheese, '21' Sauce, Tabasco, and chopped chives, served on toast.

Whether he's having lunch with the boys or a champagne and caviar supper with a beautiful lady, Neal Walsh (the man responsible for the green stripe down Fifth Avenue on St. Patrick's Day) invariably has an egg salad sandwich—with the crusts trimmed off—for his entrée. Bermuda socialite Hilda MacMartin always ordered beans and franks when she came for lunch. And always got them.

Whenever Aristotle Onassis came to '21', there was a dish of garlic pickles ready and waiting at his table, along with the ingredients for a Bloody Mary, which he preferred to make himself.

Errol Flynn, not surprisingly, also dined strictly on his own terms, arriving after lunch but before dinner, and always with a different lady. He invariably preceded his meal with a Jack Rose cocktail (Apple Jack, Rose's Lime juice, and grenadine), then dined on roast pheasant or whatever game was in season, accompanied by Bordeaux, and departed by 5:00 or 5:30 at the latest.

288

While Aristotle Onassis often dined at '21,' and even kept a private stock of wine in the cellar, he never dined in the barroom until the restaurant strike of 1972, when he and his companion dined on knockwurst and beans prepared and served by management, thereby making headlines as far away as Paris. (Courtesy of the New York Times)

When Onassis Is Hungry, Onassis Eats

NEW YORK, Nov. 23 (NYT). —Sheldon Tannen and Bob Kriendler waited on Aristotle Onassis at the "21" club yesterday. Mr. Kriendler recommended the knockwurst and Mr. Tannen fetched the order.

Mr. Kriendler and Mr. Tannen were there because they are two of the owners of "21" and it has been struck by cooks, waiters and bartenders. Mr. Onassis was at the club because he was hungry.

(Courtesy of '21')

APPLE SAGE STUFFING

SERVES 4

1 cup Chicken Stock (page 332)

3 large eggs, beaten

¼ cup whole milk

3 cups cubed French bread, fresh or day-old

1 onion, peeled, and diced (about 1 cup)

2 tablespoons unsalted butter

3 large tart apples such as Granny Smiths, unpeeled, cored, and cut in medium dice

2 tablespoons chopped fresh sage *or* 1 tablespoon dried sage

Salt and freshly ground black pepper to taste

Preheat the oven to 375°. Combine the Chicken Stock, eggs, and milk in a mixing bowl. Soak the bread cubes in this mixture until all the liquid is absorbed. Sauté the onions in the butter until translucent. Add the apples and continue cooking until the apples have just begun to soften, about 7 to 8 minutes. Remove from the heat and cool, then combine the onion and apple mixture with the bread cubes. Lightly stir in the sage and salt and pepper, and pour the mixture into a 2-quart ovenproof dish. Bake 25 minutes. Serve with Roasted Cornish Hen with Honey Mustard Glaze (page 204) or Roasted Squab (page 218).

GINGER CHESTNUT
STUFFING

SERVES 6 TO 8

1 cup Chicken Stock (page 332)

3 large eggs

3 cups 1-inch cubes whole-grain bread (about 1 1/2 pounds)

1 1/2 cups cooked, shelled, roughly chopped fresh chestnuts (vacuum-packed shelled chestnuts are an excellent substitute)

3 tablespoons grated fresh ginger

1/4 cup maple syrup

Salt and freshly ground black pepper to taste

4 tablespoons unsalted butter

Preheat the oven to 375°. Mix the Chicken Stock and eggs together in a bowl. Add the bread cubes and soak for a few moments, until the liquid is absorbed.

If using fresh chestnuts, make an incision with a sharp knife in the skin. Place them in a pot of boiling water, to cover, 20 minutes. Drain, rinse under cold water, and let them cool enough until you are able to handle them. Peel the shell away and remove any of the papery undercoating that may remain so that you are left only with a meaty chestnut. These can be broken into pieces or chopped.

Combine the chestnuts with the soaked bread, add the fresh ginger and maple syrup, and season with the salt and pepper. Place the stuffing mixture into a 1 1/2-quart baking casserole, and dot with the butter.

Bake 25 to 30 minutes. When the Ginger Chestnut Stuffing is done, allow it to rest 15 to 20 minutes before serving. Serve with Duck Breast with Balsamic Vinegar Glaze (page 208), Roast Wild Turkey (page 223), or Venison Chops (page 228).

New England
Oyster Stuffing

SERVES 10 TO 12

4 ounces fat-back pork,
    cut into $1/4$-inch cubes,
    or $1/4$ cup vegetable oil

2 large onions, peeled and diced
    (about $1^1/2$ cups)

4 stalks celery, thinly sliced
    (about 1 cup)

3 cups crumbled, unsalted water
    biscuits (about 2 pounds)

4 large eggs

$3/4$ cup whole milk

24 freshly shucked oysters, medium
    size (preferably Blue Points),
    with their juice

2 tablespoons crushed dried
    sage leaves

Salt and freshly ground black
    pepper to taste

2 tablespoons butter

Preheat the oven to 375°. Heat the cubed fat-back or oil in a large, heavy skillet over medium heat. When the pan is hot, add the diced onions and sauté until they become translucent. To the onions, add the sliced celery and continue to cook 2 minutes more.

Remove from the heat and allow to cool completely. In a mixing bowl, crumble the biscuits by hand so that when finished, they measure 3 cups. Do not overcrush the biscuits or make them too fine; leave them large. If available, you can use whole, unsalted oyster crackers.

First beat the eggs separately, then combine the eggs and milk. To the crumbled biscuits add the shucked raw oysters along with their juices, the cooked onion and celery, the sage, the salt and pepper, and the egg/milk mixture. Coat the sides of a baking dish with the butter. Pour the oyster stuffing into the dish, and bake 35 to 40 minutes. Cool several minutes before serving. Serve with Roasted Squab with Corn-and-Chili Sauce (page 218), Thyme-Roasted Chicken (page 202), or Roast Guinea Hen (page 205).

CORNBREAD AND SMOKY BACON STUFFING

SERVES 6 TO 8

3 cups crumbled cornbread, either homemade or store-bought

1 cup sourdough bread, cut into $^1/_2$-inch cubes

$^1/_2$ cup buttermilk

$^1/_4$ cup molasses

1 cup Chicken Stock (page 332)

$^1/_2$ pound smoked slab bacon, cut into $^1/_2$-inch cubes

1 cup chopped scallions

2 fresh jalapeño peppers, seeded and finely chopped

3 tablespoons chili powder

$^1/_2$ cup chopped pecans

Salt and freshly ground black pepper to taste

Preheat the oven to 375°. Combine the buttermilk, molasses, and Chicken Stock in a bowl. Add the cornbread and sourdough, and soak together. Heat a heavy skillet over medium heat. Add the cubed bacon, and cook slowly to render off the excess fat. When the bacon has browned nicely, carefully pour off and reserve the rendered grease. To the bacon, add the chopped scallions and jalapeño peppers, and cook together 5 minutes. Remove from the heat and cool.

When the bacon/scallion/pepper mixture has cooled, add it to the soaked bread along with the chili powder and chopped pecans. Season with the salt and pepper, spoon out into a baking casserole, and pour several tablespoons of the reserved bacon renderings over the top of the stuffing.

Bake 30 to 35 minutes, until the top is all browned and crispy. Remove from the oven and cool 15 minutes or so before serving. Serve with Quail with Roasted Figs (page 214), Bourbon Pepper Steak (page 179), or Chili-Rubbed Pork Tenderloin (page 194).

'21' TRADITIONAL RICE PUDDING

■

APPLE-WALNUT PANCAKES WITH CINNAMON CREAM

■

FUDGE SAUCE

■

PROFITEROLES WITH
VANILLA ICE CREAM

■

RICH FLOURLESS CHOCOLATE TORTE

■

HUCKLEBERRY AND PECAN CRUNCH PIE

■

KENTUCKY BOURBON SAUCE

■

PORT-LACED CHOCOLATE-MOCHA TERRINE

■

POACHED PEARS IN PHYLLO OVERCOAT
WITH MADEIRA ZABAGLIONE

■

CLASSIC AMERICAN STRAWBERRY SHORTCAKE

■

CHOCOLATE-COCONUT TRUFFLES

■

CHOCOLATE PECAN BROWNIES

■

LINZER TART SQUARES

■

BASIC SOUFFLÉ, FLAVORED THREE WAYS

■

FROZEN GRAND MARNIER SOUFFLÉS

■

FRESH FRUIT SORBET

■

FRESH FRUIT IN A COOL GINGER BROTH

■

'21' APPLE PIE

DESSERTS

Never eat more than you can lift.

—Miss Piggy

Desserts have always been a homey affair at '21.' As best anyone can remember, rice pudding was '21's first dessert. It has had a loyal following ever since. Apple pancakes were on the menu by 1933—and occasionally still are. Several of '21's signature desserts are true American classics: apple pie, strawberry shortcake, hot fudge sundaes. All of these are crowd pleasers and legitimately deserving of the spotlight—in our dining rooms or yours.

The desserts at '21'—and in this chapter—range from the simplicity of a quick-and-easy cobbler to the elegant tour-de-force of a hot soufflé. We've purposely spanned the gamut from light-and-healthful fruit sorbets and Fresh Fruit in a Cool Ginger Broth to the pure indulgence of Rich Flourless Chocolate Torte and Chocolate-Coconut Truffles. There's a time and place for each.

Desserts should be pure pleasure, in the making as well as in the eating. So although a few of the recipes, such as Port-Laced Chocolate Mocha Terrine and Profiteroles with Vanilla Ice Cream and Fudge Sauce, take time and involve a number of steps, we've chosen recipes where the steps don't have to be done all at once; and except for the hot soufflés, you won't have to hold your breath or tiptoe to make them come out "right."

WINE NOTES:

Almost all of the greatwine-producing countries now offer superlative "sweeter" wines that complement (or even take the place of) dessert. These fall into three general styles: wines fortified with the addition of brandy (ports and madeiras, for instance); wines made from late-harvest grapes transformed by the beneficial mold botrytis cinerea (sweet Sauternes and Rhine wines, for example); and sparkling wines that have been fortified so that they remain sweeter than the typical "brut" champagne. Each of these wine styles has some degree of residual sugar, and sweetness isa dominant quality.

The best of them—the Sauternes from France, late-harvest wines from California, and Spätlesen, Auslesen, and Trockenbeerenauslesen from Germany—have an underlying acidity that gives them a lift and backbone that is refreshing in contrast to a sweetness that would otherwise be cloying. The ideal is concentrated fruitiness, body, and the bracing acidity necessary to achieve a complex taste.

When pairing any of these wines with food, proceed with caution; they are rarely understated. Many people love these wines because of their forward natures; others shy away from them for precisely the same reason. Rather than pair specific wines with particular desserts, we suggest you explore these wines by region and discern for yourself the nuances that distinguish each area. As you browse through the recipes in this chapter, pause for brief side trips to the places most renowned for their sweet wines.

'21' TRADITIONAL
RICE PUDDING

SERVES 6 TO 8

This is the original '21' recipe for rice pudding that dates back to Prohibition days when the menu was extremely limited: a few sandwiches, chicken hash, and rice pudding for dessert. The whipped cream makes it extra-rich.

3 cups whole milk

1 teaspoon vanilla extract

$^{1}/_{4}$ teaspoon ground cinnamon

$^{3}/_{4}$ cup uncooked white rice

$^{1}/_{4}$ cup raisins

$^{1}/_{2}$ cup granulated sugar

1 cup heavy cream

Combine the milk, vanilla, and cinnamon in a heavy saucepan. Slowly bring the mixture just to the boil over medium heat, being careful not to scorch the milk. Reduce the heat to low, add the rice, and cook at a low simmer 1 hour, uncovered and stirring occasionally, or until the rice is thoroughly cooked and creamy. Remove from the heat. Stir in the raisins and the sugar and cool as quickly as possible. Refrigerate until completely cold.

Whip the heavy cream into stiff peaks with an electric mixer. Using a spatula, fold the cream into the chilled pudding, spoon into pudding cups, and serve immediately or refrigerate until needed. A nice garnish would be some dried cranberries or cherries that have been re-hydrated in brandy.

WINE NOTES:

CALIFORNIA

Some of the late-harvest wines from California are definitely world class. '21' always cellars Chateau St. Jean Select Late Harvest Riesling or Gewürztraminer. Others worth pursuing include Far Niente's "Dolce" and Freemark Abbey's "Edelwein."

APPLE-WALNUT PANCAKES WITH CINNAMON CREAM

SERVES 6

PANCAKES:

5 whole eggs

1½ cups whole milk

2 tablespoons Grand Marnier

2 tablespoons melted unsalted
  butter *or* vegetable oil *plus*
  ¼-cup melted butter to coat
  pan

1 cup unbleached white flour

¼ cup granulated sugar

1 tablespoon grated orange zest

1 teaspoon grated lemon zest

FILLING:

6 Macoun or other tart apples,
  about 1¾ pounds

2 tablespoons unsalted butter

⅓ cup maple syrup

½ cup chopped walnuts

1 teaspoon ground cinnamon

1 teaspoon lemon juice

¼ cup Grand Marnier

GARNISH:

½ cup heavy cream

2 tablespoons confectioner's sugar

½ teaspoon ground cinnamon

½ cup crème fraîche*

½ cup Fudge Sauce (recipe follows)

To make the pancake batter, whisk together the eggs, milk, Grand Marnier, and 2 tablespoons melted butter or vegetable oil. Add the flour slowly, whisking constantly to avoid lumps. Stir in the sugar and zests. Allow the batter to rest, refrigerated, at least 30 minutes before cooking.

Heat a nonstick 7-inch crêpe or omelet pan over low heat until hot. Add 1 teaspoon melted butter, using either a brush or a tiny ladle, to coat the surface lightly. As soon as the butter has started to bubble, lift the pan off the heat and pour 2 tablespoonfuls pancake batter into the pan, tilting to spread the batter evenly across the bottom. Return the pan to the heat and cook on low until golden brown on the underside, then flip and brown the second side.

As each pancake is completed, remove it to an ovenproof platter set in a 200° oven. If you fan the pancakes out on the platter, rather than stacking them directly on top of each other, they will be easier to separate later. Repeat until all the batter has been used. There should be enough batter to make at least 12 pancakes (2 for each serving).

Prepare the filling: Peel, core, and cut the apples into ¼-inch-thick slices. In a sauté pan, melt the butter, add the apple slices, and sauté over medium-high heat until they turn a rich golden color, about 6 to 8 minutes. Reduce the heat to low and carefully add the maple syrup, then the walnuts, cinnamon, and lemon juice. Cook slowly until the apples are tender at the center of each slice, but not soft and mushy. When the liquid is reduced to a syrupy quality, remove the pan from the fire and add the Grand Marnier. Then return to the heat for a moment more to integrate the flavors. The filling can be made in advance and reheated just before finishing the dish.

To assemble the pancakes, place 3 tablespoons warm apple filling in the center of a pancake, and roll into a cigar shape. Place the filled pancakes back in the warm oven until all have been completed. Whip the heavy cream, confectioner's sugar, and cinnamon together until soft peaks form. Fold in the crème fraîche. Serve 2 pancakes per person, with a dollop of the cold cream and a drizzle of hot Fudge Sauce.

*Or substitute sour cream for the crème fraîche for a similar, if not identical, result.

FUDGE SAUCE

YIELD: ABOUT 1½ CUPS

This rich, simple sauce has a myriad of uses, as you will see throughout this chapter.

½ cup heavy cream

8 ounces good-quality semisweet
   chocolate, preferably Belgian
   or French, finely chopped

Heat the cream gently in a heavy-bottomed pot over low heat. Add the chocolate, melt, and stir together with the cream. Remove from the heat and allow to cool slightly before using. This sauce can be refrigerated and gently reheated to be used again.

PROFITEROLES WITH VANILLA ICE CREAM

MAKES ABOUT 25 TO 30 MEDIUM-SIZE CREAM PUFFS

This recipe is particularly wonderful with homemade ice cream, or use a good-quality store-bought ice cream.

ICE CREAM (MAKES ABOUT 3 CUPS):

2 cups whole milk

1 whole vanilla bean

6 extra-large egg yolks

$^1/_2$ cup granulated sugar

1 cup heavy cream

CREAM PUFF BATTER (PÂTE À CHOUX):

5 extra-large whole eggs

1 cup water

1 stick ($^1/_4$ pound) unsalted butter

$^1/_8$ teaspoon salt

$^1/_4$ teaspoon granulated sugar

1 cup sifted unbleached flour

1 recipe Fudge Sauce (page 300)

EGG WASH:

1 egg combined with 1 tablespoon
    water

SPECIAL EQUIPMENT:

Ice Cream Maker

Pastry bag with a straight medium
    tip (optional)

Bakers' parchment

To make the ice cream, pour the milk into a heavy-bottomed pot. On a cutting board, split the vanilla bean down the middle and, using the tip of your knife, scrape all the seeds into the milk. Add the bean pod to the milk and bring the milk gently to a boil over medium heat, being careful not to scorch it or allow it to boil over. Lower the heat and simmer 10 minutes, uncovered. Remove from the heat and leave the vanilla bean to steep in the milk another 5 minutes.

Meanwhile, in the large bowl of an electric mixer, beat the egg yolks and sugar together at medium speed 5 minutes. Remove the vanilla bean pod from the milk, then add several tablespoons of the hot milk to the egg yolk/sugar mixture to temper the eggs. Return the pot of milk to the stove and, over low heat, add the egg yolk/sugar mixture in a slow, steady stream, stirring with a wooden spoon. Continue to cook 7 or 8 minutes, stirring constantly, until the custard has thickened and coats the back of the spoon. Remove from the heat and cool completely in an ice water bath.

When the custard has cooled completely, add the heavy cream and freeze according to the directions for your ice cream maker. While the ice cream is freezing, begin the *pâte à choux*, the classic French pastry from which cream puff shells (profiteroles) are made.

Being careful not to break the yolks, break the eggs into a measuring cup or another container from which they can be poured one at a time, and set the container beside the stove. In a heavy-bottomed pot, bring the water, butter, salt, and sugar to a boil. When the liquid boils, stir in the flour all at once, using a wooden spoon. Reduce the heat to low and stir continuously 3 to 4 minutes, until the mixture pulls together and away from the sides of the pot. Chefs call this "cooking the flour out." What you are actually doing is cooking away the raw flour flavor.

Still over low heat, add the eggs one at a time, incorporating each egg individually until it is completely absorbed by the flour before adding the next one. During this process, the mixture will take on a shiny gloss and become very elastic. When all of the eggs have been incorporated, remove from the heat, place the mixture in a stainless-steel bowl, and cool completely.

To make the profiteroles, preheat the oven to 425°. Using a pastry bag with a straight medium tip, pipe out approximately 1 rounded tablespoon batter for each profiterole onto a cookie sheet lined with lightly

'21'

CHEF'S TIP:

After the cream puffs have acquired a rich, brown color, some people like to turn the oven off, leave the oven door ajar, and allow the puffs to dry an additional 5 minutes.

buttered bakers' parchment, spacing them approximately 1 inch apart. If a bag and tip are unavailable, use a tablespoon to mound the batter on the bakers' paper.

Brush each profiterole lightly with the egg wash, place in the preheated oven and bake 15 minutes before reducing the heat to 350°. Bake until the puffs are a golden brown, about 12 minutes more. Remove from the oven and allow to cool. When they have cooled completely, cut open and fill with a small scoop of vanilla ice cream. As you fill each profiterole, place it in the freezer to keep the ice cream frozen until you are ready to serve. To serve, place 1 profiterole on each plate, top with Fudge Sauce, and serve immediately for a classic '21' dessert.

'21'

'21's pastry chef André Bonhomme directs a staff of four.
(Photo: Christopher Baker)

RICH FLOURLESS CHOCOLATE TORTE

SERVES 10 TO 12

This sinful confection is baked in a round cake pan nested in a larger pan partially full of water. After it is cooled and unmolded, it can be enrobed in ganache—yet more chocolate. One hundred percent pure indulgence.

1 cup granulated sugar

1 1/2 cups light corn syrup

20 ounces good-quality semisweet chocolate, preferably French, Belgian, or Hawaiian, cut into small pieces

2 sticks (1/2 pound) unsalted butter, plus butter for pan

10 extra-large eggs

1 recipe Fudge Sauce (page 300)

Preheat the oven to 350°. In a heavy-bottomed pot, combine the sugar and corn syrup and bring to a boil. Reduce the heat to low and cook 5 minutes. Remove from the heat.

Melt the chocolate in the top of a double boiler over simmering water. Stir the chocolate occasionally as it melts. Remove the pan from the heat and stir in the butter. Set aside to cool slightly.

With an electric mixer, beat the eggs at high speed until frothy. Lower the speed to medium and carefully pour the hot syrup into the beaten eggs. Add the melted chocolate and butter mixture and blend to a smooth consistency.

Butter a 10- to 12-inch round cake pan lightly and pour in the chocolate mixture. Set the cake pan into a larger pan (such as a roasting pan) and add hot water to rise halfway up the sides of the cake pan. Place in the oven and bake about 45 to 50 minutes.

WINE NOTES:

Loire. Try some of the sweeter and sparkling Vouvrays. For instance, in the small appellation of Coteaux du Layon, Domaine des Baumard produces a terrific late-harvest Chenin Blanc.

Being very careful not to scald yourself or get water into the torte, remove both pans from the oven, and remove the cake pan from the water bath.

Cool the torte to room temperature, then refrigerate for several hours before unmolding. Run a sharp knife around the inner circumference of the pan. Place a plate over the pan, invert, and, if necessary, tap the bottom of the pan with the knife handle to encourage the torte to release.

For a professional "finish," place the unmolded torte on a baking rack with a cookie sheet underneath, and pour 1 recipe of slightly cooled Fudge Sauce onto the center of the torte in one motion so that it will flow out in one smooth sheet over the top and sides of the torte.

Dry 30 minutes in the refrigerator. If you haven't overheated the chocolate or cream, this ganache will set and harden into a shiny *couverture* while the torte is chilling.

CHEF'S TIP:

The components of chocolate begin to break down when overheated, so always heat chocolate gently. One way is to use a double boiler. Another is to place the chocolate in an ovenproof container and place it in a 300° oven no more than 3 to 4 minutes. Remove, stir, and return to the oven for another minute to finish melting. Still another way is to use a microwave oven. Place the chocolate in a glass bowl and heat 2 to 3 minutes on low power.

HUCKLEBERRY AND PECAN CRUNCH PIE

SERVES 10 TO 12

*T*his is a large pie, perfect for parties and end-of summer barbecues. You'll most likely have to substitute blueberries in this recipe, since huckleberries are not very common, but if you can get them, they are a flavor explosion!

1/2 recipe '21' Apple Pie dough (page 326)

2 pints huckleberries

1 cup granulated sugar

3 tablespoons cornstarch

1/2 teaspoon grated fresh ginger

1 tablespoon ground cinnamon

1/4 teaspoon freshly ground nutmeg

Juice and grated zest of 1 orange (about 1/2 cup)

Juice and grated zest of 1 lemon (about 2 tablespoons)

1/2 cup day-old pound cake crumbs

1 recipe Kentucky Bourbon Sauce (recipe follows)

PECAN CRUNCH:

1/2 cup chopped pecans

1/2 cup all-purpose flour

1/2 cup granulated sugar

3 tablespoons ground cinnamon

1 stick (8 tablespoons) unsalted butter

SPECIAL EQUIPMENT:

12-inch deep-dish pie tin

Pie-dough weights or beans

Preheat the oven to 375°. Roll the pie dough out to the size and shape of the pie pan. Lay the dough into the pan and prick the bottom with the tines of a fork. Place a sheet of waxed paper over the pie dough and weigh it down with pie-dough weights or clean dry beans, and blind bake in the preheated oven 8 minutes. Remove from the oven and cool thoroughly.

Combine the berries, sugar, cornstarch, spices, and citrus juice and zest in a bowl and mix well. Sprinkle the cake crumbs on the bottom of the prebaked pie crust. Fill the pie shell with the berry mixture and bake 15 minutes.

While the pie is baking, combine the dry ingredients for the Pecan Crunch. Cut the butter into little cubes, add to the dry mixture, and, with the palms of your hands, rub together to form large nuggets—as big as peanuts, no larger than walnuts.

After the pie has baked 15 minutes, sprinkle the crunch all over the top, reduce the heat to 350°, and bake an additional 45 minutes. If the crunch begins to darken too quickly, cover with aluminum foil. Cool the pie for at least 2 hours before serving with Kentucky Bourbon Sauce.

'21'

WINE NOTES

Alsace. *We heartily recommend many of the Vendage Tardive and the Sélections des Grains Nobles'. '21' cellars Hugel, Zind-Humbrecht, and Schoffit.*

KENTUCKY BOURBON SAUCE

YIELD: ABOUT 2½ CUPS

This crème anglaise, or English custard sauce, should be made with a good-quality Kentucky bourbon. It can be made a day or two in advance of serving.

1 cup whole milk	⅓ cup granulated sugar
1 vanilla bean	½ cup heavy cream
4 extra-large egg yolks	¼ cup good Kentucky bourbon

Pour the milk into a heavy-bottomed pot. On a cutting board, split the vanilla bean down the middle and, using the tip of your knife, scrape all the seeds into the milk. Add the bean pod to the milk and bring the milk gently to a boil over medium heat, being careful not to scorch it or allow it to boil over. Lower the heat and simmer 10 minutes, uncovered. Remove from the heat and allow the vanilla bean to steep in the milk another 5 minutes.

Meanwhile, in the bowl of an electric mixer, beat the egg yolks and sugar together at medium speed 5 minutes. Remove the vanilla bean pod from the milk, then add several tablespoons of the hot milk to the egg yolk/sugar mixture to temper the eggs. Return the pot of milk to the stove and, over low heat, add the egg yolk/sugar mixture in a slow, steady stream, stirring with a wooden spoon. Add the bourbon to the sauce and continue to cook 7 or 8 minutes, stirring constantly, until the custard has thickened and coats the back of the spoon. Remove from the heat and cool completely in an ice-water bath before serving.

WINE NOTES:

Languedoc-Roussillon.
This region produces many of the "Vin Doux Naturels." The wines from Banyuls, Maury, and Rivesaltes are impressive.

PORT-LACED CHOCOLATE-MOCHA TERRINE

SERVES 8 TO 10

This elegant cake-lined terrine is especially impressive when made with homemade ladyfingers, although commercial ladyfingers may be substituted with perfectly fine results. While not a simple recipe in either case, it is a dessert worthy of its efforts.

LADYFINGERS:

4 extra-large eggs, separated

1/4 cup *plus* 2 tablespoons granulated sugar

1/2 cup sifted unbleached white flour

1/4 teaspoon vanilla extract

MOCHA MOUSSE:

1 cup granulated sugar

1/2 cup water

4 egg whites

1/4 teaspoon vanilla extract

1/4 cup dark-brewed espresso coffee

3 sticks (3/4 pound) unsalted butter, cut into chunks and softened

CHOCOLATE MOUSSE:

1/3 cup water

1/3 cup granulated sugar

8 ounces good-quality semisweet chocolate, preferably French or Belgian

1 teaspoon rum extract

2 egg yolks

1 cup heavy cream

GARNISH:

1/2 cup good-quality port

1 recipe Fudge Sauce (page 300)

Bakers' parchment	Candy thermometer
Pastry bag with a straight medium tip	3-quart springform pan (10- × 3-inch size)

Preheat the oven to 400°. Line two cookie sheets with bakers' parchment. Spread a thin coating of butter over the paper and dust lightly with flour. To make the batter for the ladyfingers, combine the egg yolks and ¼ cup of the sugar in the bowl of a mixer and whip together until golden yellow. Using a spatula, fold in the sifted flour until the mixture achieves a smooth consistency.

In a separate bowl, and setting the mixer on high speed, whip the egg whites, 2 tablespoons of sugar, and the vanilla to stiff peaks. Again using the spatula, fold this meringue gently into the flour/egg yolk mixture, taking care not to knock the air out of the mixture. (This is better undermixed than overmixed.)

Fit a pastry bag with a straight medium tip. Pour the batter into the pastry bag and pipe 3-inch-long strips (or whatever length is appropriate for the height of your pan) onto the buttered paper. Baked 10 to 12 minutes, these will produce the classic ladyfinger shape. Remove from the oven and cool.

Meanwhile, to prepare the Mocha Mousse, place the sugar and water in a saucepan over medium heat. Dissolve the sugar and cook to the soft-ball stage on a candy thermometer (234°–240°). While the sugar is cooking, whip the egg whites and vanilla in a bowl with the mixer at high speed until soft peaks form. Lower the mixer to medium speed and slowly pour the hot sugar syrup into the egg whites, creating what is known as an Italian meringue. Continue to mix the meringue 4 to 5 minutes more until it is stiff, shiny, and cool.

Shut off the mixer and let the meringue cool completely to room temperature. Then, using the slowest speed of the mixer, mix the coffee and soft butter into the meringue until both are fully incorporated. This is now a Mocha Mousse or butter cream, which can be refrigerated for later use.

To begin the Chocolate Mousse, combine the water and sugar in a heavy-bottomed pot and cook until the sugar is completely dissolved. Set aside to cool. Melt the chocolate gently in a double boiler over simmering water. Remove from the heat and add the rum extract. In a stainless-steel bowl, use the electric mixer set at medium speed to beat the egg yolks until frothy. Then, on low speed, add the sugar syrup in a slow, thin stream, to avoid scrambling the egg yolks.

With the mixer still on low, pour in the melted chocolate/rum mixture and blend until smooth. Cool this mixture to room temperature. Whip the heavy cream into stiff peaks, then, using a spatula, fold the whipped cream, one-third at a time, into the chocolate mixture. Refrigerate until needed.

To assemble the terrine, line the bottom and sides of a springform pan with plastic wrap and press snugly into the corners. Then line the bottom and sides of the pan with the ladyfingers, positioning them so that the most attractive side will be exposed when the terrine is unmolded. Using a pastry brush, paint the ladyfingers with the port, using enough for a smooth even coat without oversaturating the cake. Let this soak in and dry in the refrigerator 20 minutes before gently spooning half the Mocha Mousse into the cake-lined pan, leveling with a spatula as you go. Carefully layer half the Chocolate Mousse on top of the Mocha Mousse, again level with a spatula, and repeat until you have completed four layers of alternating mousses. Cover with plastic wrap, place in the coldest part of the refrigerator, and chill overnight (or a minimum of 6 hours).

To unmold, remove the plastic wrap covering the top of the pan. Pop open the springform, remove the terrine, and place it on a serving dish. Remove any plastic wrap that may cling to the ladyfingers. Drizzle some Fudge Sauce on top, and place the rest in a sauce boat to pass at the table. Present and slice the terrine at the table.

CHEF'S TIP:

If refrigerated, the mousses should be softened 30 minutes at room temperature before assembling the terrine.

POACHED PEARS IN PHYLLO OVERCOAT WITH MADEIRA ZABAGLIONE

SERVES 4

This is a cozy, fireside kind of winter dessert. The lightness of the fruit and flaky phyllo leave room for the rich Madeira custard sauce made in the style of a European zabaglione.

4 small, firm pears (Bosc preferred)

POACHING LIQUID:

3 cups water

1/2 cup dry white wine

1/3 cup granulated sugar

1 cinnamon stick

2 whole cloves

1 small dried chili pepper such as habañero

PASTRY:

1 (1-pound) package phyllo dough (you will need about 12 sheets), defrosted in the refrigerator overnight

1/2 cup melted unsalted butter

ZABAGLIONE:

1/4 cup granulated sugar

3 extra-large egg yolks

1/4 cup sweet Malmsey (or other Portuguese) Madeira

GARNISH:

1/2 cup dried cranberries or cherries, soaked in hot water 20 minutes

Choose firm pears that still have their stems attached. Peel the skin off with a vegetable peeler, being careful not to clip off the stem, and cut a thin slice off the bottom to create a flat surface so that the pears will stand upright during poaching.

For the poaching liquid, combine the water, wine, sugar, and spices in a pot that will be large enough to hold all the pears immersed two-thirds of the way in the liquid. Bring the liquid to a boil, lower the heat, and simmer 10 minutes. Remove from the heat and add the pears, standing each in an upright position. Return to the boil, and adjust the heat to simmer the pears gently 10 to 12 minutes, or until just tender when pierced by the tip of a knife. Remove the pears from the liquid so that they do not continue to cook. When they have cooled completely, core the pears from the bottom. Dry any excess liquid off the pears.

Preheat the oven to 400°. To prepare the pastry, allow 3 sheets phyllo per pear. Brush each of the 3 sheets with melted butter, layering them one atop the next. Place 1 pear in the center of the pastry square, pull the four corners up toward the top, and pinch the corners around the stem, leaving as much of the stem exposed as possible. If there is too much excess phyllo at the top, trim some off before pinching the pastry closed. Brush additional butter over the outside of the phyllo and bake the pears 20 minutes, or until the dough is golden brown. Cool several minutes.

While the pears are baking, make the Zabaglione: Combine the sugar, egg yolks, and Madeira in the top of a nonaluminum double boiler or bain-marie. (Using a pot with a rounded bottom makes whisking the mixture evenly easier.) Place over hot water, whisk the ingredients to a light, frothy, golden yellow, and cook until the bottom scrapes clean with each whisk stroke. The yolks should be firm but not scrambled.

Divide the warm Zabaglione among 4 dessert plates. Place a pear on each, and garnish with the cherries or cranberries.

'21'

WINE NOTES:

Rhône. Look for "Baume du Venise," a peachlike nectar with pale salmon color. This is one of France's finest sweet wines, and refreshingly inexpensive.

CLASSIC AMERICAN STRAWBERRY SHORTCAKE

SERVES 6

*T*hese shortcakes are similar in style and method to a traditional biscuit dough. For maximum flakiness, do not overmix. The dough should remain lumpy and mealy in texture in order to achieve a truly delicate cake.

SHORTCAKES:

1 cup sifted all-purpose flour

3 tablespoons granulated sugar

1 teaspoon baking powder

¼ teaspoon salt

¼ cup buttermilk

¼ cup heavy cream

3 tablespoons *cold* unsalted butter, cut into small pieces, plus 1 tablespoon butter (for the cookie sheet)

FILLING:

1 quart strawberries

TOPPING:

1 cup heavy cream

2 tablespoons confectioner's sugar

1 teaspoon vanilla extract

GARNISH:

Confectioner's sugar

To make the shortcakes: In the bowl of an electric mixer fitted with a dough hook, combine the flour, sugar, baking powder, and salt. After the dry ingredients are thoroughly blended, add the buttermilk, cream, and cold butter in quick succession, combining only briefly, to leave the mixture as lumpy as possible. Or use a food processor fitted with a dough blade. Combine the dry ingredients, pulse briefly, then add the liquid ingredients and butter, and pulse briefly.

'21'

WINE NOTES:

Jura. The vins jaunes (yellow wines) of Jura—by law aged no less than six years—are expensive, rare, and hard to find, but worth the effort. Vins jaunes from the commune of Château-Chalon are considered the best.

Turn this lumpy dough out onto a lightly floured board and flatten gently with a rolling pin into a squarish shape approximately 1-inch thick. Cut into 6 equal squares. Spread 1 tablespoon butter on a non-stick cookie sheet, place the squares on the sheet, and place the entire cookie sheet in the refrigerator to rest 20 minutes while you pre-heat the oven to 375°. Bake the chilled shortcakes 20 to 25 minutes, or until they are nicely browned.

While the shortcakes are baking, make the filling and topping. Clean and slice the strawberries. Whip the heavy cream, powdered sugar, and vanilla together into soft peaks. When the shortcakes are finished baking, allow them to cool 5 minutes. Then split them in half, slather the bottom with 2 or 3 tablespoons whipped cream and 1/2 cup sliced strawberries, cover with the top of the biscuit, and sprinkle with confectioner's sugar.

'21'

CHEF'S TIP:

I like to cut the biscuits square for this dish, but on Valentine's Day, when the Yale Whiffenpoofs come to serenade at '21,' we cut them into heart shapes. For a children's party, they can be cut into any cookie cutter shape that strikes your fancy.

CHOCOLATE-COCONUT TRUFFLES

YIELD: 70 TO 75 TRUFFLES

*T*hese are some of my favorite confections—simple, elegant, and heavenly for chocolate-lovers.

16 ounces high-quality semisweet chocolate, preferably Belgian or French, *plus* 12 ounces additional chocolate for dipping truffles

1/2 cup heavy cream, warmed

1 teaspoon vanilla extract

1 stick (8 tablespoons) unsalted butter, softened and cut into chunks

2 tablespoons rum (optional)

3/4 cup shredded unsweetened coconut

Melt the 1 pound of chocolate slowly in the top of a double boiler. Cool slightly, then combine with the heavy cream and vanilla. Stir in the butter and rum, if desired, and refrigerate until firm but still pliable, about 20 minutes. Transfer to a pastry bag fitted with a large straight tip and pipe into teaspoon-size mounds on a sheet of waxed paper; alternately, spoon out the teaspoon-size mounds. Refrigerate until firm. Working quickly to prevent melting, roll the chocolate into balls, then chill again until firm. In a food processor fitted with a metal blade, pulse the coconut briefly to make it a little finer so that it will adhere better to the truffles. When firm, roll each truffle in the coconut, pressing firmly to make sure the coconut sticks. At this point you can refrigerate the truffles for as much as a day, until you are ready to dip them.

Melt the dipping chocolate in the top of a double boiler over hot, but not boiling, water. Using a wire dipping spoon or a regular teaspoon and your fingers, dip each truffle briefly into the melted chocolate. Remove to a cake rack set over a cookie sheet until dry, and refrigerate until firm. You may scrape up any chocolate that has dripped to be returned to the dipping pot. The truffles will keep for several weeks if refrigerated in a covered container.

CHOCOLATE PECAN BROWNIES

YIELD: ABOUT 12 BROWNIES

A fudgy-cakey sort of brownie that has real character.

8 ounces good-quality semisweet chocolate, preferably Belgian or French

1 stick (8 tablespoons) unsalted butter plus softened butter to coat the pan

4 extra-large eggs

1½ cups granulated sugar

2 teaspoons vanilla extract

¼ teaspoon salt

1¼ cups unbleached white flour plus 1 tablespoon to coat the pan

2 cups chopped pecans

Preheat the oven to 350°. Butter and flour a 9- × 13-inch baking pan. Put the chocolate in the top of a double boiler and melt over simmering water. When it has melted, set aside to cool, then stir in the butter with a wooden spoon. Allow the mixture to cool to room temperature.

In a large bowl, beat the eggs with an electric mixer at medium speed, add the sugar and vanilla, and continue beating until the eggs are a light golden color. Gradually add the butter/chocolate mixture, scraping the bowl to get every last bit. Add the salt and continue mixing until the chocolate is evenly distributed.

Remove the bowl from the mixer and, using a spatula, fold in the flour and nuts. Do not overmix. The mixture should be lumpy. Pour into the buttered, floured baking pan and bake 25 minutes. Remove from the oven promptly, and cool 1 hour before cutting into squares.

'21'

WINE NOTES:

Champagne. Most Americans assume that when it comes to champagne, drier is better. While the driest (*brut*) is the most common, the sweeter champagnes—extra dry, sec, demi-sec, and doux—are wonderful dessert wines. The trick is finding them.

LINZER TART SQUARES

YIELD: ABOUT 3 DOZEN

*L*inzer torte, a traditional Viennese dessert, is simple to make and can be prepared well ahead of time. Using the best fruit jam or preserves you can find is the key. If you make your own preserves, better still. And don't limit yourself to raspberry. Try other jams too.

1 stick (8 tablespoons) unsalted butter, softened, plus softened butter to coat pan

$^{1}/_{2}$ cup light brown sugar

$^{1}/_{2}$ cup granulated sugar

3 extra-large eggs

$^{1}/_{2}$ teaspoon salt

1 teaspoon ground cinnamon

1 teaspoon baking powder

$1^{1}/_{2}$ cups unbleached white flour, plus flour for dusting

$1^{1}/_{4}$ cups ground almond flour (available from specialty stores)

1 cup raspberry preserves (jam)

Preheat the oven to 325°. Using an electric mixer on low speed, cream the butter and both sugars together to a smooth and creamy consistency. Slowly add 1 egg at a time, letting each egg incorporate fully into the creamed sugar mixture before adding the next. Stop the mixer, scrape down the sides of the bowl with a spatula, reset the machine on low, and add the salt, cinnamon, baking powder, and white flour. Continue mixing for several minutes until the flour is fully incorporated. With the mixer still running, add the ground almond flour and allow it to become fully incorporated before removing from the mixer.

Turn the dough out onto a board that has been dusted with flour. Pat the dough down using your hands and divide it into 2 pieces. Using a rolling pin, roll the first piece into a $^{1}/_{4}$-inch-thick rectangular piece that will fit on a cookie sheet or into a 9-×13-inch baking pan. Roll out the second piece of dough to the same thickness, then cut it into

CHEF'S TIP:

This dough is very delicate and will crack easily. (It also can be repaired easily with a pinch of the fingers.) To transfer the dough from the pastry board to the cookie sheet, use two spatulas and work carefully.

^{1}/$_2$-inch-wide strips with a crinkle-edge cutter. These strips will be used to form the lattice crust. Place the solid piece of dough on a lightly buttered cookie sheet or baking pan. Spread the raspberry jam evenly across the dough's surface. Use the cut strips of dough to form an open latticework crust over the top of the jam. Bake 20 minutes. Cool completely before cutting into 1^1/$_2$- to 2-inch-square bar cookies.

WINE NOTES

ITALY

Extra special: "Vin Santo" from Tuscany; Livio Felluga's Picolit from Friuli-Venezia Giulia; and Rivetti's sparkling Moscato d'Asti "La Spinetta." The exotic Malvasia from Colosi, on the island of Lipari, near Sicily, is '21' owner Marshall Cogan's favorite.

BASIC SOUFFLÉ, FLAVORED THREE WAYS

SERVES 4

*T*he most elegant of desserts may be a little tricky at first but is really quite approachable if you take the time to practice before trying it on guests. This classic soufflé base can be flavored as many ways as your imagination takes you.

SOUFFLÉ BASE:

1 cup whole milk

4 tablespoons unsalted butter, softened, plus softened butter to coat soufflé dish(es)

4 tablespoons sifted, unbleached white flour

5 extra-large eggs, separated

1/2 cup granulated sugar

SPECIAL EQUIPMENT:

1 1/2-quart soufflé dish, or 4 12-ounce dishes

In a heavy-bottomed saucepan, bring the milk to a boil, being careful not to allow it to scorch or boil over. Remove from the heat and reserve. In a second saucepan, melt the butter over low heat. Add the flour, stirring with a wooden spoon until completely combined. Pour one-third of the hot milk into the butter mixture and, using a wire whisk, incorporate it completely before adding the remaining milk. When all of the milk has been added, continue cooking over low heat 5 minutes before removing from the heat. Cool 5 minutes, then add the egg yolks, one at a time, all the while stirring with a wooden spoon. Be sure to incorporate each yolk fully before adding the next. Allow the mixture to cool completely at room temperature before finishing the soufflé. This base may be made ahead of time and will keep for up to 2 days in the refrigerator.

VARIATIONS:

For a **Chocolate Soufflé,** combine the base with 8 ounces melted (and then slightly cooled) good-quality semisweet chocolate (preferably Belgian, French, or Hawaiian).

For a **Mocha Soufflé,** combine the base with 4 ounces very strongly brewed espresso, which has been allowed to cool to room temperature.

For a **Raspberry Soufflé,** puree 1 pint raspberries and 2 tablespoons confectioner's sugar for 2 minutes in a blender, then fold into the base.

To Finish: To complete any of these soufflés, preheat the oven to 400°. Beat 5 egg whites in an electric mixer at medium speed until they form soft peaks. Add the sugar and continue to beat until firm but moist meringue peaks are formed. Gently fold the meringue into the flavored base, being careful not to beat out the air.

Butter a 1½-quart or 4 individual soufflé dish(es) lightly with softened butter. Pour the soufflé mixture to within ½ inch of the top of the dish(es). Bake in the center of the oven 18 minutes for individual soufflés or as long as 45 to 50 minutes for a large soufflé. Be careful not to jar the oven or slam the door while baking. Remove gently and serve immediately with Kentucky Bourbon Sauce (page 308), Fudge Sauce (page 300), or 1 cup heavy cream whipped with 2 tablespoons confectioner's sugar and 1 teaspoon vanilla extract.

WINE NOTES

GERMANY-AUSTRIA

Classified according to their "degrees of ripeness," the Spätlesen, Auslesen, Beerenauslesen, Trockenbeerenauslesen, and Eisweins—made from late-harvest (primarily Riesling) grapes—are some of the world's greatest wines. '21' still has Auslesen from the late 1970s. Very special indeed.

FROZEN GRAND
MARNIER SOUFFLÉS

SERVES 4

*A*ctually a frozen mousse, these wonderfully light chilled
desserts mimic the appearance of baked soufflés.

5 extra-large eggs

1/4 cup granulated sugar

1 cup heavy cream

3 tablespoons confectioner's sugar

1/4 cup Grand Marnier

TO PREPARE MOLDS:
Softened butter

Granulated sugar

SPECIAL EQUIPMENT:
4 (12-ounce) soufflé dishes

Combine the eggs and granulated sugar in the top of a stainless-steel
double boiler. Being careful not to scramble the eggs, whisk over gentle heat until the mixture is golden in color and thick enough to coat
the back of a spoon. Remove from the heat and set aside to cool.

While the egg mixture is cooling, prepare 4 (12-ounce) soufflé dishes
by cutting waxed paper long enough to encircle each dish twice and
stand 3 to 4 inches above its top. Wrap the waxed paper snugly
around the outside of the dishes and seal the edges with transparent
tape. Butter the inside of the dish with softened butter, then sprinkle
with granulated sugar, tapping out any excess sugar onto a plate.

Using an electric mixer set at medium, combine the heavy cream,
confectioner's sugar, and Grand Marnier, whipping into firm peaks.
With a spatula, gently fold the whipped cream into the egg mixture.
Pour the mixture into the buttered soufflé dishes, filling them above
the rim and into the area enclosed by the wax paper.

Place the soufflés into the freezer at least 4 hours, preferably overnight. When ready to serve, remove from the freezer and carefully remove the waxed paper collars.

FRESH FRUIT SORBET

SERVES 4

Here's a delightful way to make use of overripe fruit; a fat-free dessert you can make in an ice cream mixer or in a simple plastic container in your freezer. If you use the hand-stirred freezing technique, the result will be similar to an Italian granita.

1 cup water

½ cup granulated sugar

1 cup pureed fruit, such as
 raspberries, peaches, mangoes,
 papayas, kiwis, apricots,
 cherries, or strawberries

Bring the water and sugar just to the boil, then lower heat and simmer 5 minutes. Remove from heat and cool completely, then combine with the fruit puree. Place in an ice cream maker and follow the manufacturer's directions, or place the mixture in a plastic container, put the container in the freezer, and freeze, stirring every 10 minutes to break up the ice crystals, until completely frozen, about 1 hour.

WINE NOTES

PORTUGAL

There are a range of types and styles among the ports and Madeiras, including white, ruby, and tawny; "single," quintas, LBVs, and "Vintage." '21' sells Taylor's twenty-year old Tawny, along with many vintage ports dating back as early as 1922. Madeira comes from the volcanic island of the same name. The Sercial, Verdelho, Bual, and Malmsey Madeiras range from drier to very sweet. Some are "Vintage" and/or "Solera" dated.

Fresh Fruit in a Cool Ginger Broth
Serves 6 to 8

This is a light, refreshing dessert that is a welcome relief in warm weather, especially toward the end of summer when your guests might crave sweets yet decline richer desserts. While this is a very simple preparation, when the fruits are carefully arranged on individual plates, it makes a terrific crowd-pleaser.

For the fruit:

Use an assortment of the freshest fruits available. Some suggestions: blueberries, blackberries, sliced pitted peaches, sliced pitted plums, kiwis peeled and cut into quarters, sliced bananas, fresh currants (not too many as they are tart), mango or papaya, or any sort of tropical fruit that you can find. In short, the fruit selection is up to you.

Broth:

1 cup pineapple juice

Juice of 2 lemons (about ¼ cup)

3 tablespoons honey

2 tablespoons grated fresh ginger

⅓ cup Grand Marnier

Since this is an assortment of fruit served in a broth, count on any single piece of fruit yielding 4 portions. Two peaches, for example, would be more than sufficient. Take your time to clean and slice the fruit as neatly as possible. This is a recipe where presentation does count.

The fruits can be cut and prepared ahead of time. To keep them from discoloring, sprinkle a little lemon juice over them, cover with plastic wrap, and refrigerate until ready.

To make the broth, combine the pineapple juice, lemon juice, honey, ginger, and Grand Marnier in a saucepan. Bring quickly to a boil, reduce to a simmer, and cook 5 minutes before removing from the heat. Cool completely, either in an ice-water bath or in the refrigerator.

When ready to serve, allow 10 or 15 minutes to prepare the dishes. Use soup plates with broad, flat bottoms and arrange a mixture of the fruit in a colorful pattern across the bottom of the plate, possibly putting some of the slices in a pinwheel-type arrangement with little mounds of diced fruit or berries in the center. Once you have all the fruit divided among the plates, ladle several tablespoons of the cool broth over the fruit.

There should be just be enough broth in each plate to cover the bottom; it shouldn't be "soupy." A possible garnish might be the addition of a small scoop of sorbet in each plate and perhaps a sprinkling of grated coconut.

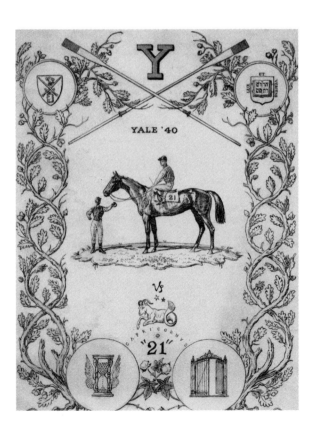

Private parties at '21' are often accompanied by programs or printed menus. In the Club's earliest days, these were generally humorous rather than serious. The private-edition 9 × 12" lithograph, with elaborate Yale, horseracing, and other symbolism, was an invitation from Mr. and Mrs. J. Frederic Byers requesting "the pleasure of your company to celebrate a 'daily double' on the joint occasion of the twenty-first birthday of that eminent sportsman Buckley M. 'Buck' Byers and the first wedding anniversary of Mr. and Mrs. J. Frederic Byers, Jr., at Jack and Charlie's '21,' Friday, January the seventh, 1938. Weather clear/Track fast/Post Time eight o'clock. (Courtesy of '21')

'21' Apple Pie

SERVES 6 TO 8

PIE DOUGH:

2 cups all-purpose flour

$^1/_2$ teaspoon salt

$1^1/_2$ sticks cold unsalted butter,
　　cut into cubes

$^1/_2$ to $^2/_3$ cup ice cold water

FILLING:

1 stick (8 tablespoons) unsalted
　　butter

12 large apples, such as Granny
　　Smith, peeled, cored, and
　　sliced into eighths (about
　　14 cups)

Juice of 2 lemons (about $^1/_4$ cup)

$^1/_4$ cup loosely packed dark brown
　　sugar

$^1/_4$ cup loosely packed light brown
　　sugar

$^1/_4$ cup Southern Comfort

1 tablespoon ground cinnamon

EGG WASH:

1 large egg beaten with
　　2 tablespoons water

To make the dough, combine the flour and salt in the bowl of an electric mixer. Mix at medium speed, then add the butter cubes, and beat at low speed to form a mealy mixture. Add ice water just until the dough pulls together. Stop the mixer. Refrigerate the dough, covered with a piece of plastic wrap, while you prepare the apples.

Prepare the filling in four or more batches. For each one, melt 2 tablespoons butter in a sauté pan until it begins to brown. Add a quarter of the sliced apples and sauté over medium heat until they begin to soften, about 5 to 6 minutes. In a bowl, combine the lemon juice, sugars, Southern Comfort, and cinnamon. Mix, and divide into quarters. Add one-quarter of this mixture to the apples and cook the mixture 10 to 12 minutes, until the apples are completely caramelized and covered with all the sugar. Remove the filling from the heat and allow it to cool. Repeat until all filling ingredients are used.

Preheat the oven to 375°. Divide the pie dough in two pieces. On a lightly floured board, roll out the first half to approximately ¼-inch thick in a round big enough to fit a 10- to 12-inch pie tin. Arrange the dough in the bottom of the tin and pierce it in several places with the tines of a fork.

Roll the second half of the pie dough into a round slightly larger than the pie pan. Fill the bottom crust with the cooked apples. Brush an egg wash coating over the lip of the dough. This is where it will be sealed to the top crust. Cover the apples with the top half of the pie dough. Trim any excess from the top crust before using both hands to crimp the edges of the two crusts together to seal. With a sharp knife, make several crosshatch slits in the top crust. Brush with the egg wash and bake 35 to 40 minutes. Remove from the oven and cool 20 minutes. Serve with Vanilla Ice Cream (page 301).

WINE NOTES

SPAIN

The sweeter sherries from Spain are absolutely not to be missed. The Amontillados, Olorosos, Palo Cortados, and PXs are a revelation. There are many fine producers.

STOCKS, BROTHS, POACHING AND STEAMING LIQUIDS, AND MARINADES

One thing is sure: while excellent stocks can be made from beef bones, veal bones, chicken carcasses and feet, tough old hares and fishheads, the stock-pot should never be treated as a rubbish bin.

—TOM STOBART, *THE COOK'S ENCYCLOPÆDIA*

A well-made stock is a wonderful way to enrich the flavor of all your cooking. Sadly, stock-making is a lost art in the culinary repertoire of too many American cooks—even otherwise adventurous ones. Our busy lives appear to be the culprit. Granted, some stocks benefit from many hours of simmering, but they are perfectly happy to do so on their own, while you go about your life. And though you wouldn't want to leave home with the stove on, electric crock pots may be a perfect way to simmer a stock while you go off and earn the daily bread.

In general, stocks are cheerfully pragmatic. It is far easier to prepare vegetables and herbs for the stock pot than for the serving bowl. Fresh herbs can be tossed in with no more ado than a rinse. Peeling vegetables is usually unnecessary (even undesirable in the case of roasted onions). If they're not going to be peeled, of course, they must be well rinsed or scrubbed clean. But chopping needn't be precise or pretty. Peppercorns can go in whole, and garlic cloves after just the smack of a knife blade.

The actual cooking process is usually as simple as heat to a boil, reduce to a simmer, and let it be until it's done. Timing is less critical than in most other areas of cooking. While an undercooked stock may be weaker and less flavorful than a properly cooked one, it always can be reduced to concentrate its flavor.

If cooled quickly in an ice-water bath and refrigerated in a clean, airtight container, stock will keep nicely for at least a week. Frozen stocks retain excellent quality for months. Although a good-quality, low-salt canned broth can be substituted in most recipes calling for stock, the rewards of making your own are as ample as those of cooking from scratch rather than subsisting on TV dinners.

Poaching and steaming are quick, simple ways to impart a lot of flavor in very little time. We have included a selection of both traditional poaching liquids such as Court Bouillon, and contemporary alternatives such as Ginger-Soy Broth. All are moist, flavorful, low-fat alternatives to oil-based cooking techniques.

Although some of the traditional reasons for marinating food—to tenderize tough meats and disguise "off" flavors and aromas—may no longer be imperative, marinades are becoming more popular than ever for a whole set of good new reasons. In keeping with today's lifestyles, marinades can be made ahead of time, working their magic while you're off at work or play. And unlike traditional fat-laden sauces, marinades are a light, healthful, low-salt way to add flavor. They also help keep foods moist when subjected to the high heat of grilling, broiling, and sautéing.

Marinades also can be used to baste meats or vegetables during cooking. Unused marinades can be stored, refrigerated, in a clean sealed container for as long as two weeks. Do not attempt to reuse marinades that have been drained from meats, fish, or poultry.

FISH STOCK

YIELD: 1 TO 1½ QUARTS

*O*f the various kinds of stock, fish stock is one of the simplest and quickest to make. A good fish stock is a wonderful addition to your supply of kitchen "basics." Not only is it essential for some fish and soup recipes, but it can enhance flavor in many other recipes without adding fat.

2 pounds fish bones from nonoily fish*

1 large onion, peeled and diced

2 stalks celery, washed and chopped, including leaves

1 leek, split, washed, and sliced

¼ cup chopped flat-leaf parsley, leaves and stems

1 tablespoon dried thyme

2 bay leaves

1 teaspoon white peppercorns

¼ teaspoon salt

2 quarts water

½ cup dry white wine, such as Chardonnay

Wash the bones in cold water to remove any scales or unwanted materials, then combine all ingredients in a large pot. Quickly bring just to a boil, then lower the heat to a slow simmer and cook 1 hour. While the stock simmers, skim and discard any coagulated proteins from the fish bones that rise to the surface. Remove from the heat, pour the stock through a fine-mesh sieve lined with cheesecloth, and then cool as quickly as possible in an ice-water bath. Refrigerated and covered, the fish stock should keep well for up to 1 week. The stock can also be kept frozen for as long as 6 months.

*Use only fish bones that come from nonoily fish, such as red snapper, flounder, sea bass, or sole. Avoid salmon, pompano, tuna, and other fish with strong and fatty flavors.

CHEF'S TIPS:

1. Cover the ingredients in your stock pot with an extra 2 inches water, and make sure they remain covered throughout the time they are cooking, even if that means adding more water at various intervals.

2. Avoid cooking the stock at a boil, as this will result in a cloudy stock.

CHICKEN STOCK

YIELD: 1 GALLON

A good generic poultry stock can be made with chicken and/or turkey or other poultry bones. Chicken stock is preferable in recipes that require an especially mild-flavored stock.

8 pounds raw or roasted chicken or other poultry bones

6 quarts water

3 carrots, washed and chopped

2 large onions, peeled and chopped

4 stalks celery, including leaves, washed and chopped

2 leeks, split, washed, and sliced

2 tablespoons dried thyme

2 bay leaves

3 cloves garlic, peeled and crushed

1 tablespoon each salt and black peppercorns

Wash the chicken bones with cold water. Put all of the ingredients together in a large stock pot and bring to a boil. Reduce to a simmer and continue to cook 4 hours. Skim any foam as it collects on top since this contains impurities that will cloud your stock. Remove from the heat and cool the stock slightly before straining it into a bowl through a fine-mesh sieve lined with cheesecloth. Continue to cool the stock as quickly as possible in a cold water bath. After the stock has cooled sufficiently, use a spoon to skim off the fat that has risen to the top. Refrigerate promptly.

'21'

CHEF'S TIP:

The stock pot is an excellent way to make the most of every last bit of a roast turkey, chicken, duck, or goose. The results here will be a darker and fuller-flavored stock. Of course a turkey, duck, or goose stock won't taste exactly like a chicken stock. Who cares? Each is delicious in its own right.

BEEF AND VEAL STOCK

YIELD: 1 GALLON

A long and slow-cooking stock like this one should not be intimidating even in a fast-paced world. This stock requires a full day of cooking, but if you allow a weekend morning and afternoon to make it, the quantity it yields will last for months in the freezer. This particular stock is used in small quantities to finish a dish, so its original preparation time can be amortized over numerous meals. If veal bones are unavailable, double the quantity of beef bones for a rich stock.

8 pounds each, veal and beef soup bones

2 large onions, washed but unpeeled, stem and root ends cut off

4 carrots, washed and roughly chopped

4 stalks celery, washed and chopped

3 leeks, split, washed, and sliced

1 cup canned crushed plum tomatoes

4 cloves garlic, peeled and crushed

2 tablespoons dried thyme

3 bay leaves

1 teaspoon each salt and black peppercorns

6 quarts water

Preheat the oven to 375°. Roast the bones and the vegetables 1 hour before placing all ingredients in a large stock pot. Cover with water to a depth of 2 inches above the bones, and quickly bring to a boil. When the water reaches a boil, lower the heat to a simmer, and continue to cook 8 hours. If more time is available, you can cook 10 to 12 hours to extract the maximum flavor from the bones and vegetables. When the stock has finished cooking, remove from the heat, strain the liquid through a fine sieve, and cool rapidly in a cold water bath before refrigerating. The solids may be discarded and the cold stock frozen in small batches.

GAME STOCK

YIELD: 1 1/2 QUARTS

Although a perfectly satisfactory game stock can be made using the Beef and Veal Stock recipe, this more elaborate method— which incorporates wine and another stock—will bring you one step closer to a finished sauce in the minimum amount of time. It is not necessary to tackle a recipe calling for Game Stock all at once. Instead, prepare the Chicken Stock one day, the Game Stock another, and the finished dish on yet a third.

2 pounds mixed game bones (quail, squab, venison, or duck, in any combination)

1 onion, washed but unpeeled, stem and root ends cut off

2 carrots, washed and chopped

2 stalks celery, washed and chopped

2 tablespoons dried thyme

1 bay leaf

1 tablespoon crushed dried juniper berries

1 teaspoon each salt and black peppercorns

1 cup dry red wine

1 quart Chicken Stock (page 332) or other poultry stock—or, for a richer style, Beef and Veal Stock (page 333)

Water to cover bones plus 2 inches

Preheat the oven to 375°. Roast the bones and vegetables for 1 hour before placing all ingredients in a large stock pot. Cover with wine, stock, and water to a depth of 2 inches above the bones. Bring to a boil, then lower the heat to a simmer, and continue to cook 2 hours (up to 4 hours if the time is available). Strain into a bowl through a sieve lined with cheesecloth and use immediately, or cool quickly in an ice bath and store, refrigerated, for up to a week or, frozen, for up to a year.

COURT BOUILLON

YIELD: 2 CUPS

*T*he name of this traditional poaching liquid translates
in English as "short broth." Typically it is used to poach
salmon, shrimp, or lobster.

1 teaspoon whole white
  peppercorns

1 teaspoon dried thyme

2 bay leaves

1½ cups water

¼ cup white wine vinegar

¼ cup dry white wine

1 small onion, peeled and chopped

1 carrot, washed and chopped

2 stalks celery, washed and chopped

1 leek, washed and chopped

Tie the peppercorns and dry herbs together in a little bundle of
cheesecloth. Combine the liquids in a saucepot and bring to a boil.
Add the vegetables and the herb bundle, and simmer together 20 to
25 minutes. This will result in a flavored broth that can be used to
poach fish or shellfish.

VEGETABLE STOCK

YIELD: 5 TO 6 QUARTS

Use this full-flavored vegetable stock to make meatless stews, soups, or chili. Reserve the remaining vegetable solids to thicken sauces and soups.

2 large Spanish onions

1/4 cup pure olive oil

1 head celery (including leafy parts), washed and roughly chopped

2 large leeks, including green tops, split, washed, and sliced

4 carrots, washed and roughly chopped

1 (15 1/2-ounce) can crushed plum tomatoes

1 cup cleaned and sliced fresh mushrooms (any mixture is fine, the more variety the better)

1/2 cup roughly chopped kale

2 medium turnips, peeled and chopped

1 parsnip, peeled and chopped

2 starchy potatoes (such as Russet or Idaho), washed but not peeled, diced

1/2 cup chopped flat-leaf parsley, leaves and stems

2 cloves garlic, crushed

1 teaspoon dried thyme

1 bay leaf

2 whole cloves

1/2 teaspoon each salt and black peppercorns

6 quarts water

Wash the unpeeled Spanish onions, trim the root and top ends, cut in half and roast in a 350° oven 1 hour, until browned. This caramelizes both the flesh and the skin, adding color and richness to the stock.

Heat the olive oil in a large soup kettle or stock pot. Add the onions and all of the remaining ingredients except the water. Cook the vegetables over medium heat approximately 15 minutes, or until they have wilted. Add the water and bring to a boil, then lower to a simmer and cook 2 hours. Skim any foam as it collects on top since this contains impurities that will cloud your stock.

Strain the stock through a sieve, pressing against the vegetables to extract as much of their juices as possible. (The solids can be pureed in a food processor and frozen in small batches to be used later to thicken soups, stews, and sauces.) Cool the stock as quickly as possible, preferably in a cold water bath, before refrigerating. For freshest flavor, unfrozen stock should be used within a week. Stock also can be frozen in smaller containers to be used as needed. This stock may be used as a substitute in recipes that call for more traditional meat-based stocks, but with different results in taste and consistency.

GINGER AND SOY
BROTH

YIELD: 1½ CUPS

*W*ith the popularization of Pacific Rim cuisines, a larger variety of soy sauces has become available in America, including low-salt soy sauces and a mushroom soy that is particularly flavorful. A good-quality soy sauce is a worthwhile staple for every kitchen.

1 cup Fish Stock (page 331) or low-salt canned chicken broth

¼ cup dry (*not* cooking) sherry or vermouth

¼ cup mushroom or low-salt soy sauce

2 tablespoons peeled and chopped fresh ginger

2 stalks fresh lemon grass, crushed

1 chili pepper *or* ¼ teaspoon crushed red pepper

GARNISH:

¼ cup chopped scallions

½ cup sugar snap peas

Heat the Fish Stock or chicken broth until just below the boil. Add the remaining ingredients and simmer gently 10 minutes. The broth can be used immediately to poach fish such as Sea Bass (page 138) or shellfish, or cooled and refrigerated for later use. The broth also can be served with any fish or vegetables you might like to cook in it for a light but flavorful dish. If you intend to serve the broth as part of a dish, add some fresh chopped scallions and perhaps some finely shredded sugar snap peas as garnish.

ENRICHED VEGETABLE CONSOMMÉ

SERVES 4

*T*he key ingredient here is a well-made vegetable stock. The effort required to make the stock in the first place will be rewarded by its usefulness in so many different dishes and styles of cooking. Here the stock is enriched by the addition of fresh vegetables. The resulting vegetable broth, or consommé, is a light starter for a meal or—when reduced in volume—a light sauce for fish, chicken, or vegetables. Naturally low in fat, it is deceptively rich-tasting and has the virtue of allowing the true flavors of other foods to shine through.

2 1/2 cups Vegetable Stock (page 336)

1/4 cup dry (*not* cooking) sherry

1/4 cup sliced fresh shiitake mushrooms

1/4 cup finely diced peeled carrots

1/4 cup finely diced celery

1/4 cup finely diced leeks

1 small sweet red or yellow pepper, diced

1 large clove garlic, peeled and finely chopped

1 tablespoon each, chopped fresh thyme and basil leaves

Heat the Vegetable Stock thoroughly and add all of the ingredients. Bring to a boil, reduce to a simmer, and cook 30 minutes. If you want to reserve this consommé for use at some later time, cool in an ice bath and refrigerate.

ROASTED SHELLFISH BROTH

YIELD: 3½ QUARTS

*T*his richly flavored broth is an excellent way to get more mileage from the shellfish you buy for other uses. Save shrimp and lobster shells, cooked or uncooked, in the freezer, or make this broth right away and then freeze it to use another time. You also may purchase lobster bodies from any good fish dealer, but expect to pay more than you would for fish, chicken, or beef bones. This is not a stock in the true sense of the word because it stands on its own as a simple but elegant soup—a delightful lunch when served with garlic bread and a salad. Shellfish broth can be used to poach fish and is the base for our bouillabaisse-style Fulton Market Fish Chowder (page 90).

3 pounds cleaned lobster bodies and/or shrimp shells*

2 carrots, washed and peeled

3 stalks celery, washed

1 large leek, split and washed

2 medium onions

3 large cloves garlic

1 (15½-ounce) can plum tomatoes, drained

¼ cup pure olive oil

½ teaspoon saffron threads

1 tablespoon dried thyme

1 tablespoon dried oregano

2 teaspoons salt

1 teaspoon whole black peppercorns

2 bay leaves

1 cup dry white wine

4 quarts water

Preheat the oven to 350°. Roast the shrimp and lobster shells 1 hour to give them a good rich flavor. Meanwhile, put the vegetables in a food processor fitted with a metal blade and pulse to chop fine.

Heat the olive oil in a large stock pot over medium-high heat until just before it smokes. Add the vegetables and sauté them 5 minutes to caramelize. Add the roasted shells, the saffron and other seasonings, and continue to cook 5 minutes more to meld all the flavors. Stir to ensure that nothing burns or sticks to the bottom of the pot. Add the white wine and reduce it by half to concentrate its flavor. Add the water and bring to a boil. Reduce to a simmer, and cook $1\frac{1}{2}$ hours. Skim any foamy particles that rise to the surface during cooking to ensure a clear, not cloudy, broth. Strain into a bowl through a cheesecloth-lined sieve and cool in an ice-water bath. Will keep about 1 week, refrigerated.

*Before roasting, split the lobster shells and clean by removing the light green tomalley (liver) in the body cavity and the feathery gills at the head section.

LEMON AND GARLIC MARINADE

YIELD: 1 CUP (ENOUGH FOR 2½ TO 3 POUNDS OF CHICKEN OR FISH)

A refreshing marinade for chicken, guinea hen, fish, shellfish, and vegetables that you plan to grill, sauté, or oven-roast. Caution: Don't overmarinate fish or poultry for so long that you may mask its natural flavors.

Juice of 2 lemons

4 tablespoons finely chopped garlic

¼ cup fresh basil leaves

1 tablespoon fresh thyme leaves

¼ cup flat-leaf parsley

1 teaspoon dried oregano

1 teaspoon dried rosemary

½ teaspoon fennel seeds

¼ teaspoon ground cardamom

½ cup pure olive oil

Combine all of the ingredients *except* the olive oil in the bowl of a food processor fitted with a metal blade. Pulse to blend. While still pulsing, *slowly* drizzle in the olive oil to create a creamy emulsion. Brush on the meat, fish, or vegetables you wish to marinate and refrigerate at least 30 minutes. Meat and poultry can be marinated in the refrigerator overnight; fish for no more than 2 hours. This can be used to marinate Thyme-roasted Chicken (page 202) or Roasted Cornish Hen (page 204).

GINGER-PEPPER
MARINADE

YIELD: 2½ CUPS

An Asian-inspired marinade that subtly enhances the flavor of chicken and fish.

1 cup canola or vegetable oil

Juice of 3 limes (approximately ¼ cup)

3 fresh jalapeño peppers, seeded

2 cloves garlic, peeled

¼ cup fresh cilantro leaves, lightly packed

1 teaspoon cracked black peppercorns

¼ cup grated fresh ginger

¼ cup unsweetened coconut milk

Combine all ingredients in the bowl of a food processor fitted with a metal blade and pulse to combine. Use to marinate swordfish, salmon, tuna, or red snapper for several hours before cooking, or marinate chicken, beef, or lamb overnight. This is a great marinade for grilling over smoky wood chips.

SHERRY-SOY MARINADE

YIELD: 1 ½ CUPS

½ cup canola, vegetable,
or peanut oil

½ cup dry (*not* cooking) sherry

¼ cup low-sodium soy sauce

2 tablespoons Oriental sesame oil

2 tablespoons peeled and finely
chopped fresh ginger

2 cloves garlic, peeled and
finely chopped

¼ cup coarsely chopped cilantro
leaves, tightly packed

3 whole scallions, sliced

3 tablespoons rice wine vinegar
(or white vinegar)

1 tablespoon annatto (achiote)
paste

2 tablespoons ground cumin

Combine all ingredients in a saucepan and heat to just below the boil. Remove from the heat. Cool. This marinade may be stored in refrigerator up to 2 weeks. Use to marinate chicken, shrimp, or pork for several hours before grilling.

RED WINE AND THYME
MARINADE

YIELD: 1½ CUPS

*U*se a full-bodied red wine with good varietal character. Wine for cooking should not be expensive but it should always be good enough to drink. "Leftover" table wines, stored in the refrigerator, can be put to excellent use as cooking wines.

1 cup dry red wine

¼ cup pure olive oil

3 tablespoons finely chopped shallots

½ cup crushed fresh thyme sprigs

2 cloves garlic, peeled and finely chopped

2 teaspoons coarsely ground black pepper

2 teaspoons fennel seeds

2 bay leaves

Juice of 1 lemon (about 2 tablespoons)

Combine all the ingredients in a bowl and allow the flavors to blend several hours before using. Brush on chicken 2 hours before, lamb or pork the night before, grilling or broiling. If brushed on during outdoor barbecuing, the marinade will cause the fire to smoke more, giving the meat extra smoked flavor.

"Dry" Rub Marinade for Lamb, Beef, or Pork

Yield: ½ cup

¼ cup pure olive oil

3 cloves garlic, peeled

1 tablespoon cracked black peppercorns

1 bunch parsley, washed, dried, and stemmed

Juice of 3 lemons (about 6 tablespoons)

2 tablespoons dried thyme

2 tablespoons dried rosemary

Combine all of the ingredients in the bowl of a food processor fitted with a metal blade and pulse to a paste. Spread the marinade on the meat being marinated, rub it in, and refrigerate overnight. Grill over a medium fire to the desired degree of doneness. Serve with Roasted Corn and Tomatillo Salsa (page 356).

'21'

Chef's Tip:

Fresh herbs can be wonderful to use but you'll need twice as much as the dried herbs.

"DRY" CHILI RUB

YIELD: ³/₄ CUP

This is a wonderful way to marinate foods such as beef, pork, and chicken for roasting or grilling. This bold combination of spices imparts flavor and aroma as memorable as the beautiful color produced by the annatto seeds. Annatto, also called achiote, is found in many Latin markets. You can substitute achiote oil, which is the ground seed blended with oil, but achiote oil is often heavily salted.

2 ounces dried ancho chili peppers

5 or 6 fresh jalapeño peppers

2 tablespoons cumin seed

1 tablespoon coriander seed

¹/₂ teaspoon allspice berries

¹/₄ teaspoon annatto seeds (achiote)

¹/₄ teaspoon ground cinnamon

2 cloves garlic, peeled and finely chopped

¹/₄ cup dark brown sugar, firmly packed

¹/₄ cup canola or vegetable oil

Stem and seed the dry and fresh chili peppers, using rubber gloves to protect your skin from the hot volatile oils. Grind all of the ingredients in a food processor fitted with a metal blade to form a thick paste. Using approximately 2 tablespoons per portion, rub into red meats the night before cooking; for fish and poultry, spread on several hours before roasting or grilling. Unused rub can be refrigerated in a clean, sealed container up to 2 weeks.

BARBECUE BEFORE, DURING, AND AFTER SAUCE

YIELD: 1½ CUPS

To Texans and certain other purists, barbecue sauce is strictly a table condiment. But many others use it as a marinade or slather it on during cooking. Whichever approach you prefer, this recipe adds a lot of sizzle to chicken, beef, or pork.

½ cup ketchup

½ cup red wine vinegar

¼ cup firmly packed dark brown sugar

1 onion, peeled and chopped

2 cloves garlic, peeled and crushed

1 tablespoon dark molasses

3 fresh hot chili peppers, such as jalapeño, or hotter if desired, seeded

2 tablespoons hot dry Coleman's mustard mixed with 1 tablespoon water

2 tablespoons Worcestershire Sauce

2 tablespoons ground cumin

2 tablespoons chili powder

Combine all ingredients in a saucepan and simmer over low heat 20 minutes. Cool, then puree in a blender or food processor fitted with a metal blade until smooth. This sauce can be stored in the refrigerator up to 2 weeks in a covered container.

" '21,' and Hurry!"

(© KFS)

HORSING AROUND AT '21,' PART III

America's great racing stables are immortalized at '21' by the restaurant's signature jockey hitching posts, which line the wrought-iron grilled stairs and balcony out front. Each is painted in the "colors" of one of the famous racing stables, like Calumet and Glenriddle farms, which bred such immortals as Whirlaway, winner of the 1941 Kentucky Derby, and War Admiral, winner of the 1937 Derby. No one seems to remember who donated the first of these jockeys to '21.' But whether it was Jock Whitney, Alfred G. Vanderbilt, or another member of the horsey set catered to by '21,' the tradition snowballed from there. "If we had one of anything," remembers Jerry Berns, "pretty soon we had a collection." All of the greatest stables, mounts, and riders of their day were represented, until the entire facade threatened to collapse from the weight, and management had to begin declining further offers.

APPLE AND BERMUDA ONION RELISH

■

CRANBERRY-ORANGE RELISH

■

PINEAPPLE CHUTNEY

■

SPICY PEAR CHUTNEY

■

ROASTED CORN AND TOMATILLO SALSA

■

CHILI PASTE (PUREE)

■

CHILI MAYONNAISE

■

GREEN HERB MAYONNAISE

■

HOT CHILI OIL

■

BASIL OR CHIVE OIL

CONDIMENTS

Condiments are like old friends—highly thought of,
but often taken for granted.

—MARILYN KAYTOR

As butter-rich sauces and artery-clogging gravies have given way to leaner, healthier ways of eating, low-fat condiments have come to the rescue of flavor and variety. Given this more essential role for condiments, it's not surprising that more people are making their own pickles, chutneys, and salsas, rather than settling for what's on the grocer's shelf. Where oil *is* called for, I offer some options that dress up a dish without running up the cholesterol count.

APPLE AND BERMUDA ONION RELISH

YIELD: 1 QUART

A terrific accompaniment to grilled rabbit or pheasant. Perfect with pork, turkey or squab and even shrimp.

2 pounds Granny Smith apples

2 tablespoons fresh lemon juice

1 large red Bermuda onion, diced

1 sweet red pepper, diced

1 yellow pepper, diced

2 tablespoons canola oil

2 tablespoons curry powder

1 teaspoon cayenne pepper

1/2 cup firmly packed brown sugar

1/2 cup cider vinegar

1/2 cup fresh cilantro leaves, loosely packed

Core and slice the apples into thin wedges. Place in a bowl, toss with the lemon juice, and reserve. Put the diced onion, peppers, and oil in a nonstick 3-quart saucepan and sauté over medium heat until the vegetables are soft and wilted. Turn the heat to low, add the dry spices, and stir to coat the vegetables evenly and release the full flavors of the spice mixture. Add the sugar, and continue cooking until it melts and begins to bubble. Add the vinegar slowly and carefully to avoid splashing. Continue cooking 5 minutes. Stir in the reserved apples and their juice and cook no more than 2 to 3 minutes, watching to be sure the apples don't overcook and become mushy. Remove from the heat and set the pan in an ice-water bath to cool the relish as quickly as possible. Chop the cilantro leaves coarsely and add to the relish at the last moment before serving. Without the cilantro leaves, the relish will keep 1 to 2 weeks in the refrigerator, longer if properly stored in air-tight jars.

CRANBERRY-ORANGE RELISH

YIELD: 5 CUPS

A traditional holiday treat to serve with roast turkey. Frozen cranberries make it possible to enjoy this relish any time of year.

1/2 cup granulated sugar

1/4 cup loosely packed dark brown sugar

1/4 cup maple syrup

3/4 cup water

1 tablespoon ground cinnamon

1 teaspoon freshly grated nutmeg

1 pound fresh or frozen cranberries, cleaned

4 navel oranges, peeled and divided into segments

1/2 cup coarsely chopped walnut pieces

Bring the sugars, syrup, water, cinnamon, and nutmeg to a boil. Reduce to a simmer and cook gently 5 minutes. Add the cranberries and continue to simmer, uncovered, until half the berries "pop." Remove from the heat and stir in the orange segments. Cool, stir in the walnut pieces, and serve.

PINEAPPLE CHUTNEY

YIELD: 4 CUPS

This recipe also works well with peaches, plums, nectarines, or other fresh fruits you may have in seasonal abundance.

1 large pineapple, peeled, quartered, and grilled on an outdoor grill until slightly charred on all sides

$^1/_2$ cup peeled and diced red onion

$^1/_2$ cup diced sweet red pepper

3 tablespoons chopped fresh ginger

1 teaspoon chopped garlic

1 tablespoon unsalted butter

$^3/_4$ cup firmly packed dark brown sugar

$^1/_2$ cup white wine vinegar

$^1/_2$ cup raisins

$^1/_2$ teaspoon salt

$^1/_2$ teaspoon cayenne pepper

Cool the grilled pineapple quarters and dice into $^1/_2$-inch cubes. Sauté the onion, sweet pepper, ginger, and garlic quickly in the butter. Add the sugar and vinegar, and bring to a boil. Lower the heat, add the pineapple, raisins, salt, and cayenne pepper, and simmer 25 minutes. Remove from the heat and cool before serving. The chutney can be stored in the refrigerator up to 1 week, or preserved for longer storage using accepted canning methods.

SPICY PEAR CHUTNEY

YIELD: 3 CUPS

$^1/_2$ cup cider vinegar

$^3/_4$ cup loosely packed light brown
    sugar

$^1/_4$ cup peeled and chopped onion

$^1/_4$ cup chopped sweet red pepper

$^1/_2$ cup raisins

1 tablespoon chopped garlic

3 tablespoons peeled and chopped
    fresh ginger

$^1/_2$ teaspoon salt

$^1/_2$ teaspoon cayenne pepper

6 pears, peeled, cored, and sliced
    $^1/_4$-inch thick

In a saucepan, bring the vinegar and sugar to a boil. Add all remaining ingredients except the pears and simmer 5 minutes. Add the pears and simmer an additional 5 minutes before removing from the heat. Cool 15 minutes, then transfer to a clean container and refrigerate up to 2 weeks.

ROASTED CORN AND TOMATILLO SALSA

YIELD: 4 CUPS

*W̲onderful with Chili-rubbed Pork Tenderloin (page 194),
Venison Chops (page 228), or Grilled Quail Salad (page 212).
A good use for the bounty of sweet corn available in late summer.*

4 large ears fresh sweet corn

$^1/_2$ pound fresh tomatillos, papery
    skin removed

1 medium red onion, peeled and
    finely diced

$^1/_4$ cup coarsely chopped cilantro
    leaves

2 tablespoons chopped garlic

1 teaspoon ground cumin

Juice of 2 limes (about $^1/_4$ cup)

2 tablespoons pure olive oil

1 jalapeño pepper, stemmed,
    seeded, and finely chopped

2 fresh plum tomatoes, diced

2 tablespoons balsamic vinegar

Salt and freshly ground black
    pepper to taste

Prepare a barbecue grill of hot coals. Husk the corn, then roast it on
the hot grill 5 minutes, turning often to cook evenly. At the same
time, roast the whole tomatillos on the grill until they begin to soften.
Remove the corn and tomatillos when they are done. Cut the corn off
the cob. Dice the tomatillos. Combine all ingredients in a bowl and
marinate several hours at room temperature. Serve at room temperature with grilled meats or fish. This delicious salsa will keep several
days in the refrigerator.

CHILI PASTE (PUREE)

YIELD: 1½ CUPS

This simple operation will yield a delightful and flavorful result, well worth the effort. Dried chiles are often sold in 2-ounce packages, hence the scale of this recipe. The "heat" of the paste will depend on the variety of chili or chiles you use. In addition to the several recipes in this book that call for chili paste, you can use it in any recipe that calls for chili powder.

Any combination of: 6 ounces
    dried ancho, chipotle,
    cascabel, or other chiles

Remove the stems and seeds from your choice of dried chiles. Pour boiling water over the chiles to cover and soak 30 minutes. Drain the chiles and puree them thoroughly in a food mill or food processor fitted with a metal blade. If you use a food mill, the result will be a smooth paste. If you use a food processor, you may want to press the paste through a sieve to produce a totally smooth paste. The paste can be stored, covered and refrigerated 10 days to 2 weeks; if covered with oil, it will keep in the refrigerator several months.

CHILI MAYONNAISE

YIELD: ABOUT 1 CUP

An oh-so-simple idea, useful in many dishes.
Even if you're forced to substitute chili powder for the paste,
do give this a try as a sandwich spread.

1 cup prepared mayonnaise   2 teaspoons Chili Paste (page 357)

Stir together and store in a covered container up to 2 weeks. Serve
with the Soft-shell Crab Club Sandwich (page 163), roast beef, grilled
steaks, or roasted chicken; or use as a bread spread for a tuna salad
sandwich; or a dip for crudités or tortilla chips.

GREEN HERB
MAYONNAISE

YIELD: 1½ CUPS

lso called sauce verte or watercress sauce, Green Herb Mayonnaise is the classic accompaniment to Cold Poached Salmon (page 134). It is also great with chilled shrimp or Lobster Salad (page 115). Try it on a tuna sandwich for a tasty surprise.

1 cup fresh spinach leaves, washed and destemmed

1 small bunch fresh watercress, bottom stems removed

1 small bunch flat-leaf parsley, bottom stems removed

1 cup prepared mayonnaise

3 tablespoons extra-virgin olive oil

Juice of ½ lemon (about 1 tablespoon)

½ teaspoon cayenne pepper

1 teaspoon salt

Blanch the spinach leaves in boiling water just until they barely wilt. Remove and shock in ice-cold water. Dry the spinach leaves, and wash and dry the watercress and parsley. Place all ingredients in the bowl of a food processor fitted with a metal blade, and process until smooth. Store in the refrigerator for 4 to 5 days until needed.

HOT CHILI OIL

YIELD: 1 CUP

Infusing oils with herbs and seasonings is a dazzling way to add a burst of flavor and color to a dish. These oils are almost always used as a final touch, rarely during cooking. Sprinkled on at the last moment, they serve not only as a culinary crescendo, but as an alternative to a traditional sauce. With discreet use, flavored oils can highlight taste and keep fat grams lower than using traditional finishes such as butter or cream. The FDA recommends keeping all herb oil refrigerated. This will cloud them between uses, but a few minutes at room temperature will rectify that. There are also some wonderful herb oils available in better markets, and these will be as delicious as homemade.

2 ounces dried chiles, such as ancho, chipotle (smoky), or New Mexico

1 cup canola or olive oil

1 teaspoon salt

Place the chiles, oil, and salt in a saucepan and simmer 5 minutes on very low heat. Remove from the stove and steep the chiles in the oil another 30 minutes, as you would tea. Strain the oil and store covered. It will keep in the refrigerator for several months. Refrigerate and reserve the chiles for another use, such as adding to a marinade or even to purée for chili paste.

'21'

CHEF'S TIP:

I prefer to use pure olive oil (or even canola oil) instead of extra-virgin olive oil in making flavored oils, since the oil is meant to carry the added flavor, not overpower it with its own fruity taste.

BASIL OR CHIVE OIL

YIELD: 1 CUP

½ cup fresh basil leaves *or* chopped fresh or frozen chives

1 cup canola or pure olive oil

1 teaspoon salt

Blanch the basil leaves or chives in salted, boiling water 30 seconds. Remove the leaves to a bowl of ice water to shock. Drain and dry them on paper towels. Place the basil leaves or chives and oil in a blender and puree. (If you had to, you could use a food processor, but it doesn't work quite as well for this application.) Strain the oil, refrigerate, and let rest overnight to let any remaining solids settle to the bottom. A beautiful, clear oil will be your reward for patience. This should be kept refrigerated and used within 1 or 2 days.

CHEF'S TIP:

Blanching the basil leaves or chives gives the resulting oils a jewellike clarity and brilliant pastel color.

Entertaining in the '21' Tradition

Jerry Berns escorted them to a table upstairs, where they were surrounded by beautiful antiques and Georgian silver. The food and service were superb.

—Sidney Sheldon, *Rage of Angels*

Every year '21' caters hundreds of parties in private rooms as intimate as the Wine Cellar (maximum capacity twelve guests) or as spacious as the sixty-foot-long Main Dining Room. We've served Wine Cellar dinners for two, and Grammy Awards dinners for 2,000. (We had to go around the block to the Museum of Modern Art to handle that crowd.) No matter the scale or the cause for celebration, being entertained at '21' is a memorable experience.

We hope the recipes, chef's tips, and wine recommendations contained in this book will inspire you to share the '21' experience with friends and family in your home as well. To that end, we offer a selection of menus for a variety of events: some casual and homey, others elegant and grand in scale. All the menus are intended only to illustrate how thoughtful menu planning serves to make any event go more smoothly. There are few rules in home menu design except eat as you like with an eye toward balancing flavors and textures and bring a sense of style to each meal. Cook with warmth and friendship, and the love will truly shine through. I believe cooking for others can be the most selfless and rewarding experience. Bon appétit.

21's elegant Main Dining Room is a favorite of brides. At the Rehearsal Dinner preceding the wedding of Stephanie Cogan and John Golfinos, Best Man Tom Nagorski offers a toast. (Photo: Denis Reggie)

A FAMILY HOLIDAY
MENU

*When the family comes for the holidays,
it's more than a meal, it's an all-day event.*

First, hors d'oeuvres, arranged as finger food on platters and served around the fireplace:

TEQUILA-CURED SALMON GRAVLAX
(PAGE 52)
■

MIXED GRILLED VEGETABLE CROSTINI
(PAGE 64)
■

TUNA KEBABS WITH WASABI DIPPING SAUCE
(PAGE 63)
■

Later, at the table:

PUMPKIN SOUP WITH APPLE SCHNITZ CROUTONS
(PAGE 92)
■

ROASTED OYSTERS WITH COUNTRY BACON
(PAGE 58)
■

STANDING RIB OF BEEF
(PAGE 180)
■

ROASTED SHALLOT-POTATO CAKE
(PAGE 244)
■

TOMATO AND ZUCCHINI GRATIN
(PAGE 255)
■

ROSEMARY-SEARED SPINACH WITH
OLIVE OIL AND GARLIC
(PAGE 251)

∎

ENDIVE, WALNUT, AND BLUE CHEESE SALAD
(PAGE 105)

∎

'21' APPLE PIE
(PAGE 326)

∎

CHOCOLATE-COCONUT TRUFFLES, CHOCOLATE
PECAN BROWNIES, AND LINZER TART SQUARES
(PAGES 316–319)

'21'

*It wouldn't be Christmas at '21' without the Salvation Army. This improbable sing-along, a '21' tradition for more than half a century, attracts so many people it is now scheduled on several consecutive days.
(Photo: Barrett Gallagher)*

A BLACK TIE AFFAIR

*Why wait for a special event when you can create your own?
All it takes is invitations that encourage festive dress and
food that's equally elegant.*

AMERICAN CAVIAR IN SIMPLE PASTRY CUPS
(PAGE 48)

■

'21' TRADITIONAL COLD POACHED SALMON
WITH PRESSED CUCUMBERS
(PAGE 134)

■

ROASTED SCOTTISH PHEASANT WITH
APRICOTS AND DATES
(PAGE 220)

■

WILD RICE WITH SPICY PECANS
(PAGE 286)

■

BRAISED EXOTIC MUSHROOMS
(PAGE 268)

■

MÂCHE AND ENDIVE WITH
STILTON CRUMBLE AND PORT
(PAGE 107)

■

FROZEN GRAND MARNIER SOUFFLÉS
(PAGE 322)

AFTER-OPERA SUPPER

A late-night supper to make ahead of time and enjoy with guests after a show, a concert, or an evening at the movies.

**YELLOW PEPPER GAZPACHO WITH
SEARED SHRIMP AND HOT CHILI OIL
(PAGE 84)**

■

**'21' TRADITIONAL STEAK DIANE
(PAGE 174)**

■

**MATCHSTICK POTATOES
(PAGE 240)**

■

**ENDIVE, WALNUT, AND BLUE CHEESE SALAD
(PAGE 105)**

■

**PROFITEROLES WITH
VANILLA ICE CREAM AND FUDGE SAUCE
(PAGE 301)**

A Celebration
Grand Buffet

These are all dishes that work well to serve twenty or more from an elegantly set buffet table.

SMOKED SALMON AND TROUT WITH CHIVE OIL
(PAGE 56)
■

POLENTA CORN CAKES WITH
WILD MUSHROOM PAN ROAST
(PAGE 68)
■

MICHAEL'S CAESAR SALAD
(PAGE 102)
■

WARM FRESH TUNA SALAD WITH
ROASTED PEPPERS
(PAGE 116)
■

GRILLED SHRIMP ON SKEWERS
(PAGE 160)
■

ROASTED FILLET OF BEEF WITH
ROASTED SHALLOTS
(PAGE 177)
■

DUCK BREAST WITH BALSAMIC VINEGAR GLAZE
(PAGE 208)
■

SAFFRON BASMATI RICE
(PAGE 287)
■

TOMATO AND ZUCCHINI GRATIN
(PAGE 255)
■

Sweet Potato and Parsnip Casserole
(PAGE 250)

■

Poached Pears in Phyllo Overcoat with Madeira Zabaglione
(PAGE 312)

■

Huckleberry and Pecan Crunch Pie with Kentucky Bourbon Sauce
(PAGE 306)

■

Port-laced Chocolate-Mocha Terrine
(PAGE 309)

■

Chocolate-Coconut Truffles
(PAGE 316)

■

Linzer Tart Squares
(PAGE 318)

'21'

EMI Records chairman Charles Koppelman chats with Bonnie Raitt during Grammy Awards Dinner he hosted at '21' in 1992. By 1994, the event had grown so large the feast was moved to the Museum of Modern Art—but was still catered by '21.'
(Photo courtesy of EMI)

'21'

A LITTLE CATERING ON THE SIDE

Although '21' has never officially had a catering division, the lengths to which the club always has been willing to go for its customers has taken it off premises more than occasionally. During Prohibition, Jack Kriendler reportedly made booze deliveries to customers on Park Avenue, Sutton Place, and Fifth Avenue riding in a Ford convertible and dressed in full Western regalia, including Stetson, boots, holsters, and six-shooters.

Who could forget the oh-so-Grace-Kelly scene in *Rear Window*, where she waltzes into Jimmy Stewart's apartment swathed in tulle with her favorite '21' waiter in tow, bearing a carry-out feast of lobster and all the trimmings?

In the late 1960s, while General David Sarnoff, then chairman of the board of RCA, was recovering from mastoid surgery in a New York hospital, '21' delivered lunch and dinner to his bedside daily.

Several nearby law firms order working lunches sent in on a fairly regular basis. And David Letterman, who has featured Michael Lomonaco on his program several times, has had '21' burgers sent over to him at the studio on a number of occasions.

'21' also participates in a quite different form of carry-out made possible by a wonderful organization called City Harvest. City Harvest collects still-edible leftovers from many of New York's restaurants and recycles this good, nutritious food to soup kitchens, senior centers, and shelters around the city.

A Window-Shopping, Gallery-Hopping, or Bird-Watching Brunch

A refreshing fix-ahead meal to follow a brisk weekend walk in the city or country.

Roasted Corn Chowder with Country Cheddar Cheese
(PAGE 94)

■

'21' Traditional Crab Cake
(PAGE 46)

■

'21' Traditional Sunset Salad
(PAGE 100)

■

Fresh Fruit in a Cool Ginger Broth
(PAGE 324)

DINNER IN THE WINE CELLAR

Some of '21's most exclusive private dinners are held in our historic Wine Cellar. Re-create the romance and elegance at home with candlelight and these menu suggestions.

FOIE GRAS WITH SWEET AND SOUR CABBAGE
(PAGE 74)
*DOMAINE DES BAUMARD
"COTEAUX DU LAYON"
1990 BOTRYTISED CHENIN BLANC*

■

SEA BASS POACHED WITH
LEMON GRASS AND CHILI COCONUT BROTH
(PAGE 138)
CALERA "VIOGNIER" 1991 CALIFORNIA

■

GIANT BLUE PRAWNS WITH GARLIC RISOTTO
(PAGE 158)
*CHABLIS GRAND CRU "VALMUR"
J. COLLET 1988*

■

QUAIL WITH ROASTED FIGS
(PAGE 214)
*CROZES-HERMITAGE
"DOMAINE DE THALABERT"
P. JABOULET 1983*

■

RACK OF LAMB WITH MUSTARD SEED CRUST
(PAGE 190)
CHÂTEAU DUCRU-BEAUCAILLOU 1970

■

VARIETY OF RIPE CHEESES
TAYLOR "VINTAGE" PORT 1945

■

CHOCOLATE SOUFFLÉ
(PAGE 320)
RIVETI MOSCATO D'ASTI "LA SPINETTA" 1994

'21'

'21's historic wine cellar is available for special private wine dinners featuring numerous small courses, each served with a notable accompanying wine. (Photo: Christopher Baker)

A Sunday Buffet to Celebrate Spring

*T*hrow open the windows or, better yet, carry the buffet table out
of doors to celebrate the return of warmth and sunshine.

MIXED GREEN SALAD WITH
SHALLOT AND CHAMPAGNE VINAIGRETTE
(PAGE 123)

■

SOFT-SHELL CRAB CLUB SANDWICH
(PAGE 163)

■

BONELESS ROAST LEG OF LAMB WITH
FETA CHEESE, OLIVES, AND BABY EGGPLANT
(PAGE 192)

■

COUSCOUS WITH ROASTED TOMATO
(PAGE 277)

■

TUSCAN WHITE BEANS WITH OLIVE OIL
(PAGE 256)

■

CLASSIC AMERICAN STRAWBERRY SHORTCAKE
(PAGE 314)

HALFTIME SPREAD

A casual, make-ahead meal that leaves the cook free to enjoy friends, family, and all the action.

WHITE BEAN AND CABBAGE SOUP
(PAGE 95)
■

'21' TRADITIONAL HUNTER SALAD
(PAGE 101)
■

GRILLED SHRIMP ON SKEWERS
(PAGE 160)
■

QUICK-COOKING RED VENISON CHILI
(PAGE 230)
■

STUFFED POBLANO PEPPERS
(PAGE 258)
■

'21' TRADITIONAL RICE PUDDING
(PAGE 297)
■

CHOCOLATE PECAN BROWNIES
(PAGE 317)

A Romantic Evening for Two

A Valentine dinner prepared with heart, shared with love, and fondly remembered.

Roasted Oysters with Country Bacon
(Page 58)

■

Whole Maine Lobster Salad
(Page 115)

■

Pan-roasted Quail with Port Sauce
(Page 210)

■

Rich Flourless Chocolate Torte
(Page 304)

HARVEST MOON
DINNER

*I*n late September, the first hints of fall turn our thoughts
from the salads of summer to heartier fare.

PROSCIUTTO AND PORT-POACHED PEARS
(PAGE 76)
■
PUMPKIN SOUP WITH APPLE SCHNITZ CROUTONS
(PAGE 92)
■
GRILLED MUSHROOM SALAD
(PAGE 108)
■
ROASTED SQUAB WITH CORN-AND-CHILI SAUCE
(PAGE 218)
■
NEW ENGLAND OYSTER STUFFING
(PAGE 292)
■
MAPLE-GLAZED ROOT VEGETABLES
(PAGE 269)
■
APPLE-WALNUT PANCAKES WITH
CINNAMON CREAM AND FUDGE SAUCE
(PAGE 298)

ANTIDOTE FOR A COLD WINTER'S NIGHT

When the holidays are long gone but spring still seems years away, sharing the comfort foods of winter with friends warms body and spirit alike.

DINNER AL FRESCO

Whether you call it a picnic, a cookout, or a barbecue, everything eaten outdoors seems to taste that much more delicious.

COBB SALAD
(PAGE 104)

■

GRILLED SWORDFISH SALAD
(PAGE 117)

■

GRILLED QUAIL SALAD
(PAGE 212)

■

CHOCOLATE PECAN BROWNIES
(PAGE 317)

■

LINZER TART SQUARES
(PAGE 318)

AND FINALLY, LADIES AND GENTLEMEN . . .

*H*ow do bathroom stories fit in a cookbook? Well, like every other square inch of '21,' the bathrooms have fascinating tales to tell—particularly the men's room. Until the expansion and remodeling at the end of World War II, necessities for the ladies were hardly more than an afterthought. From the barroom level, powdering a lady's nose meant trudging upstairs. But the bar-level men's room was something else. Illustrator Charles Baskerville painted the walls with bawdy murals so charming that although the 1987 renovation required tearing down the walls, the murals were carefully cut out, restored, and remounted after the restoration.

*L*orenzo "Rev" Robinson continues family traditions both as a Baptist minister and at '21.' Behind him, a Dean Cornwell painting banished to the men's room during the 1987 renovations. (Photo: Christopher Baker)

In contrast to the murals' earthiness, at least half a dozen members of a family that includes thirty-seven Baptist ministers have stood guard over '21's masculine inner sanctum for most of the past half century. Scion of the dynasty was Otis Coles, nicknamed "Deacon" (although not himself an actual minister), who presided over '21's men's room for forty years until his death in 1989 at the age of eighty. Not a man passed through Otis's men's room without a little sermon and a "God bless you." And whenever a president of the United States visited his domain—as several did—Otis would stand guard outside the door and not let anyone in until the President emerged.

Today, Otis's nephew, "Rev" Lorenzo Robinson, commutes from North Stanford, Connecticut, every day to deliver the sermons in '21's men's room, and travels as far as Jersey City, New Jersey, to preach in church on Sunday mornings.

RESOURCES

Although we encourage you to support your local retailers and try to persuade them to order (and ultimately stock) hard-to-find ingredients for you, we realize that this will not always get you what you need in the short run. In some instances, mail order may be your only recourse to secure particularly rare ingredients.

Several of the suppliers listed here are primarily wholesalers who cater to restaurants such as '21.' We have included only suppliers with which we have had positive experiences. While everyone listed has indicated a willingness to respond to orders from individuals, some do have requirements for the minimum-size order they are willing to handle. The cost of special overnight shipping also can add significantly to the ultimate cost of the items ordered. Getting friends to order with you could help reduce your share of the costs.

GAME

Broken Arrow Ranch　　　　　　1-800-962-4263
P.O. Box 530,　　　　　　　　　　(210) 367-5875
Ingram, Texas 78025
An authentic source for wild Texas venison and other game items. Call for a catalog.

D'Artagnan　　　　　　　　　　1-800-DARTAGN
399 St. Paul Avenue
Jersey City, NJ 07306
D'Artagnan is '21's primary supplier of fresh game, foie gras, and specialty poultry. It also publishes a catalog and ships direct to individual customers.

International Home Cooking　　　1-800-ADSPICE
305 Mallory Street
Rocky Mount, NC 27801
Offers a wide variety of exotic game—from alligator to rattlesnake—as well as "staples" such as farm-raised pheasant, foie gras, and venison. Owner Earl Peck will also help track down "impossible-to-find" items. Call for a catalog.

MEATS

DeBragga & Spitler, Inc.   (212) 924-1311
826-D Washington Street
New York, NY 10014
'21's supplier of aged Black Angus beef and other fine meats. No catalog or 800-number, but it will ship to individuals. Call for a price list.

SEAFOOD

Jordan Lobster and Seafood Company   (516) 889-3314
Reynolds Channel
Island Park, NY 11558
'21's supplier of fresh Maine lobsters. Again, no catalog or 800-number, but it will ship to individuals anywhere overnight by FedEx. Call Steve or Mike to check availability and current market prices.

Nantucket Specialty Seafood Company   1-800-344-BAYS
Box 487
Nantucket, MA 02554
We serve these fresh Nantucket Bay scallops all winter at '21.' Call for a catalog.

"Sweet-Water" Aqua Farms, Inc.   1-800-477-2967
P.O. Box 1807
San Benito, TX 78586
Farm-raised cultured seafood, including the giant blue prawns in the recipe on page 000. Call for the catalog.

The '21' Club   1-800-721-2582
21 West 52nd Street
New York, NY 10019
Fresh Russian malossol beluga, osetra, and sevruga, and American caviar shipped on request.

PRODUCE

Aux Delices Des Bois   1-800-666-1232
4 Leonard Street (212) 334-1230
New York, NY 10013
Wild and exotic mushrooms, truffles, and fresh herbs. Call for a catalog.

Lloyd Harbor Greens　　　　　　　(516) 845-8057
56 Central Drive
Farmingdale, NY 11735
'21's supplier of baby greens, mâche, fresh herbs, and specialty produce. Reasonable minimums required for individual orders. No catalog. Call for availability and prices.

GENERAL

Balducci's　　　　　　　　　　　1-800-572-7041
424 Sixth Avenue
New York, NY 10011
A New York landmark. Impeccable standards for fresh produce, prime meats, and specialty products, including fine cooking chocolates. Ask for the catalog.

Dean & DeLuca　　　　　　　　　1-800-221-7714
560 Broadway
New York, NY 10012
Famous for gourmet groceries and specialty items, including fine cooking chocolates. Its own-brand spices also are carried by upscale retailers nationwide. Catalog available.

Paprikas Weiss Importers　　　　　(212) 288-6117
1572 Second Ave., New York, NY 10028
Enormous variety of spices and seasoning mixtures, from Asafetida to Zubrovka. The forty-four-page catalog includes many other Hungarian and European delicacies as well.

Zabar's　　　　　　　　　　　　(212) 787-2003, or
2245 Broadway, New York, NY 10024   (212) 496-1234
A revered New York tradition, particularly famous for its smoked and cured salmon. Ask for a catalog.

INDEX